## WHAT OTHERS ARE SAYING

*A Jesus Mission Life* is a challenging read for a Jesus follower. It is an honest look at what it takes to live a life focused on serving the Lord, but it does not stop with the challenge. It fills in the gaps with real-life and honest stories that are both focused and, at times, intimate accounts of Leonard's life.

Leonard is a man of faith; he is also a man of action who is not afraid of saying yes to the leading of the Lord. I have served with him and his wife; you will see their faith in real life as you embrace the ideas of *A Jesus Mission Life.*

I recommend this adventure to all believers as a way to deepen their pursuit of kingdom living. It helps the reader to look at the Scriptures through a new lens.

***—Gary Fox***

My favorite passage in the entire Bible is in Luke chapter 15. In the parable of the lost sheep, we read of God's shepherd-heart for all who are separated from Him. Moreover, He places a missional emphasis on those of us who are secure in Christ to reach those who are disconnected from Him.

Pastor Leonard Lee has written a book that I'm praying goes viral inside and outside of the Kingdom. In *A Jesus Mission Life*, Pastor Lee explains why every human being needs to center everything they do in life around Jesus and the mission He has called each of us to. I can personally attest to the fact that my friend Leonard has successfully done this.

***—Bob Balian***
***Founding pastor of Midtown Church Sacramento, CA***
***Chaplain to the Sacramento Kings***

I have had the privilege of calling Leonard a friend and a spiritual father. We have shared more than thirty years of friendship and life together and hundreds, if not thousands, of hours over the years serving and talking about Jesus. As I read this book, I was reminded of different conversations over campfires, coffee, and more meals than I can remember. I have traveled the world with him to serve Jesus. I have heard him teach across cultures. All the ministry I do is very much a product of his leadership and teaching. With all of that being said, this book isn't just words on a page. *A Jesus Mission* Life is Leonard's life. He lives and breathes every word of it.

***—Justin Orr***
***Life Groups Pastor Heights Church***

I have had the privilege of knowing Leonard Lee as both a mentor and a friend for the past decade. Throughout this time, he has exemplified what it means to lead a life dedicated to a mission with Jesus. Almost every conversation we have had has centered on this topic, as it is the core of the gospel and a fundamental aspect of Leonard's life. No one I know is more qualified to speak about it with such clarity and depth of experience. Leonard effectively communicates the essential truth that Christians should live a life focused on the mission of Jesus. He does this with his characteristic humor, compassion, and unique ability to challenge others gently and directly. I highly recommend this book for anyone who wishes to follow Jesus seriously or for those seeking to understand what it means to walk with Him.

***—Cory Johnson***
***Lead Pastor of Bayside Woodland***

I have known Leonard Lee since 2011, and it's an honor to call him friend, mentor, and co-laborer for Christ. In the last five years, I have studied a great deal on disciple-making, and I have learned more from Leonard than anyone else—it's not even CLOSE! Leonard is the executive director of 4GENetwork, and his sole purpose in life is to make disciples who make disciples and to train church leaders around the globe to create a disciple-making culture not only in the churches they lead but for them to become disciple-makers themselves.

If you want to know the mission of Jesus and the heart of Leonard Lee, you must read *A Jesus Mission Life*. Leonard's book is not based on any theory one might learn in a classroom; instead, it's based on real-life experiences, and the teachings and examples of Jesus put into practice by Leonard himself. If you or a group of friends are looking for a book on living your life on mission to make disciples, look no further—*A Jesus Mission Life* is for you!

***—Patrick Lightfoot***
***Church Planter and Lead Pastor of Traverse Christian Church***

*A Jesus Mission Life* offers a fresh perspective on the mission Jesus has given us, with practical applications for living it out daily. Through personal stories, thought-provoking questions, and strong scriptural connections, this book will challenge you to deepen your relationship with Jesus and embrace your role in His mission. Not only does it provide guidance and insight, but it also serves as a constant reminder of the mission Jesus has for you, His Church, and the Kingdom.

Each chapter extends beyond the page, offering prayers, reflective questions, and actionable steps to apply in daily life. By exploring the difference between purpose and mission and how these concepts apply in today's world, this book equips you with tools for ministry, community, and living as a follower of Jesus. Its content is deeply valuable and essential for today's Christians and beyond.

I have had the honor and privilege of knowing Leonard Lee for twenty-two years. He is a brother, a friend, a mentor, and a partner in ministry. From hours-long coffee shop chats to missional adventures overseas, Leonard has always been ALL IN—he is and always has been fully committed to encouraging others toward God's best and to living a Jesus mission life. He exemplifies this devotion while humbly recognizing that this is not his mission but Jesus's mission. I couldn't be more excited for his new book's release and its impact on the Kingdom moving forward.

***—Scott Shaull Jr.***
***Special Needs Coordinator, Mount Hermon Conference Center***
***Founder and Director of Emmanuel's Light***

I have had the privilege of knowing Leonard Lee for thirty-four years since we first worked together in youth ministry. Over the years, Leonard has served as a guest speaker at many of our youth events and worship services and has led discipleship training for church leaders at our project sites in Ambo, Ethiopia. He is a man of impeccable integrity, great wisdom, and genuine humility.

Leonard has been making disciples who make disciples since his high school days—it's not just a calling but a passion. I can't think of a conversation with him where I didn't jot down something to remember and apply. *A Jesus Mission Life*: Finding Your Why in the Mission of Jesus is the book I have been waiting for—one that Leonard is uniquely qualified to write. If you want to know how to follow Jesus into the mission life you were meant to live, read this book now!

***—Ronald J. Hunt***
***Pastor, Church of God of San Jose***
***Executive Director, 4others***

Leonard Lee has given us a definitive mission-driven discipleship guidebook. In it, he invites the follower of Jesus to go "All In" and to reorient their life's purpose to reach the world with the Good News through making disciples who make disciples. He insists that God can use whoever goes "All In" as an effective witness and dynamic disciple-maker.

Lee's penetrating examples of peculiar encounters and personal experiences are seamlessly coupled with biblical exegesis and practical exercises that are clear, concise, and conceivable. In every chapter, I was drawn back to biblical passages, asking myself, "Why didn't I see that there before?"

***—Dr. Rich Frazer, President, SOS International***

I love this book. I have been a Jesus follower for almost forty years and a pastor for almost thirty. I was hooked when I sat down with *A Jesus Mission Life* and read the introduction. Part of what makes it so compelling is that Leonard lives it. I have known and worked with him in different capacities for the last seventeen years. He never writes or teaches anything that hasn't first worked its way through his life and faith, and this book is the culmination of a lifetime spent daring to follow Jesus wherever He leads. Leonard embodies the message and truth of this book.

I believe that what you're holding in your hands could change your life. A Jesus Mission Life simply and effectively cuts through so much of the noise that can surround and fill Christianity. It goes to the heart of what's missing for many Christians today. Maybe what I love most about this book is that, whether you're new to faith or a long-time believer, *A Jesus Mission Life* will inspire, encourage, illuminate, challenge, equip, and empower you to follow Jesus authentically, not just settle for believing in Him. Leonard weaves powerful biblical truth with everyday language, stories, and examples in a way that puts skin on what it looks like to live out your faith and join Jesus on His mission. If you're anything like me, you will want to mark up the book and make notes on every page. Read and internalize every word, then follow Jesus into a life on mission full of faith.

***—Randy Sherwood***
***Pastor of South Hills Church, Idaho Campus***

I love Leonard Lee! As you read the book you now hold in your hands, you will be drawn closer to Jesus if you are not careful. Leonard has a beautiful way of writing and showing others how our Lord calls us to join him in reaching his people. My experience serving alongside Leonard happened when I joined him to serve pastors in West Africa by sharing the ministry of Celebrate Recovery. As I read this book, I was impressed by how God showed Leonard what his WHY was by serving pastors all over the world. To me, this book is Leonard's legacy. Holy Spirit inspired, God led Leonard to write *A Jesus Mission Life* all because Leonard said YES!

***—Jeff Redmond***
***Bayside Celebrate Recovery Pastor***
***USA West Regional Director Celebrate Recovery***

*A Jesus Mission Life* is a powerful invitation to embrace the transformative adventure of following Christ—to say "yes" to Jesus's invitation to do, see, be, and become more. Written with warmth, wisdom, and a deep understanding of the human heart, Leonard's book masterfully blends conversation with discovery, drawing readers into a deeper relationship with Jesus. It's not just about knowing Him—it's about experiencing the joy and fulfillment that comes from living in His purpose for your life.

Each page is filled with practical insight and soul-stirring encouragement, showing us how to move beyond routine faith to a dynamic, mission-driven life that honors God and transforms the world around us.

Whether you're new to the faith or have walked with Jesus for years, A Jesus Mission Life will ignite your passion for His calling and empower you to live a life that is exciting, fulfilling, and fully aligned with God's perfect plan. If you're ready for a deeper, more vibrant walk with Christ, A Jesus Mission Life is a wonderful roadmap. Prepare to be inspired, challenged, and, most importantly, changed along the way.

***—Billy Ivey***
***Director of Story, Small Stories Studio***

This book is written by a deeply formed practitioner. Leonard Lee not only talks about the Mission of Jesus, he lives it. I have witnessed how it seeps into every aspect of Leonard's life—his family, ministry, extended relationships, resources, and presence wherever he goes. Leonard lives "all in," as he describes in his book.

Long before Leonard received degrees and recognition, he committed himself to listening to Jesus through the Word and the Spirit. As written in this book, he has studied and seen how God's mission weaves throughout history and is active in the time in which we find ourselves. If you desire to deeply live the Mission of Jesus, fully embrace His teachings, and passionately multiply His Mission in others, READ THIS BOOK.

***—Bud Locke, Lead Pastor, Hope Center Covenant Church***

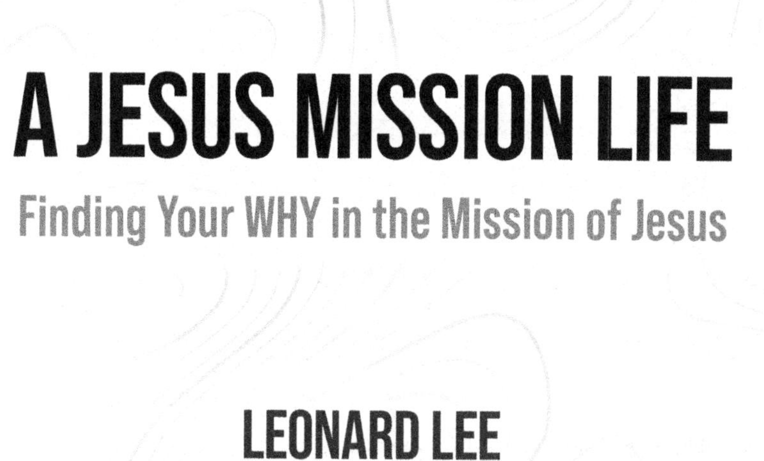

# A JESUS MISSION LIFE

## Finding Your WHY in the Mission of Jesus

LEONARD LEE

*A Jesus Mission Life: Finding Your WHY in the Mission of Jesus*



Published by Lee Resources, 531 Briarhill Road, Lebanon, TN 37087. For more information about this book and the author, visit LeonardLee.com.

Copyediting and production by Jennifer Edwards (jedwardsediting.net)

Cover design by Lacy Wilson

Interior design by Ben Holman

ISBN Paperback: 9781735772349

ISBN Ebook: 9781735772356

ISBN Audiobook: 9781735772363



*Disclaimer:* The author has tried to recreate events, locales, and conversations from memories of them. In order to maintain their anonymity, protect their privacy, and ensure their safety, some names of individuals and places, identifying characteristics, and other details such as physical descriptions, occupations, and places of residence have been changed.

Library of Congress Control Number: 2025900685

PRINTED IN THE UNITED STATES OF AMERICA

# DEDICATION

*This book is dedicated to the best person I know who is not Jesus:*

Merrily Lee, you are my true hero and example of what it means to follow Jesus and to live a Jesus Mission Life. In my life, no human being has been more trustworthy and faithful, and I love you more and more each day. Thank you for enduring the hours of me wrestling through the content and tone of this book. Thank you for your wisdom that made this book better. Also, thank you for the sacrifices you have made to build a Jesus Mission Marriage. We have been together since 1989. Let's see if we can get another twenty-five years under our belt.

And Katey and Mason, I love you more than I love my own life. You both mean the world to me.

# CONTENTS

# ACKNOWLEDGMENTS

I stand on the shoulders of so many people.

Gary Fox, my executive director at Youth for Christ, thank you for the ways you let me lead, grow, fail, learn, and lead again. Thank you for modeling what a Jesus Mission Life looks like in the everyday world.

Jim Holst, you trusted me with responsibilities and leadership I did not deserve. Thank you.

Ray Johnston, thank you for challenging me to grow my leadership in kingdom work.

Pastors Merle Booth and David Einer were the two pastors who called me to a Jesus Mission Life as a child and teen.

Roy Clark, who led me to Jesus in 1966, you have shaped my love for Jesus and His Word.

Ron Hunt, Dean Crist, and Mark Maniord, I am so grateful for your friendship in life and ministry.

Scott Friesen, you left way too soon, but while you were here, no other friend loved me better. Thank you, and I will see you when I finish here.

My late parents, thank you.

My brother Cliff Lee and my sister Lois Johnson whose prayers and support humble me. Thank you for loving your baby brother so well.

My staff, my board, and the team that makes up the ministry of the 4GENetwork, thank you.

Eric Joppa, Justin Orr, Cory Johnson, Scott Shaull Jr., Patrick Lightfoot, and Mike Cook, thank you.

Thank you to the thousands of people who rally to pray for me, my family, and the ministry.

The people whose financial support has been invested to shape both heaven and earth, thank you.

Thank you to the pastors and leaders around the world who have taken our training and, as of 2024, influenced over 40,000,000 people with the Gospel.

If I did not mention you, that is not because your life has not influenced mine, I just ran out of space—thank you, too.

# ABOUT THIS BOOK

The title of this book was hard to come by. I had about a dozen other titles. I brainstormed with friends and even did an AI search. My friends who read large parts of the book could not come up with a title either. Finally, after reading the book four or five times without a title, I kept circling back to what I believe God had placed on my heart before I wrote it—*A Jesus Mission Life: Finding Your WHY in the Mission of Jesus*—for that is what Jesus wants for each of us.

Living a Jesus Mission Life is my "why." It is why I get up each day, why I treat people the way I do, and why I invest my time and resources the way I do. By building a life around Jesus and His Mission, I have found my "why," and I pray this for you, too.

A Jesus Mission Life is one that is built around the Mission of Jesus, which is "to seek and save the lost" (Luke 19:10) and "to give His life a ransom for many" (Matthew 20:28). It is expressed when Jesus people see it as their mission to make disciples who make disciples. This Jesus Mission Life is what we were made for and how God's image is expressed in us. It becomes our "why."

As you read, you will find that God's expressed image as it relates to mission looks different for each of us. Here is why I want you to read this book:

### MISSION BRINGS HEALING

Literally every good thing in my life has come from my friendship with Jesus that has been forged in mission. The healing from traumatic wounds in my childhood and those experienced along the way have been both healed by God and then, by His grace, used to love others. Jesus once said, freely you have received, freely give. This was not about money but about grace and truth. When we live a Jesus Mission Life, we are in perfect harmony with Jesus's own words. I want that for you.

### MISSION BRINGS LIFE

You are made for Mission. We all are specifically and wonderfully made for mission, the kind of mission that can only come from a deep and abiding friendship with Jesus. The abundant life Jesus said He came to give us is found as we live out the life HE has authored for us. Our lives become what He designed them to be when we join Him in His Mission.

### WE ALL GOT PEOPLE

Every Jesus follower I know has a person they want to know and love Jesus more. We pray for them, we hint at them, we invite them to our gatherings, and this book will give some very useful and practical ways in which to invite the people you love to know the God you love.

This book is made up of two parts. In Part One, we will see that we are very loved by God and that this love is foundational to living a Jesus Mission Life. One of the struggles in our current Christian culture is that many people might know much about Jesus and are saved by His grace through faith but still do not know Jesus deeply enough to embrace His single and only Mission fully—the Jesus Mission Life. Together, we will be reminded that it is the love of Jesus that sends us, and we will also discover that the Mission Jesus had and still has is active and awaiting each of us. We will trace how God has carried out His Mission throughout history and how this mission translates to the Church today. Essentially, Part One provides insight into how Jesus's Mission is also our mission.

In Part Two, we will dive into the many ways we can enter fully into the process of a Jesus Mission Life. We will also see how God the Holy Spirit is our chief partner in building this life. At the end of this book is an invitation from God to you. It is an invitation to be His, to follow Him, and to live a life beyond your ability to imagine

At the end of every chapter, I've included three important responses. First, **A Prayer You Can Pray Today.** Take time to pray the words and, more importantly, the *heart* behind the prayer. Write it out and take it with you. Pray it several times a day and throughout the week. Second, **Some Questions to Move You Forward.** These questions can be a personal way to take a spiritual inventory of how you are doing in living a Jesus Mission Life. Third, **Steps to Take as You Go.** These are practical suggestions to build your Jesus Mission Life.

There are a number of ways to use this book. You can read it personally and embrace the Mission of Jesus with your life, what I like to call being ALL IN. You can also use it in a small group setting by reading a chapter each week and discussing the questions at the end of each chapter to start a conversation about living a Jesus Mission Life. I encourage you to share this book with a friend and give them a copy to start a discipling relationship. And if you lead a ministry, please share *A Jesus Mission Life* with your team or staff. Either way, the goal is that each of us learn to embrace a Jesus Mission Life and take the mission Jesus gave us to make disciples who make disciples. This book is a great starting place.

Then you will know the truth, and the truth will set you free. (John 8:32)

# INTRODUCTION

## Finding Your WHY in the Mission of Jesus

I wonder if Matthew, the disciple who left his tax collector booth so he could follow Jesus, imagined that following and embracing the Mission of Jesus would take him from being hated by his people to writing the Gospel of Matthew. I wonder if Thomas, the guy we label as "Doubting Thomas," imagined that following and embracing the Mission of Jesus would lead him away from his beloved home of Israel so he could bring the Gospel of Jesus to India. When I think about Peter, whose name was Simon when he met Jesus, I wonder if he thought that accepting Jesus's invitation to leave his nets and follow Him would open the door to such an impactful life. Do you think he ever considered that following Jesus would include walking on water, raising the dead, feeding the masses, preaching the sermon that launched the Church, healing the sick, training countless other disciples, and eventually dying in Rome for the Jesus he loved and followed?

What about the two brothers, James and John, whose nicknames were Sons of Thunder? Did James think that following and embracing the Mission of Jesus would give him the honor of giving his life for Jesus? I wonder if John thought that as a part of following Jesus, he would get to spend about thirteen years caring for Mary, the mother of Jesus. Did he know that he would eventually become known as the apostle who best taught Jesus's message of love? I cannot fathom that he thought his journey would make him the author of five New Testament books, including the Gospel of John and the book of Revelation.

The apostle Paul embraced Jesus's Mission and took His message throughout the Roman world. I wonder if he imagined that in following Jesus and embracing His Mission, God would use him to launch churches that would transform cities and nations. Did he think his letters to these churches and regions where he served would become thirteen New Testament books and that we would still read them almost two thousand years later, revering them as God-breathed? Did Paul know the price he would pay to follow Jesus and embrace His Mission?

Before meeting Jesus, Paul was on the fast track to becoming one of the most powerful people in the Jewish religion and his country. Meeting Jesus caused Paul to exchange his own mission for a Jesus Mission Life. Paul's new mission became Jesus's Mission, the mission to take the Gospel of Jesus everywhere he went. This exchange led to shipwrecks, attacks, beatings that left him for dead, abandonment, prison, and more. Paul was eventually beheaded in Rome because he was embraced and loved by God and immersed himself in a Jesus Mission Life.

These are just a few of the countless stories of people who followed Jesus and lived a Jesus Mission Life. I cannot imagine any of them knew what was coming, but I am sure every one of them was convinced that knowing Jesus was worthwhile.

When I met Jesus, I had no idea what He would do with me. When you met Jesus, you most likely had no idea what He would do with you, either. I was a kid whose dad had abandoned him, which left a giant hole in the heart of a little boy. One day, I asked Jesus into my life. I asked Him to forgive my sins and told Him I would follow Him for the rest of my life. I had no idea what this new friendship with Jesus would bring. It is possible you once said words similar to these, making a request for Jesus to help you and then committing to follow Him. If not, cut to the "A Note to the Reader" part at the end of this book any time and see why this matters.

I could not have imagined the full and fruitful life that following Jesus and embracing His Mission has given me, which, by the way, is a Jesus Mission Life. It still overwhelms me to think that Jesus lets me go where I go, do what I do, say what I say, and live how I live. A common question that runs through my mind is, "How in the heck did I get here?"

I remember asking this question in West Africa, where I was training pastors to live a Jesus Mission Life. Bombs were being delivered to churches and exploded by extremists, and my friends felt it necessary to hide me for a few days. Tucked away in my hiding place, I sat in a small room where the windows were covered with metal bars, almost like a prison cell. The door to my room also had metal bars as an added level of security. If that were not enough, my room was in a compound surrounded by cement walls that were fifteen feet tall and ten inches thick. The top of each wall was embedded with jagged pieces of glass and metal, topped off with razor wire, and there were two iron gates that were barred, padlocked, and guarded by a man stationed at the gates.

My mind was racing as I sat on my bed, but the most dominant thought kept coming back in the form of a question, "How in the heck did I get here?" This question was not a fear question but rather one of gratitude to Jesus. I was grateful that He let me serve in this place. How did I get picked to be here, to open God's truth to these amazing friends in West Africa, and to share Jesus's Mission? (FYI, I often feel like the least likely guy to do most of the things that embracing a Jesus Mission Life has opened doors for me to do.)

That afternoon, sitting on the edge of my bed in a compound tucked away on the other side of the world, I asked, "Jesus, how did I get here?" I sat there feeling grateful; I was praying, reading my Bible immersed in wondering, when I heard the gentle voice of Jesus say, "You followed Me here. My son, when you invited Me into your life and asked Me to forgive you, I did, and you are here because this is what you said you would do—you are following."

I lost it. I cried the ugly kind of cry. I had no idea following Jesus would take me to Africa where I would sit in a compound, being hidden and protected by my dear African brothers as I worked to train pastors, but I wouldn't have had it any other way.

Here is the reason I am writing this book and the reason I really want you to read it. Like me, you most likely have no real idea where or to whom following Jesus will lead you. That is how a Jesus Mission Life works. None of us are fully aware of how embracing the Mission of Jesus and declaring with our whole lives that Jesus is worth everything will impact our lives or the lives of others as we live on mission—Jesus's Mission.

Following Jesus will probably not lead you to Africa, but it might. Following Jesus most likely will not lead you to India, Cuba, Asia, Central or South America, but it might. I promise you one thing, though: Follow Jesus, and HE will lead you. Embrace His Mission, and the world around you changes. Jesus will lead you to places you never thought you would go. Jesus will lead you to people you never thought you would meet. Jesus will lead you to say words you never thought you would say. Jesus will lead you to act in compassion, serve communities, know truth, and speak grace. Follow Jesus, and the freedom that enters your life—because you are following—is the freedom Jesus promises when we embrace a Jesus Mission Life (John 8:32). Following Jesus and embracing His Mission is what it really means to be a Christian.

The majority of people in churches scattered across the world have yet to experience what it is to embrace a Jesus Mission Life. If you want to know the adventure of living fully into the Mission of Jesus because of the love of Jesus, please keep reading.

I am praying for each of you. If God speaks to you, send me a note at leonardl@4-gen.net. I would love to hear your story.

With much love and prayer and, of course, HOPE,

Leonard Lee

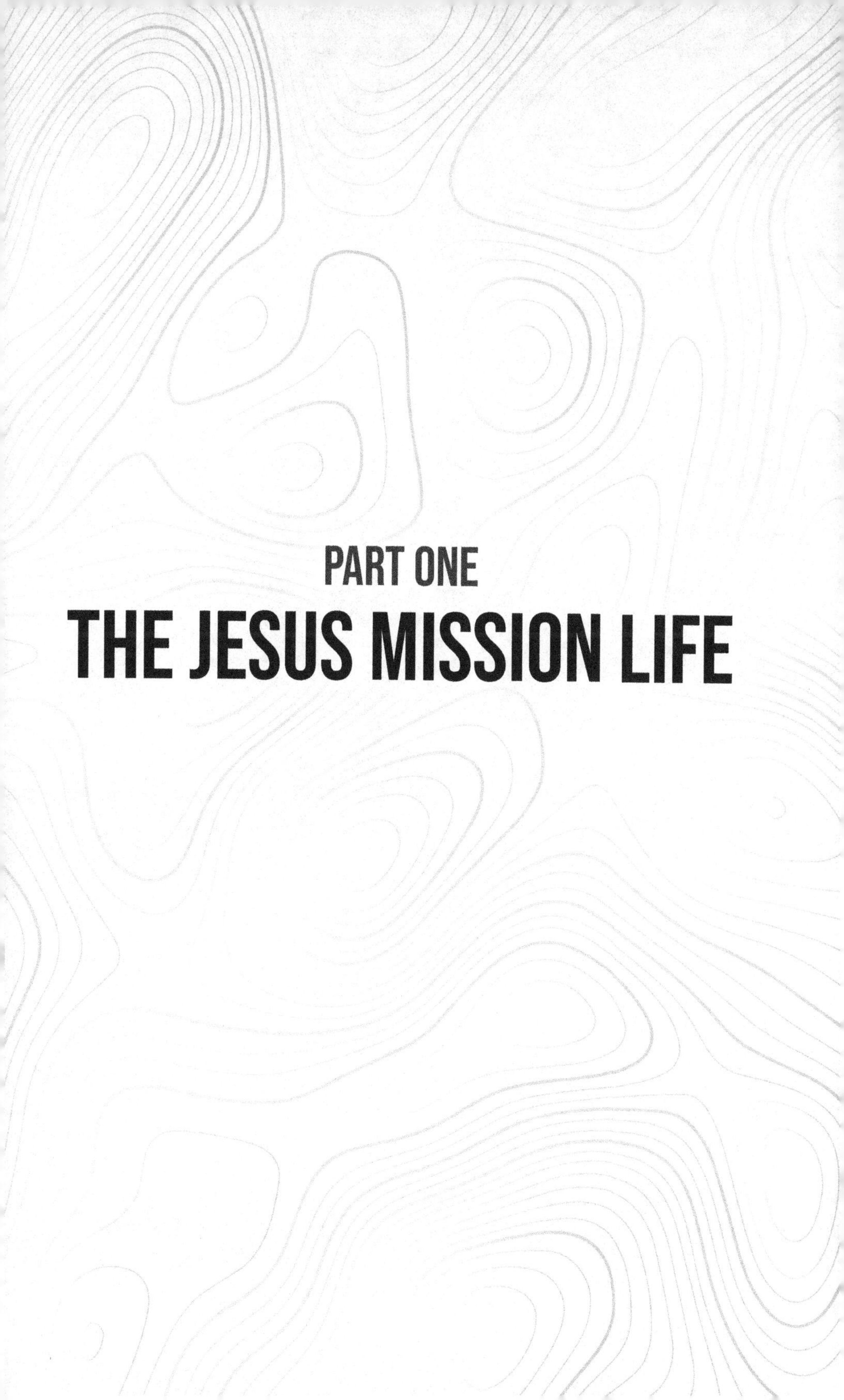

PART ONE

# THE JESUS MISSION LIFE

For I am convinced that … nothing can separate us from the love of God that is in Christ Jesus our Lord. (Romans 8:38–39)

Chapter 

# Breathing New Air

*What is that smell?*

This was the question that came flying at me in my early days of learning to cook. It was the smell of burnt. Burnt everything. Smoke filled the house, doors were wide open, and fans were trying to blow out the old air so we could breathe new air. There is no shortage of life moments when the air we breathe is smoky, stale, and pungent with odors that make us long for new air. As a teen, my buddy and I drove past a home on fire and helped evacuate people from the smoky death trap. Once outside in the fresh air, our instructions were to breathe.

Breathing new air is a must, especially when the air carries more than scent but is also toxic. New air saves us, gives us vitality inside, helps our brains function, and carries health to our lungs, hearts, and the rest of our bodies. Anyone who has spent time with a loved one attached to an oxygen tank has seen firsthand how quickly bad air harms and good air helps.

You and I live in a pretty broken world, and we are pretty broken people, too. The "air" we breathe is filled with lies and hate. We breathe air that pushes fear into our spiritual lungs, crippling the healthy flow of God's grace to our minds and hearts. The air of politics, self-doubt, anger, past hurts, and sinful choices is thick and makes our need for new air desperate.

I was in India, and it was over a hundred degrees and pouring rain; the air was thick and hard to breathe. Another time, I was serving villages in the Himalayan mountains, and we were at 18,000 feet above sea level. The air was thin, and it was very hard to breathe. Both situations made for the need to breathe new air, for without new air, all of my activity was limited. How about a million-dollar question to launch into a book on building a Jesus Mission Life:

**What is the air we must breathe if we are to live a Jesus Mission Life?**

It is very rare in my ministry experience that someone follows Jesus because of a final piece of information that was provided. Rarely do I see a person follow after Jesus primarily because of facts and statistics. The people who are healthiest in life and ministry all have one common "air" they breathe: *the love of God.*

Knowing is important. Truth matters in every way. The need for others to know Jesus is a strong driver in my life. Satisfaction, joy, peace, and meaning in my life all play a factor in a Jesus Mission Life, but by far, the air I breathe most deeply is the love of God. These other motives might be contributors to knowing and relying on the love God has for me, but the "new air" I am desperate for, the air that fills my spiritual lungs and gives me life, is God's love.

Paul the Apostle was the worst. As Saul the Pharisee, he arrested, killed, and jailed Christians with a fury and drive the world has rarely seen. His truth was offended. His religion was challenged. His whole commitment to life was threatened, and he was determined to stop these new followers of Jesus. What he found was that he couldn't stop them from breathing the new air of God's love, which made him even more furious.

Once Saul met the living Christ in person, this new air also filled his lungs. The God of Heaven, instead of crushing Saul for his sin, loved and welcomed him into his family, forgave his sin, and gave him a new name and a new mission (Acts 9). As Paul, he was never the same again. He went on to write thirteen books of the New Testament, the love of God compelling him to give every ounce of his being to a Jesus Mission Life.

In one of Paul's letters, the book of Romans chapter 8, Paul stops to give a personal view of God's love for him and for each of us. He laid out in detail God's beautiful rescue plan, writing of the overwhelming love of God and His inclusive grace. Jesus's sacrifice on the cross makes it possible for us to know God, and the resurrection of Jesus seals forever the satisfaction of God for all who come to Him by faith. The very moment we trust Christ, we begin a friendship with God that leads each of us to the most fulfilling partnership with Him. This is a plan that has been in the loving heart of God before creation, and now we can call God our Father because the Spirit of God lives in us. In the end, all will be just as God desires.

In response to these truths, Paul asks four questions and provides "new air" answers to each one. These questions and answers are the "new air" Paul breathed and the air we are to breathe, too:

> What, then, shall we say in response to these things? If God is for us, who can be against us? He who did not spare his own Son, but gave him up for us all—how will he not also, along with him, graciously give us all things? Who will bring any charge against those whom God has chosen? It is God who justifies. Who then is the one who condemns? No one. Christ Jesus who died—more than that, who was raised to life—is at the right hand of God and is also interceding for us. Who shall separate us from the love of Christ? Shall trouble or hardship or persecution or famine or nakedness or danger or sword? As it is written: "For your sake we face death all day long; we are considered as sheep to be slaughtered." No, in all these things we are more than conquerors through him who loved us. For I am convinced that neither death nor life, neither angels nor demons, neither the present nor the future, nor any powers, neither height nor depth, nor anything else in all creation, will be

able to separate us from the love of God that is in Christ Jesus our Lord. (Romans 8:31–39)

These questions are not just a quiz we take to confirm our understanding of grace; rather, these questions are the springboard for shouting a truth that is our new air. So what shall we say in response to these things? Let's look at the four foundational questions Paul asked for us to have a friendship and partnership with Jesus.

## QUESTION ONE: "WHAT, THEN, SHALL WE SAY IN RESPONSE TO THESE THINGS? IF GOD IS FOR US, WHO CAN BE AGAINST US?"

Romans 8:31 sets the expectation of great love that those who are loved can respond. And our response is a bold and clear declaration that "If God is for us, who can be against us?" Pause, read that again, and replace the word "if" with the word "since" and read it out loud. Pause, read it again, remove the rhetorical question mark at the end, and put an exclamation mark. Now, let's write a power sentence together:

**GOD IS FOR ME!**

These four words answer the question, "What shall we say in response to all of these things?" God is for me! Oh, man, what a powerful four words! **GOD IS FOR ME!** Go ahead and shout it if you want. Considering all that Jesus has done to reach you, **"GOD IS FOR ME"** seems to be the appropriate thing to say in response to all of these things. Breathe the new air!

Once, when I was speaking to several hundred students, I noticed that sitting right in the center of the room were six young men who were self-described Satan worshippers. They came to make a show and frighten people. These guys were dressed in their black clothes, had darkened eyes, fingernails all painted black, and wore upside-down crosses and pentagrams around their necks. "Satan is our God" was displayed for all to see. During my talk, they were trying to curse me, and possibly their greatest intention was that they were trying to intimidate and frighten the people around them.

When the distraction grew too much, I paused and stood directly in front of them. Speaking directly to these six boys now, I said, "Do you not know who my God is? Do you not understand how great and powerful He is? Do you not see that your god was created by my God, and when your god rebelled, he was kicked out of heaven by my God—showing my God to be greater? Your god wants to destroy you, to hold you in captivity to shame, fear, and anger, but my God came to rescue me, make me His own, and set me free from sin and death. I am not afraid of you; none of us are. It does not matter who your god is—ours is Jesus Christ! This is what we say to you: **OUR GOD, JESUS CHRIST, IS FOR US,** so who cares who is against us?"

With that, everyone in the room was stunned and silent, especially the six Satanists. One by one, the rest of the students grew in their confidence and began to clap, cheer, and applaud. Why? Because what we say in response to all of these things is, **"GOD IS FOR ME!"**

One struggle many Jesus followers seem to have is that our words are in more response to life, pain, sickness, brokenness, or our wounds. Fear, shame, and anger have surrounded us, keeping us from a growing confidence in the God who loves us. **Don't miss this!** In Romans 8, we are not asked to say words of response to sin, but rather to say words in response to God and His love. We are asked to respond to what God has done and is doing, not what life or the enemy is doing. I recently heard a preacher telling a frenzied audience, "Speak to your shame and tell it to go away. Speak to your pain and tell it to stop. Speak to your sickness and tell it to be gone." Stop it! God is saying, "Speak to what I have done, not what sin or Satan can do." Breathe the new air—**GOD IS FOR ME!**

I have a friend who was diagnosed with lung cancer. He did all the treatments he could possibly do, all of the surgeries, chemo, and radiation, and in the process, his eyes were on defeating cancer. The treatments nearly killed him, but when the words "You are in remission, today you are cancer-free" were spoken by the doctor, none of his past pain and struggle mattered. What do you say in response to this? I was his second call, and our conversation began with these four words, "I am cancer-free!" He spoke those words like they came from breathing new air.

The Bible tells us that each of us is dead in sin, broken, and unable to fix the mess into which we were born and now choose to live. In one sense, we have a spiritual cancer and need treatment. God's plan from before creation was to become our treatment, to heal the spiritual death sentence in our souls. Jesus is so incredible! He took all the treatments on Himself, which He knew would only end in one thing—His death. This is what the cross is about: Jesus taking on the treatment for our spiritual sickness, our sin, and the death sentence of our souls.

So if God is for us, who can be against us? Okay, so just how *for us* is He? How much can He do? How much is He *willing* to do? **Everything!** What Jesus accomplished on the cross opened the door to an eternal promise God made that when we come to Him by faith—we are adopted into His family, made new in His likeness, given His life, and sealed with the gift of God the Holy Spirit, who, by the way, now takes up residence within us. Let's add to our sentence:

**GOD IS FOR ME! WHO CARES WHO IS AGAINST ME? GOD IS FOR ME!**

How do we know? God started the process by giving us His only Son, not sparing Him from taking the treatment for our sin! And since this is the starting place, how will He not also make every advantage and benefit of His love available to us? Or as Paul said, "give us freely all things." Jesus spared nothing, so why would He leave us there? The answer? *He won't.* When God gave us His Son, Jesus, He gave us everything else that would make knowing Jesus worthwhile.

For each of us, the love of God is a compelling entry point to knowing Jesus. But the love of God is also an overwhelming moment-by-moment way of living our lives each day. The apostle John, one of

Jesus's best friends, said it this way: "And so we know and rely on the love God has for us" (1 John 4:16). Like Paul, John is confirming that the love of God is much more than getting into heaven; it is something that is real, and we rely upon it as we invest each day in the Mission of Jesus. God's love is the air we breathe.

There is so much more that comes with Jesus as we live our lives. If God gives us His life, adopts us into His family, and fills us with His Spirit, doesn't it make sense that there is more? That is Paul's argument for new air.

As a kid learning to swim, I would take a deep breath and kick my way across the pool. But what I quickly discovered was that to keep swimming, I needed a regular dose of new air. Good news! Jesus is not about teaching us just to swim across a pool; He is teaching us to swim everywhere. "He who did not spare his own Son, but gave him up for us all—how will he not also, along with him, graciously give us all things?" (Romans 8:32). We breathe new air every day.

Before I move to the next "breathe new air" question," here is a short list describing what knowing Jesus continually brings into our lives. This is the air we breathe.

*I am loved.*
*I am forgiven.*
*I am strengthened.*
*I have His Mission.*
*I am a child of God.*
*I have a home in heaven.*
*I am healed.*
*I am comforted.*
*I am set free.*
*I am made whole.*
*I am strong.*
*I am sealed.*

*I am used.*
*I am given God's wisdom.*
*I am fruitful for eternal impact.*
*I am protected.*

### QUESTION TWO: "WHO WILL BRING ANY CHARGE AGAINST THOSE WHOM GOD HAS CHOSEN?"

In Romans 8:33, Paul asks a second new air question. "Who will bring any charge against those whom God has chosen?" Stop the presses. I know the answer to this question, and so do the people and the devil, too! Get in line because we are about to make a list. It is not hard to find accusers making charges against me. I have voices in my head shouting, "Guilty as charged!" Guess what? I did the sin, and I am guilty. Shhhh, your secret is safe with me, but you are guilty, too; we all are. Or are we? In Christ, the new air answer is no. Why? As Paul answers, "It is God who justifies."

The work of Jesus is complete, and because of Jesus, we are not guilty anymore. Read those eight words again. **Because of Jesus, we are not guilty anymore.** In Bible words, Romans 5:1 says, "Therefore, since we have been justified through faith, we have peace with God through our Lord Jesus Christ." To be "justified by faith" is a legal term that more than makes us acquitted of the crime but actually declares us as no longer accused. When we are justified by faith, it's as if we never did the sin. Why? Because Jesus took all our guilt and sin upon Himself when He died on the cross. One of my favorite sentences in the Bible is from 2 Corinthians 5:21, "God made him who had no sin to be sin for us, so that in him we might become the righteousness of God."

Paul writes that God took the one without sin (Jesus) and made Him to be sin for us. Wait, just breathe that in. That is new air! What love God must have for us that He would take on all our sin by becoming our sin. Why? So that in Jesus, we become the righteousness of God. So that in Jesus, when the Father looks at us, all He sees is the righteousness of His Son.

Jesus traded our sin for His righteousness, and by faith, this trade applies to each of us, so we can answer with 100 percent confidence the second question: "Who will bring any charge against those whom God has chosen? No one! Because in Christ we are justified. Because Jesus became sin on our behalf, in Christ and in the eyes of the Father, we are in possession of the righteousness of Christ Himself. Thank you, Jesus! Because of Him there is nothing left to accuse us of. All our sin—past, present, future—was placed on Jesus. This is why Paul answered the second question, "It is Christ Jesus who justifies."

Jesus's life, death, and resurrection mean that by faith, we are clean and free from the impact, power, and effects of sin. Amazing grace, right? His love does not just liberate us and make us better people; His love settles the debt our sin accrued by giving us the righteousness of Christ instead. His love paid that debt and made us forever clean before God. We became friends of God. This is the new air we breathe.

The answer to the question, "Who will bring any charge against those whom God has chosen?" is no one because the only one who has every right to bring this charge chose to take the charges upon Himself. Whenever I teach these verses, I often get two questions:

**First, "What do I do about the sins I commit every day?"** The apostle John answered this question in his first letter:

> If we confess our sins, he is faithful and just and will forgive us our sins and purify us from all unrighteousness. (1 John 1:9)

The word *confess* is a word that means to agree with what is true. When I confess my sin, I agree that what I did was wrong. Confession is the simple act of being in full agreement with God about sin, and this involves repenting, too. When I confess, I turn away from my sin to God. Confession also agrees that God's solution to my sin is enough. It is not a three-steps-to-feeling-better formula. I agree that what Jesus did was enough and that I am truly, and in every way the righteousness of Christ in His eyes.

Confession aligns our hearts and minds to what God has already done in Christ, giving our conscience a chance to be clean, too. Confession clears the air we breathe and allows us to breathe in deeply the new air of God's love, grace, and truth. Confession makes our hearts right with God, helping us agree with God that Jesus could condemn us, but instead, He took all the condemnation upon Himself.

**The second question I get is: "If I am forgiven for all my sin, past, present, and future, why do I feel bad about my sin?"** In short, the answer has to do with the grace of God at work in you by God the Holy Spirit. When you first believed in Christ, God sent the Holy Spirit to live inside you (Ephesians 1:13–14). Of the many reasons for this, one is to help give you a right response to the sin we seem to do far too often. This right response is to be convicted of three things: sin, righteousness, and judgment, for Scripture tell us, "When He comes, He will prove the world to be in the wrong [convict] about sin and righteousness and judgment" (John 16:8:).

First off, the bad. Sin brings death and destroys. Sin hurts God, hurts me, and hurts others. Sin drives a relational wedge between friends. For Jesus followers, sin cuts us off from the promise of freedom and joy, robbing us of the life we have been made for by Jesus. God, in His great love for us, wants to bring full alignment to who we are in Christ with how we live in Christ. We have been given God the Holy Spirit to make this happen. It is in this alignment that we find our freedom and joy. God the Holy Spirit convicts my conscience of sin to show me where to grow and where the Jesus life I have been given could be diminished by sin. Confession and repentance are how God the Holy Spirit brings realignment with Jesus and His followers. When I sin as a Jesus follower, sin does not break the relationship, but it certainly impacts the alignment of who Christ has made me and how I live.

I have no fashion sense at all. None. My only fashion rule is "it has to be comfortable." Sometimes, when I get dressed, I hear a voice that says, "Nope. Go change because that doesn't work. That does not fit you. You shouldn't wear that; it is not your best." God the Holy Spirit speaks this way about my sin. "Leonard, lies do not fit you—tell the truth." "Leonard, you never look good in envy—confess that and change." "Leonard, you were made for more than the temporary joy your sin can provide; don't get comfortable in wearing that." This is the sin-convicting role of the Holy Spirit in a Jesus Mission Life.

Second of all, righteousness—the very place where things are right with God. The Holy Spirit reveals to Jesus followers what is righteous in the eyes of God and then convicts us when we are not living in that place. When I sin, I miss the beauty and sweetness of the gift of LIFE in the places where God's grace has planted me. I miss who I am in Christ. I miss who God is making me and the very mission He has planned for me.

Sin robs me of confidence in the love of Jesus that reaches me, and when His love reaches me, it sends me on a mission in this world. God tells us over and over again that we have been set free for a reason. The Holy Spirit shows us how to live more consistently and confidently into His righteousness. He produces in us the very life of Jesus by convicting, revealing, and then strengthening us to live fully immersed in the love and Mission of Jesus. Take a minute now to read Galatians 5:22–23 to see what living with the Holy Spirit can be like.

God the Holy Spirit convicts us of judgment, too. When we sin, the Bible says that Jesus stands as our advocate before the Father, interceding (speaking on our behalf) and declaring us righteous before God. I sometimes find this truth hard to apply in my daily life, so my response to sin is to hide it, deny it, or change the rules and call what God calls sin not sin. Whenever I hide, deny, or change the rules in response to sin, I have forgotten how God has already judged sin. When I hide, deny, or replace the rules, in a very real sense, I act as the advocate for my sin (speaking on my behalf about my sin) by doing or saying something other than what Jesus has already done and said. Jesus took my sin. God the Holy Spirit reminds me of this truth and convicts my heart in such a way as to immerse myself in the death and resurrection of Jesus.

God's love is so great, and truthfully, I am so small that in order for me to actually answer question number two, I need God the Holy Spirit to convict me of my sin, of my righteousness provided by Christ, and of the judgment poured out on Jesus to make this true. *Breathe in the new air.*

## QUESTION THREE: "WHO THEN IS THE ONE WHO CONDEMNS?"

Oh, man, verse 34 is so good! Who condemns us? The word *condemns* here means to render worthy of judgment. This question is about who gets to decide we are worthy of God's judgment and punishment.

The answer? *No one.* Not you, not me, not anyone. In Christ, there is **NO CONDEMNATION.**

> Therefore, there is now no condemnation for those who are in Christ Jesus. (Romans 8:1)

As Jesus followers, we are not able to be condemned once we are in Christ because the work of Jesus has removed everything we could be condemned for. The death of Jesus was our condemnation. The resurrection of Jesus seals God's satisfaction with this truth. In Christ, we are not condemned anymore. Read those last seven words again out loud, applying them to yourself.

**IN CHRIST, I AM NOT CONDEMNED ANYMORE!**

The raising of Jesus is how He executed the truth that "In Christ, I am not condemned anymore!" The resurrection guarantees that this truth stays "true" in two places. First, in heaven. Jesus stands forever as proof that I am no longer condemned. Second, in me. Jesus intercedes for me. He is my advocate and speaks on my behalf, saying to the

Father and to me through the Holy Spirit—**NO CONDEMNATION**! Breathe the new air. In Christ, we are now un-condemnable.

### QUESTION FOUR: "WHO SHALL SEPARATE US FROM THE LOVE OF CHRIST?"

Cue the lights and sirens, get the band on the field, and start them a marching. Get the parade rolling and start skywriting with planes. This question matters—a lot. Verse 35 asks, "Who shall separate us from the love of Christ?" Paul's answers to these four questions move from the theological to the personal because of the theological. The first three answers are found in simple good gospel theology. This one is found in a personal friendship with Jesus, one based on Him and His great love.

Who shall separate us from the love of Christ? Can circumstances? Nope! When Paul listed these things, he spoke from his own experience of what happens when the love of God reaches you and then sends you. Paul suffered hardship—he was stranded in the sea for days and experienced loss of food, loss of status, and loss of relationships and dreams, all in the service of the God who loved him.

> I have been crucified with Christ and I no longer live, but Christ lives in me. The life I now live in the body, I live by faith in the Son of God, who loved me and gave himself for me. (Galatians 2:20)

Because of the love Christ had for him, Paul was beaten, whipped, stoned, left for dead, left naked and bleeding, imprisoned, and threatened with the sword. But despite these things, look again at how he described his life.

> Shall trouble or hardship or persecution or famine or nakedness or danger or sword? As it is written: "For your sake we face death all day long; we are considered as sheep to be slaughtered." (Romans 8:35–36)

Verse 36 is a quote from another Scripture in Psalm 46, a psalm that declares that when we are loved by God, and that love sends us on His

Mission, it is always worthwhile, no matter the struggle.

Being loved by God and then being sent by God were the reasons for Paul's hardships, but they were the new air that sent him forward. Paul suffered great persecution at the hands of many as he lived a Jesus Mission Life. With great boldness, he says that in all these things, we are more than conquerors. He is NOT saying that we are super-conquerors. He is NOT saying we are "take names and kick backside champions." He is NOT saying that the devil doesn't have a chance with us on the field. Paul IS saying that we are much, much more than conquerors.

In Christ, we are much more than an overcomer or a conqueror; we are children of the living God. We are sons and daughters who cry "Abba, Father." We are friends of Jesus with the mind of Christ. We are temples in whom Jesus lives by the Holy Spirit. We are ambassadors who speak the very words of Christ. Why? Because Jesus has already conquered. He already declared, "It is finished." He already took down the wall separating people from God. He already defeated sin and death. Jesus is more than a conqueror; He is God with skin, full of grace and truth. We are also more than conquerors because we are children of God, in whom the Spirit of God lives. We are set aside for the Mission of God because of the love of God. We are something much more than a conqueror—we are friends and partners with God. Breathe this new air.

Because this is true, Paul wrote some of the most incredible words ever written. This truth had a profound impact on his life, and it convinced him of God's love.

> For I am convinced that neither death nor life, neither angels nor demons, neither the present nor the future, nor any powers, neither height nor depth, nor anything else in all creation, will be able to separate us from the love of God that is in Christ Jesus our Lord. (Romans 8:38–39)

What does it take to convince you that you bought the right car? You drive it, and it performs amazingly. It brings you joy. It gets you where you want to go. What convinces you that you have the right job? You like it, you are fulfilled, it pays your bills, and it provides for the family, just to name a few things. We become convinced of something over time and with experience. This is what the word means when Paul boldly states, "I am convinced." He meant, "I have come to know through experience and testing and life that NOTHING can separate us from the love of God. God loves me, and God loves you, and the love of God is bigger than we know. Once loved as a friend, always loved as a friend" (paraphrase mine).

Do you know what convinced people do? They breathe different air. I was in a small cave when I was a kid, nothing dangerous but certainly smelly. The scent of every animal that relieved itself was in that cave, some of the substance, too. I couldn't wait to breathe different air. Once, while traveling in North India, my room had a sewage leak, and I couldn't wait to breathe different air. I have driven behind gross polluter trucks and cars that blow exhaust into every corner of my open-air Jeep, and I couldn't wait to breathe different air. I have had times in my life when I was uncertain of a medical test, a grade I needed to pass a class, a friendship that seemed to be crumbling, and the air I was breathing was suffocating and smothering my confidence.

When we lack the confidence that God indeed loves us, we will struggle to know how real and useful God's love is. God's love is the air we are supposed to breathe. When this "Air" gets diluted or polluted, we are limited in so many ways. Stale and loveless air limits our ability and often our willingness to love others. Stale air limits our friendships, keeping us from growing. Stale air hides and keeps us from experiencing just how loved we really are. Breathing stale air never helps. But when we are convinced, we breathe different air.

Convinced people breathe the air of freedom and joy. Convinced people breathe the air of being fully known and fully loved at the same time. Convinced people are more generous. Convinced people have more courage. Convinced people see life with different eyes. Convinced people get unstuck from the same ruts of faith that have trapped them before. Convinced people have a different strength because they breathe different air. Convinced people live Jesus Mission Lives. This is the air Paul breathed.

What can we do if we were truly convinced these sentences are 100 percent true that "nothing can separate us from the love of God"? Try finishing this sentence a few times for application:

"Because I am convinced NOTHING can separate me from the love of God that is in Christ Jesus my Lord, I can … I will … I have … I must … ."

For Paul, all of these words are his way of saying that we are more loved than we know. He prays in Ephesians 3 that we would come to know this love that surpasses knowledge. This is Paul's prayer because he knows that when we breathe the new air of God's love, we will also be sent by God to love others. Only when we love others will the depth of God's love be known by us.

The starting place for a Jesus Mission Life is the love of God! God's love is a personal part of His rescue Mission for you and is also how you become a part of His rescue Mission for others.

In the Gospel of John, Jesus gives us a command that essentially says we have been loved by Him, so we should also love others. This is not a simple encouragement to be nice but an actual call to mission, the Mission of Jesus.

> A new command I give you: Love one another. As I have loved you, so you must love one another. By this everyone will know that you are my disciples, if you love one another. (John 13:34–35)

I grew up hiking, fishing, and hunting in the Sierra Mountains in Northern California. As I would trek these mountains, I would often come upon a small body of water and try to find it on my map. One reason I wanted to find it on my map was because if it was on my map, it was fresh water; if it wasn't on my map, it was a runoff pond and on its way to being stale. The difference between a runoff pond and a small lake was that water flowed into and out of the body of water. That difference, water flowing in and flowing out, was the difference between water that was filled with life and water that was stagnant. The crazy part of my high mountain adventures is that some runoff ponds looked more alive and had more beauty than small lakes.

When it comes to the love of God, the plan of God is to be lakes and not runoff ponds. What God desires is that our lives have places where the love of God enters and is seen by us. These four questions help us see the height, depth, width, and breadth of God's love. These four questions show us the places where God's love flows into our lives. When God's love arrives, it brings new air, fresh water, life, and refreshment.

But the love of God, by design, is too good to keep to ourselves. The love of God is too good for me to hold on to, and it mandates me to have a place in my life where it also flows to others. In order for me to breathe in fully the new air of God's love, I must exhale that love to others. This is a Jesus Mission Life—a life being filled with God's love and releasing that love to others. What God so generously causes to flow to me must also flow through me.

As you will read throughout this book, the Mission of Jesus is to seek and save the lost (Luke 19:10). Jesus did this by giving His life as a ransom for many (Matthew 20:28). This was His Mission even before creation. To get His rescue Mission accomplished, He suffered and died on the cross and then rose again. To make His Mission a global one, Jesus recruited disciples who would make disciples, whose disciples would also make disciples. Then Jesus said, "Here is your mission. Everywhere you go, make disciples" (Matthew 28:19, paraphrase mine).

Jesus told His disciples they would become disciple-makers as they followed Him. He loved them, trained them, and commissioned them to make disciples because now they were disciple-makers. Disciple-making is not a task we do because Jesus is awesome; it is someone we become because we are loved by God.

Let me finish this chapter by encouraging you to contemplate the four foundational questions for friendship and partnership with Jesus for yourself, using the answers Paul gave in Romans 8:31–39.

- What, then, shall we say in response to these things?
- Who will bring any charge against those whom God has chosen?
- Who then is the one who condemns?
- Who shall separate us from the love of Christ?

# *Stepping into Jesus's Mission*

## A prayer you can pray today:

*Dear Jesus,*

*Thank You for loving me so well. Your love really is the air I need. Will You help me grow my confidence in the ways You have loved me? Will You help me share with others the love You so freely give? I am so grateful to You for your love.*

*Amen*

## Some questions to move you forward:

What is something you discovered in this chapter about breathing the new air of God's love?

What does it mean to you that God loves you?

Share a time in your life, past or present, when breathing the new air of God's love was or is a struggle.

Which of Paul's four questions and answers resonate most with your heart and why?

When you need to breathe the new air of God's love, what is your "go-to" to find this new air?

What or when was a time when God's love for you gave you new air?

What is one thing you will begin to do daily to find and breathe the new air of God's love?

## A step to take as you go:

Take some time this week to write down on a 3" x 5" card Romans 8:31–39. Do your best to memorize it. If you are reading this book in a group or with another person, try to quote it from memory when you sit together.

The fear of the Lord is the beginning of wisdom, and knowledge of the Holy One is understanding. (Proverbs 9:10)

# Chapter 2

## If You Know, You Know

There are several common and some less-common sentences that talk about what we do know and what we do not know. "God only knows" has found its way into a conversation or two. Business leaders and coaches say, "You don't know what you don't know." They usually follow it up with, "You learn what you don't know, and then you know what you know."

"I know it like the back of my hand" usually means that I am very, very familiar with the topic. In my heart, I just know. I know that I know. I know everything about them (best-friend speak). "You never know." "Nobody knows." "I only know this one thing." When a hunch pays off, we say, "I knew it!" And when it doesn't, we say, "Well, what do you know." Of course, one of my favorites is "I just don't know." Whenever my dad was about to have a serious conversation with me, he always started the conversation with these words, "Well, son, I don't know …" or "Don't tell your mother I said this," but that is a different subject.

When I use the word "know" in this chapter, I am not talking about compiling information. I am referring to gaining through experience actual and useful knowledge that can be used in such a way that impacts others and can be passed on to other people. One of the Bible words for *to know* is to gain assurance of something through experience. Another is *to know* because of closeness, sometimes used to describe intimate relations between a husband and wife.

Did you know that God places a lot of importance on knowing? He says that wisdom begins when we know Him. He says that Jesus came so we might truly know God. Jesus told His friends that knowing the Father would be very important for their lives and mission and knowing Jesus is the will of the Father. The apostle John wrote five books of the New Testament with the stated purpose that we would know Jesus. In fact, all of the writers of the New Testament wrote with the same goal: that we would *know* God and that in *knowing* God, we would also *know* and live a Jesus Mission Life.

Peter, one of the people who knew Jesus best, wrote that God had actually provided everything we need for life and godliness through our **knowledge** of Jesus:

> His divine power has given us everything we need for a godly life through our knowledge of him who called us by his own glory and goodness. (2 Peter 1:3)

Once, while training a group of pastors and leaders in West Africa, I asked if they knew Jesus. The immediate response was "Yes," and a few were shocked that I would even ask such a question. I paused for a few seconds, sat down, and said, "Tell me what you know." It was interesting because most of the answers were facts about Jesus, "He lived in Israel." "He died." "He rose again." "He did Miracles." "He had disciples." Very little was about knowing Jesus. "He rescued me." "He forgives me daily." "His love strengthens my soul and gives me courage." "He is the voice in creation." "He is the redeemer of the world."

I was in another country and asked the group of leaders to take ten minutes and brag on Jesus. I said, "Tell me how great He is, how amazing He is, how big He is," and the room fell silent. I was confused because these men and women had great faith. I came to realize that so much of our faith in Christ is focused on what Jesus can do for us rather than who He is. I've had this very same experience in the USA. I often get more of what Jesus did in the first century than who Jesus is now.

In 1 John, Jesus's friend begins his letter with an invitation, you guessed it—to know Jesus. Check out how he puts it:

> That which was from the beginning, which we have heard, which we have seen with our eyes, which we have looked at and our hands have touched—this we proclaim concerning the Word of life. The life appeared; we have seen it and testify to it, and we proclaim to you the eternal life, which was with the Father and has appeared to us. We proclaim to you what we have seen and heard, so that you also may have fellowship with us. And our fellowship is with the Father and with his Son, Jesus Christ. We write this to make our joy complete. This is the message we have heard from him and declare to you: God is light; in him there is no darkness at all. (1 John 1:1–5)

In summary, John's simple invitation is, "We know Jesus, and He is so amazing; we want you to know this amazing Jesus, too." When you know Him, really know Him, there is eternal life, community, relationship with the Father, and joy and light—the kind of light that can only come from THE LIGHT OF THE WORLD. Oh, and don't forget fellowship that is driven by our common love and knowledge of Jesus.

If you dig deeper into this idea of knowing God throughout the whole Bible, you will see the impact knowing God has on lives. Words like wisdom, confidence, assurance, boldness, hope, trust, faith, love, peace, and joy directly flow from truly knowing Jesus. Our salvation, our navigation in life, our fruitfulness, and our eternity all center on the kind of knowing the Bible describes, both experiential and personal. You will also discover the impact of not knowing God. Fear, isolation, lostness, and living without a compass or wisdom are all byproducts of not knowing God. Second Thessalonians says that those who leave this life without knowing Jesus will be cut off from the presence of God forever (1:9). So you see, knowing Jesus is essential to our whole life here and into eternity.

Over the next few pages, I want to focus more intently on the impact of truly knowing Jesus. I hope some words will bless you and give you the feels. I pray some words will encourage you in your pursuit of knowing Jesus better and challenge you to examine whether you really know Him and, if you do, how well you know Him. The goal is to take your "knowing" on an impactful journey from your head to your heart to your hands and then to your feet. This is a Jesus Mission Life. As Peter says, when we know Jesus, and this knowledge is increasing, we become fruitful and stable.

> For if you possess these qualities in increasing measure, they will keep you from being ineffective and unproductive in your knowledge of our Lord Jesus Christ. (2 Peter 1:8)

## GOD'S PLAN IS THAT WE KNOW HIM AND JOIN HIM

From creation until now, God's desire is for people to really know Him. The heartbeat of Jesus is that we would become children of God and know the Father. **God expressed this desire by giving us a soul—the place inside of us where Jesus is most able to be known and heard.** The soul is the eternal part of people that connects our hearts and minds to Jesus so that we can willingly choose to love Him and know Him. By giving us a soul, God demonstrated His desire that we know Him forever, not for just ten, twenty, fifty, or eighty years.

**God also expressed His desire that we know Him by making us in His image.** To bear the image of God is to be *like* Him, not to be Him. His image in us gives humanity a unique ability to connect with Him because He shared a part of Himself with people. He did not share His image with anything else in creation. The image of God is what makes us creative. It's what gifts us with emotions and why we have free will. His image is what allows us to love and be loved. It makes our work meaningful, offers us hope, and lets us become both friends and partners with God.

When sin entered the world, death came physically and spiritually, and this death affected our bodies and all of creation. Sin entered and distorted the very image of God within us. So God gave us another gift, the greatest gift of all—Jesus, whose Mission is to heal our souls by taking away our sin and restoring the image of God within us.

The entire Bible was written to explain God's plan. It is God's invitation for mankind to know Jesus, and in knowing Him, we can become friends with God. As God's friends, we join Him in what HE wants to be done, and we become His partners, too. The Bible is about Jesus and His Mission, serving as an invitation to God's image-bearers to come close to Him and join Him on His Mission. Chapter 3 will say much more about this.

Some of the most shocking words Jesus said while on the earth is that there will be a time when people will come before Him, and His response to them will be, "Go away because we do not know each other." As a kid, I remember reading these words and feeling really nervous, as if there was a chance of me going to hell and not knowing I was "out" until I got there. In other passages, Jesus told stories of people who didn't know Him but thought they did.

One story is about a rich guy who gave three not-so-rich guys some gold and then took a trip. The expectation was that the three not-so-rich guys would invest the gold, and upon the return of the rich guy, a report would be given. Long story short, two of the not-so-rich guys doubled the original investment, and the third not-so-rich guy did not invest or even make any interest in a bank; instead, he buried the gold in the ground and did nothing. The reason the third not-so-rich guy gave for not doing anything with the gold was centered on what he thought he knew about the rich guy. You can read this story in Matthew 25:14–28.

My point is not to make us question if we are in or out but rather to invite each of us to examine if what we think we know about Jesus gets in the way of actually knowing Jesus. Like my friends in West Africa, what they thought they knew was so wrapped up in tradition and religious activities they struggled to tell me about the Jesus they actually knew. So, what does Jesus say is the evidence that we actually know Him?

Let's look at four ways God measures how well we know Jesus. Three come from the words of Jesus Himself, and the final one comes from the book of Wisdom, Proverbs.

### One—Knowing Jesus Means Loving Others Everywhere We Go

> A new command I give you: Love one another. As I have loved you, so you must love one another. By this everyone will know that you are my disciples, if you love one another. (John 13:34–35) (Take time to read all of John 13.)

Jesus spoke these words as He shared a last meal with the disciples before He was arrested and nailed to the cross. The disciples were in the room where Jesus washed their feet and commanded that they imitate Him. This took place on the night Jesus was betrayed. As they sat together, Jesus told His disciples that people would know they were really His disciples by how they loved one another. *Stop.* I hope we can see that it is very important to Jesus that His disciples are known as His disciples. How does this happen? They are known as His disciples by the way they love others.

Many Rabbis in Jesus's day had disciples, and Jesus was teaching His friends that what would convince people that these guys were HIS disciples was love. Jesus's words were much more than them name-dropping and saying they were close with Jesus. Jesus was saying that He wants everyone to know that His guys share the same mission, heart, passion, and practice as their Rabbi. How will this become known? The evidence is love.

This was Jesus's last night with His disciples, and He was preparing them to live the rest of their days with His Mission as their mission. Jesus was preparing them to live a Jesus Mission Life, telling them, "As you go from here and live on mission, the new commandment is to love as I love" (paraphrase mine). This whole night was strangely upside-down from what they were expecting. Jesus was acting in a way no other Rabbi in Jerusalem was acting. In this final Passover meal with His friends, Jesus was saying words and making claims that no other leader of disciples had ever made.

For nearly 1,500 years prior, the Passover had been a celebration of Israel's miraculous exodus from Egypt. The people had never celebrated any other meaning to the bread, the wine, or the meal. But Jesus, on this Passover, seized His final moments before the cross and resurrection to equip His disciples for His Mission.

The meal began with feet-washing. Not one Rabbi in all of Israel was washing the feet of his disciples because masters do not wash feet. But on this night, Jesus did, and in doing so, He gave His disciples an example of how to love others. The bread they shared represented suffering, escape, and freedom for the people of Israel. But that night, only in this room, the bread also represented Christ's body, which would soon be broken for them. The wine they drank represented a celebration of deliverance from Egypt, but only in this room was it a picture of the New Covenant—a new way of living with God.

I imagine the disciples' heads were spinning. Thoughts of "What the heck!" and "Did he just say that?" had to have filled their heads. "How could bread be your body?" "What do you mean broken for us?" "How could wine represent a New Covenant?" "What about the Old Covenant?" No person on that night in all of Israel was saying words like Jesus, except in an upper room in Jerusalem. Jesus, the Savior of the world, was speaking, and NOTHING was as it seemed.

Now, try to imagine the disciples' surprise when Jesus said, "Here comes a new commandment." "Wait, what about the other commandments?" "What about the Law?" Jesus's words and actions were turning everything upside down.

---

Side Note: The traditional Passover meal, as beautiful and rich and symbolic as it was, from that night on, was never the same for the disciples and their disciples. Because of Jesus's final Passover with His friends, to this day the Church models Jesus's words and teaching every time it breaks the bread and drinks the cup during communion.

---

In just a few hours, Jesus would be arrested, and not long after that, Jesus would be dead. In the crux of the moment, Jesus said, "People will know that you know Me and are on My Mission by how you love." If that was not enough, he added the measurement of "As I have loved you, now you go love others." By the way, there are tons of Scriptures that tell us this same truth. We know Jesus when we love others.

### Two—Knowing Jesus Means We Know His Voice

> The gatekeeper opens the gate for Him, and the sheep listen to His voice. He calls his own sheep by name and leads them out. When He has brought out all His own, He goes on ahead of them, and His sheep follow Him because they know His voice. (John 10:3b–4)

I was in the Himalayan mountains and saw a large sheep pen on the side of a hill. I discovered that it was often used by several shepherds at one time and that the sheep in the pen came from many flocks. In the morning, a shepherd would shout, give a whistle, and make a noise, and only his sheep would follow. His sheep knew his voice, and they followed. I immediately thought of Jesus's words from John 10.

What does Jesus sound like? Do you know? Is His voice loud and echoey like in the movies? Is His voice soft and whispery and hard to hear? Does Jesus even talk today? How can I be sure the voice I hear is really the voice of Jesus? These are such great questions to ask. Serving in ministry over the years, this topic has opened the door to countless personal and encouraging conversations about the voice of Jesus. I turn to John 10 often and read the words about how Jesus's sheep follow Him because they hear and know His voice.

In reality, sheep know the shepherd's voice because they are close to the shepherd and depend upon him for food, leading, and safety. I imagine that the more I depend upon Jesus as my Shepherd, the better I will know His voice. In fact, He identifies the people who know Him as one who hears His voice and follows.

In John 10, Jesus is speaking to the shepherds of Israel—the Pharisees and Sadducees. These religious leaders would have immediately known that Jesus was referring to the corruption of the priests written about in Ezekiel. In Ezekiel 34, the prophet condemns the shepherds of Israel and announces that God will someday come and be the Shepherd of Israel and beyond. Those listening that day would have this condemnation in mind from the prophet Ezekiel, and they would have recognized that Jesus was claiming to be God, the promised Good Shepherd.

Jesus's words in John 10 form the backdrop for Jesus saying that HIS sheep know HIS voice and they follow HIM. Time and time again, Jesus said that hearing should lead to doing; it should lead then to following, and it must lead to His Mission. His call to listeners, "Whoever has ears to hear, let him hear," stands as an invitation for people to pay closer attention to what He is actually saying.

Jesus is asking each one of us to learn His voice and listen to Him. He promises that when we do, He will lead us because He is the Good Shepherd. The closer I get to Him, the better I know His voice and the closer I follow. To follow Him is to live with Jesus as our King, His Kingdom as our kingdom, and His Kingdom Mission as our mission. As you will see in the next chapter, the Mission of Jesus is clear, and it is also clear that His Mission is to be ours.

### Three—We Know Jesus When We Live in Obedience to His Kingdom's Ways and Mission

The most famous sermon Jesus ever preached is called "The Sermon on the Mount," and His words are recorded for us in Matthew 5–7. This sermon marks out the mission and values for His Kingdom. The Sermon on the Mount serves both as an invitation to His Kingdom as well as an invitation to the mission of His Kingdom. For the next few pages, we will take a quick look at Jesus's words about His Kingdom and how living in His Kingdom evidences we know Him.

In context, Jesus is sitting, which is a posture a Rabbi would take when He was about to speak with authority. He calls His disciples close to Him and begins to teach them. There is also a crowd listening in as He speaks. His sermon is filled with words of contrast, wisdom, warnings, hope, and perspective. This message gives us words from King Jesus about His Kingdom.

Some of the most frightening words Jesus speaks while on earth are contained in the Sermon on the Mount:

> Not everyone who says to me, "Lord, Lord," will enter the kingdom of heaven, but only the one who does the will of my Father who is in heaven. Many will say to me on that day, "Lord, Lord, did we not prophesy in your name and in your name drive out demons and in your name perform many miracles?" Then I will tell them plainly, "I never knew you. Away from me, you evildoers!" (Matthew 7:21–23)

These are such heavy words, and reading them sometimes makes me want to say, "Stop it, Jesus, you are scaring me. It feels like you are telling me that I can be loyal to you all my life and still get the rejection notice in the end!" No, that is NOT what Jesus is saying. There is a greater context provided for us in both the ministry and Mission of Jesus and most directly in the sermon itself. These words were not written to be used against sincere people who fall short but to let His disciples know that His Kingdom has a standard and a mission.

To understand the Sermon on the Mount, it is essential to understand the Mission of Jesus. Jesus is on Mission, and one of the ways He defines His Mission is in terms of the kingdom of God. The kingdom of God is the place where Jesus rules and reigns, and according to Jesus, the kingdom of God has landed right here in the middle of the kingdom of people. Specifically, in this context, the kingdom of men is where religion has ruled and reigned in the name of God. Many of the people in this kingdom of men are subject to the religious leaders' piety and religious expression. The people in the kingdom of men are weighed down by the religion and power of the religious elite.

The religious elite got rich off the backs of the people and established themselves as nearly untouchable by controlling the definition of "God's Best People." Their definition of "God's Best People" meant following all the rules or at least their interpretation of the rules. Enter Jesus, and in this section of the Sermon on the Mount, Jesus starts by defining who is the "best" in His Kingdom in Matthew 5:1–12. We call this passage the Beatitudes, and it describes who Jesus considers to be the "best." Blessed are the poor in spirit, blessed are those who mourn, blessed are the meek, blessed are those who hunger and thirst for righteousness, blessed are the merciful, blessed are the pure in heart, blessed are the peacemakers, blessed are those who are persecuted for His Name's sake. None of these descriptions for being blessed were being shouted as the standard in the kingdom or men. Only in God's Kingdom, where Jesus is King, are these the "best" people.

As Jesus continues to teach His disciples, He tells them that in His Kingdom, there is a Mission—to light the world, salt the earth, and point people to the Father. Being in His Kingdom makes us salt, so we are to do what salt does. Being in His Kingdom makes us light, so we do what light does. We glorify the Father so others will see Him. We show we know Him by accurately pointing to Him (Matthew 5:13–16).

Jesus answered the question on everyone's mind: "What about the Law?" Jesus says what only a perfect Savior could say: "I did not come to destroy the Law, but rather I came to keep the Law perfectly." Later, His friends would understand Jesus's keeping the Law perfectly qualified Him to be the perfect sacrifice for all sin. The religious elite affirmed the Law by using it as a hammer; Jesus affirmed it by living up to its standards and then giving His life on the cross for all who could not meet its standards (that is everyone, by the way). (Matthew 5:17–20)

Jesus then finishes this part of His sermon in Matthew 5 with a series of authority-taking comments about what they hear from the religious elite and what God really meant. Six times, Jesus makes Himself the Kingdom authority by saying, "You have heard it said, but I say to you." Jesus points out that the standards of His Kingdom cannot be measured by keeping rules but are actually measured by our hearts, which turns out to be a much higher standard (Matthew 5:21–48).

In Matthew 6, Jesus gives some upside-down views of how God measures faith and practice in the kingdom of God. Instead of showboat faith, He encourages personal connection to the Father, who rewards what we do in secret. Jesus teaches that in His Kingdom, we get to address God as our own Father. Jesus reminds us that in His Kingdom, it is impossible to serve two masters; singular devotion is required. Finally, Jesus shares with His disciples what might be some of the most challenging thoughts in this chapter when He describes **the divine exchange** His Kingdom requires.

**The divine exchange** shows itself when Jesus commands that in His Kingdom, our mission changes. "Therefore I tell you, do not worry about your life …" (v. 25). This is not a simple message about stress, worry, or God's provision. This is a statement that in the kingdom of God, our mission shifts. In His Kingdom, we move from the mission of satisfying our own life and meeting our own needs to something entirely different. I love how the King James Version of the Bible says it: "Take no thought for your life" (Matthew 6:25). In fact, this instruction is given three times. Sprawled against the backstop of Jesus and the Father and the kingdom of God, we are told that in the old kingdom, thinking about your life is common, but in the new Kingdom, the one where Jesus is King, and His Mission is central, we are told to exchange the mission of our lives and ourselves to the Mission of His Kingdom.

If you keep reading Matthew 6, you will see that **God's people get**

**God's care in God's Kingdom so God's people can focus on God's Mission—His Kingdom Mission.** This truth is why Matthew 6:33 commands us to "seek first the kingdom of God and his righteousness." The divine exchange is the kingdom of me for the Kingdom of Jesus. Take no thought for yourself; instead, seek first Jesus's Kingdom and righteousness. The expectation is a shifting of mission from me first and how I live to how I will live seeking His Kingdom first and how I can advance His Kingdom.

This is not a passage about defeating worry; it is a passage about embracing God's Kingdom Mission. It is about embracing His righteousness. The righteousness of God is the place where things are made right with Him, where the justice of God is invited to replace the injustice of man. This is a missional swap, and the promise is that in the kingdom of God, we can make this swap because of what our King knows—He knows what we need.

Jesus's disciples are sitting right in front of Him; the eye contact is both loving and awkward, and He is saying to them, "On our Mission to become fishers of men, this swap must take place." They made the change of mission, and it is also a must for us. I am supposed to seek first the kingdom of God because the King has a Mission. If I belong to the King, if I am loved by the King, if I am a part of His Kingdom and love the King myself, then I can do nothing else but seek His Mission most if I seek first His Kingdom.

Finally, in Matthew 7, Jesus moves effortlessly between warning and wisdom. He warns against the old kingdom that has the habit of being hypocritical in its judgment, finding fault only in others instead of judging ourselves first. Jesus warns His disciples not to give what is holy to pigs. (By the way, the pigs in this sermon are the religious elite, not pagans.) In wisdom, Jesus, knowing that the standards of God's Kingdom are impossible without the King, instructs His disciples to ask the King and to keep on asking; to knock and to keep on knocking; to seek and to keep on seeking.

His wisdom reminds the disciples that Kingdom-of-God living requires persistence. This wisdom shouts that God is good and will answer the prayers of all who come to Him. Jesus declares that if in a broken kingdom, broken fathers know how to meet the requests of their sons for fish and bread with actual fish and bread, not snakes and stones, then how much more in God's Kingdom will the Father give good things to His kids and answer their prayers?

Jesus warns that the road paved by the religious elite will lead everyone on it to destruction, but His road, narrow as it might be, leads to life. Jesus adds to His warning to be careful of those people who speak God-like words but do not have God-like hearts. In wisdom, Jesus instructs how to discern the difference between these false prophets. It is in the fruit their lives produce. Another way to say this could possibly be that you can tell the difference by the mission they possess. Enter Jesus's shocking words. Read them again.

> Not everyone who says to me, "Lord, Lord," will enter the kingdom of heaven, but only the one who does the will of my Father who is in heaven. Many will say to me on that day, "Lord, Lord, did we not prophesy in your name and in your name drive out demons and in your name perform many miracles?" Then I will tell them plainly, "I never knew you. Away from me, you evildoers!" (Matthew 7:21–23)

One of the things that made people run to Jesus was how His words and actions often made space for those who didn't feel like they fit. These words, when understood in the context of the moment, make that space. The people Jesus is specifically calling out are the religious elite of Israel who are focused on building the wrong kingdom. Jesus is saying that the people who belong most in His Kingdom are not the ones whose religion makes a show but the ones whose faith drives them to accomplish the will of the Father.

Accomplishing the will of the Father, according to Jesus, is to enter into the Mission of Jesus's Kingdom.

> "My food," said Jesus, "is to do the will of him who sent me and to finish his work. Don't you have a saying, 'It's still four months until harvest'? I tell you, open your eyes and look at the fields! They are ripe for harvest." (John 4:34–35)

Accomplishing the will of the Father, according to Jesus, is to rescue humanity from their sin.

> And this is the will of him who sent me, that I shall lose none of all those he has given me, but raise them up at the last day. For my Father's will is that everyone who looks to the son and believes in him shall have eternal life, and I will raise them up at the last day. (John 6:39–40)

The religious elite used their faith to accumulate power and grow their own kingdom. They did so by adding to the spiritual burdens the people carried. These faith leaders set themselves as the standard of God's Kingdom. Jesus is challenging the false confidence that entering the kingdom of heaven is measured by human standards.

Jesus is making the entry point to God's Kingdom relational, not religious. He is saying, "You can all come, and all qualify for the kingdom of heaven because, in my Kingdom, the Father's will is seeking first the kingdom of God through Me" (paraphrase mine).

Jesus is not trying to make you and I feel insecure as we approach the last day and stand before Him. He is saying one trait of knowing Him is living in obedience to the King and investing in His Kingdom and Mission. The evidence of knowing Him is not power but faithfulness to the Father's will—knowing Jesus.

Jesus wraps up His sermon by telling the people that the foundation matters if you want your house to last. Kingdom-of-God people build on the great foundation of hearing and then doing Jesus's words. Kingdom-of-men people have a weak foundation because even though they hear, even though they are religious, even though on the surface they seem to wield the power of God, their house cannot stand—it has no real foundation because they still do not do Jesus's words.

Pay attention to Jesus's warning because Jesus is building a Church that is "gates-of-hell proof." It is both hearing and doing the Mission of Jesus that He uses to build His Church, to build His followers, to build each of us. Matthew 5–7 instructs that we KNOW Jesus when we obey His Kingdom words and live out His Kingdom Mission and values.

**Four—Knowing God Begins with Fearing God**

> The fear of the Lord is the beginning of wisdom, and knowledge of the Holy One is understanding. (Proverbs 9:10)

Merrily and I were at the Grand Canyon for our thirtieth wedding anniversary, and we were both awed by its size and beauty. Did you know the Grand Canyon can be seen from space with the naked eye? That is big! We would get up early to watch the sun rise over the Grand Canyon, and a couple of nights we stayed late just to watch it set. Both the sunrise and sunset were awe-inspiring. I have traveled the world, and there is nothing in nature that takes my breath quite like the Grand Canyon.

One of the most helpful tools we found while visiting the Grand Canyon was found on a large five-foot wide and three-foot tall picture on a wall. It was a map of the Grand Canyon. What made this one of the most helpful tools for us? We could see the whole canyon, but more than that was the little yellow arrow with the words "You Are Here." Those words acted as a starting place for us to see how giant the Grand Canyon really is (it lives up to its name) and helped us get our bearings while experiencing it.

Did you know that according to the Bible, the kind of wisdom and understanding that bring us to really knowing Jesus has a starting place? The Bible provides a "You Are Here" sign for each of us who desire to really know God, and that sign is the "fear of the Lord." Wait a minute, Leonard Lee, God is loving and kind, His mercies are new every morning, He is faithful and forgiving, so why the fear? Why is the fear of the Lord the "You Are Here" sign? Glad you asked.

In short, we are unable to take in all that God is and all that God does. It is impossible, not because God is unknowable but because we are limited. For me to know a perfect God, I need instructions—a map that both tells me where I am and where I am supposed to go. The fear of God is the starting place on the map; it is the little "You Are Here" arrow on the map.

What does it actually mean to fear the Lord? Today, we explain the word fear to mean reverential awe. This is not a bad understanding, but it is incomplete because the word also means terror and fright. Without both ends of the definition, we will miss the "You Are Here" arrow, and while we might appreciate the size of God, we will never really be overwhelmed by who God is.

A few years back, I was privileged to meet and spend some time with the Pope of the Orthodox Church in Ethiopia. The Orthodox Church in Ethiopia has over fifty million people and makes up about 60 percent of the population of Ethiopia. This was kind of a big deal, and it was amazing! As we spoke, we talked about history and theology and life and mission. During our time together, I realized that he was a regular guy who held a powerful title. I am not diminishing his status or character, nor am I elevating myself in comparison with him. His authenticity and humor made him relatable, and I was inspired to think about how God could use me. Great men and women of God have this effect on us.

As a kid, I wanted to sing like John Denver, play the guitar like Johnny Cash, run like Willy Mays, hit a ball like Babe Ruth, and be as funny as Steve Martin. As I got older, I wanted to preach like Billy Graham or E.V. Hill. I wanted to write like A.W. Tozer or Max Lucado and be taller than a fifth grader. My point is that none of these people made me feel awe—they just told me that I could do better. Good heroes do that. Right now, I usually experience awe as appreciation for someone who is better than me at something I like. Because of our cultural understanding of what it means to have awe, I do not think we are equipped to experience awe today. At least not in the "You Are Here" way.

I often meet people whose courage, faith, and obedience ratchet up my awe. But the truth is, I still can see myself in them and wonder if I could do that, too. Would I be so brave? Would I remain faithful? Would I be so wise? With these questions, there is an inkling of hope, a "maybe I could," or even a solid "Yes, I can!" Again, I experience awe as an inspiration to be as brave, courageous, faithful, and wise, but this is still too small an understanding for the word awe in reverential awe.

I was at the Notre Dame Cathedral in Paris, and as a guy who loves both art and history, this was a special treat. From the outside, I experienced some awe. The architecture and beauty were magnificent. When I entered, I saw artwork in paintings, stories told through stained glass, wood carvings, and beautiful statues, and my sense of awe increased again. When I sat in the middle of the Notre Dame Cathedral, I had a moment of reflection and wondered, "What did people in 1350 AD say to God when they sat here? What did people say in 1450 AD say to God when they sat here? Today, my awe for the Notre Dame Cathedral has faded and is a whisper of what it was when I was there. My awe for the Notre Dame Cathedral is now mostly contained in a memory that I write about to make a point.

---

Side Note: The people who gave tours had no awe because the beauty of the Notre Dame Cathedral had become familiar and routine. Is it possible we lack the awe needed to really know God because we are too familiar with a view of Jesus that is short-sighted?

---

Here is my problem: I use the word awe for how I experience art, history, and people I admire, people who inspire me, and so my definition of this word becomes my default filter for how I experience being in awe of God. I am never undone when I meet a hero. I am never wrecked when I see a mountain. My understanding of what it means to be in awe of God is limited by me. The result is that when I equate the fear of the Lord to only mean reverential awe, I miss the grandeur of God, I miss the depth of the wisdom of God, and I miss knowledge of the Holy One. Not because my heart is bad but because both my capacity to take it all in and my definition of awe is too small.

To fear the Lord is to be terrified of being in the presence of someone who is so unlike me in size, power, wisdom, knowledge, and holiness, and you could add a few more words here to describe God. It is in the presence of this God that I am completely undone. But it is more than that because, in my undone posture, I am revealed in every part of my soul—nothing is hidden. It is in this moment of seeing God and fearing what I see that I submit to Him and His Mission. In this moment of seeing Him like He is, I am transformed into His image.

> Dear friends, now we are children of God, and what we will be has not yet been made known. But we know that when Christ appears, we shall be like Him, for we shall see Him as He is. All who have this hope in Him purify themselves, just as He is pure. (1 John 3:2–3)

The fear of the Lord is my entry point to knowing God. When the fear of the Lord is fully at work in me, I am not inspired to be a better version of myself; I am crushed under the weight of who HE is, and my only response is to silently shift the posture of my life to absolute stillness and wait for Him to speak.

When the fear of the Lord is my entry point, I understand that God owes me nothing, that He owes me no explanation, no mercy, no grace—nothing. My entry point is to recognize I am not worthy to stand, sit, kneel, grovel, or be in His presence. My entry point is to let who He is strip away any part of me that does not look like Him, no matter the price, so He can remake me fully into His image. My entry point is to know that apart from Him, I truly can do nothing. This entry point also gives me an awe-inspiring view of the grace and love of Jesus. The God who doesn't owe me or need me loves me and wants me to be His own.

Let's go back to the Grand Canyon for a minute. What if I stood on the edge of the Grand Canyon and shouted, "I am huge, look at me!"? Silly, I know, because no one stands next to such overwhelming size and beauty and declares themselves big. Yet, we often do this with God because we do not properly fear Him. Consider Jesus's words to His disciples in Matthew 10.

> So do not be afraid of them, for there is nothing concealed that will not be disclosed, or hidden that will not be made known. What I tell you in the dark, speak in the daylight; what is whispered in your ear, proclaim from the roofs. Do not be afraid of those who kill the body but cannot kill the soul. Rather, be afraid of the One who can destroy both soul and body in hell. (Matthew 10:26–28)

In Jesus's own words, He says that people often fear man more than they fear Him and that if they are to live out the Mission of Jesus, they need to think less about what people can do to their body and fear more the One who can condemn both body and soul to hell. The entry point to mission is the rightly placed fear of God. Why? Because healthy fear leads to wisdom, understanding, and knowledge of God.

Our "You Are Here" arrow is knowing God, and our "You Are Here" arrow for knowing God is to actually fear the Lord.

We have a God who is loving, kind, and tender and invites us to come to Him. And in coming to Him, we are forgiven and freed, and we discover everything we were made for. We also have a God who is so big, who is so NOT like us, and who is so powerful that in His presence, people fall to their faces as though dead. How can I experience both sides of this God at the same time?

More than once the disciples found themselves experiencing both sides of God through Jesus. Mark 4:41 reminds us that when Jesus calmed the storm with just a word, they were terrified at the One whose words could calm a storm, yet they loved and followed Him, too. It is healthy faith that lives in the tension of a good and gracious God who is also great and mighty and frightening. A healthy sense of awe is how we can stay in this tension.

The writer of the book of Hebrews gives us some insight into living in the tension of having a frightening but safe place with Jesus. The first followers of Jesus were mostly Jewish, and to follow Jesus meant persecution and sometimes great suffering. After a while, many of these Jesus followers began to question if following Jesus was worth it and were tempted to go back to their old religion. Hebrews was written to them and for us. The message of Hebrews is that Jesus is always better.

Wrapping up Hebrews, the writer recounts the story of the Jewish people after they left Egypt and were headed to the promised land of Israel, and the parallel is remarkable. In the wilderness, the people experienced the *goodness* of God, who delivered them from slavery. The people had experienced the generous *provision* of God when He fed and watered them in a place where food and water were scarce. These people experienced the *leadership* of God with a cloud by day and a fire by night. They experienced the *protection* of God from enemies who would attack. They experienced the *care* of God in giving them clothes that did not wear out. In every way, the *kindness* of God was present for these people. At the same time, the fire and smoke coming from the mountain as God spoke and gave His Law made them tremble and fear and close their eyes and cover their ears. They saw God move a sea, open the earth, and shake the earth, and it terrified them. For these people, the most frightening place for them to be was also the safest place to be.

I should mention that this entire generation did not move into the promised land because they failed to live in this very real tension of fearing God and embracing the love of God. This generation failed to enter into the Mission of God because they could not see God correctly. When they saw the greatness of God, they demanded that

God do more, and the most common trait describing these people in their failure was a lack of gratitude and obedience stemming from a skewed view of God. These people failed to take their place in the mission and plan of God because they failed to fear God. They saw a really big God and said, "Look how big we are, give us more."

They failed to understand we need a God who is frightening and scary and loving and good at the same time; otherwise, we become ungrateful for His generosity and demanding of His care.

> Therefore, since we are receiving a kingdom that cannot be shaken, let us be thankful, and so worship God acceptably with reverence and awe. (Hebrews 12:28)

Paul the Apostle adds for us what he did to live in the reality of a God who is to be feared and completely safe, too. He embraced a Jesus Mission Life. Look at what he wrote in 2 Corinthians 5, a chapter that is 100 percent about living in the Mission of God.

> Since, then, we know what it is to fear the Lord, we try to persuade others … For Christ's love compels us, because we are convinced that one died for all, and therefore all died. And he died for all, that those who live should no longer live for themselves but for him who died for them and was raised again. (2 Corinthians 5:11, 14–15)

Paul understood that the fear of the Lord is the starting place, and the love of God is the landing place. He lived in this space by being immersed fully in the Mission of Jesus. This is a Jesus Mission Life.

Let me wrap up this chapter with two stories. When I was in Ethiopia training pastors, on the morning of our third of five days of training, I came down to the dining room from my room at the hotel where I was staying to get a cup of coffee, an egg, and a piece of toast. Looking out the windows at the hotel, I saw several young men with hoodies and face masks, carrying AK-47s, crouching and sneaking through the streets. Within a few moments, gunfire erupted and continued throughout the morning. The hotel guests were now in a panic, making calls, and trying to get out of this danger zone. My perspective on the fear of the Lord actually provided me a blanket of peace.

"What are you going to do?" guests asked with great urgency. "I am going to eat an egg and toast and drink some coffee," I replied. "What? Why are you not trying to get away; why are you not panicked?" I responded, "I am not panicked because I fear the ONE who can take both my soul and body more than the ones out there who can only harm my body. I will stay on mission because, although this is a frightening moment, I know and am confident in the ONE who keeps me in His hand. I believe that I am so much safer in the hands and plans of Jesus than if I panic and fail to trust Him." The fear of the Lord is the beginning of understanding and wisdom and leads to the knowledge of the Holy One (Proverbs 9:10).

The church where we were training pastors was about a mile away from my hotel, and after breakfast, I noticed about forty pastors waiting for me by the side door of the hotel. These dear brothers, in the midst of gunfire and explosions, surrounded me as we walked to the church, taking back streets and alleyways.

When we arrived at the church, we were met with another fifty or so pastors, and they asked, "Should we cancel our training?" I told them, "I am here to train pastors to live a Jesus Mission Life, and I will do whatever you want." We paused to pray and commit ourselves to fearing God more than men, even men with guns. After prayer, with one voice, the pastors said, "Let us continue the training." I need to add that I am not extra brave; it is just that in this moment, the Holy Spirit made the "You Are Here" arrow very clear. I knew in the moment who to fear most, and with the fear of the Lord comes the knowledge, wisdom, and understanding I need to know God.

Let me tell my second story and wrap up this chapter. A part of the enormity of God that is meant to undo us is His grace and love. God's love for us is meant to make us like Peter when he met Jesus on the shore, and Jesus overwhelmed him with fish.

> When he had finished speaking, he said to Simon, "Put out into deep water, and let down the nets for a catch." Simon answered, "Master, we've worked hard all night and haven't caught anything. But because you say so, I will let down the nets." When they had done so, they caught such a large number of fish that their nets began to break. So they signaled their partners in the other boat to come and help them, and they came and filled both boats so full that they began to sink. When Simon Peter saw this, he fell at Jesus' knees and said, "Go away from me, Lord; I am a sinful man!" For he and all his companions were astonished at the catch of fish they had taken, and so were James and John, the sons of Zebedee, Simon's partners. Then Jesus said to Simon, "Don't be afraid; from now on you will fish for people." So they pulled their boats up on shore, left everything and followed him. (Luke 5:4–11)

I have three observations about this passage. First, how do you love a fisherman? Give him a ton-o-fish. Jesus's miracle was a specific use of His power to grace and love Peter. Second, the love of God, as shown by Jesus, made Peter see his sinfulness and be afraid. Jesus's love and grace gave Peter a "You Are Here" arrow and caused him to fall on his knees and say to Jesus, "Depart from me, I am sinful man." You can use the word FEAR here. Third, it was through this act of love that Peter was undone, and from a place of fearing the Lord, Peter entered the Mission of Jesus.

Knowing God, really knowing God, is a process. We know we are in the process when we love like Jesus, know the voice of Jesus, and follow Him to live out His Kingdom Mission and values wherever we go.

Where do we start? The fear of the Lord.

# Stepping into Jesus's Mission

## A prayer you can pray today:

*Dear Jesus,*

*Thank You that You can be known and that You want me to know You. Help my life to reflect what it means to know You by loving others, knowing Your voice, and living out Your Kingdom Mission. Let me know what it means to fear the Lord, and use that knowledge to draw me closer to You. I appreciate Your patience with me.*

*Amen*

## Some questions to move you forward:

As you read this chapter, was there anything new or fresh that you discovered about truly knowing God?

Jesus said knowing Him means you will love others, know His voice, and live in obedience to His Kingdom ways and Mission. Which of these three evidences of knowing Jesus do you find most challenging?

How has knowing Jesus brought these three evidences into your faith journey so far?

Why do you think that the "You Are Here" arrow for knowing God is the fear of the Lord?

Where do you see the struggle in today's faith culture with true reverential awe when it comes to Jesus?

Share any Scriptures used in this chapter that were a particular challenge or a specific encouragement to you.

What is something you will begin to do as a result of reading this chapter about knowing Jesus?

## A step you can take as you go:

This chapter was a lot and could easily be overwhelming. This week, try to focus on one place where God spoke to you most through this chapter. Make an action plan to take one step toward knowing Jesus better.

All who dwell on the earth will worship
Him, whose names have not been written
in the Book of Life of the Lamb slain from
the foundation of the world.
(Revelation 13:8 NKJV)

# Chapter 3

## God's Original Mission

The entire story of God, as told in the Bible, is primarily a story of mission. God has a mission, and Revelation 13:8 tells us exactly what it is. Read the Scripture verse on the left again … slowly, this time. It says the Mission of God is the rescue of humanity, which actually began before the creation of the world. This reality was spoken by Peter, too, when he wrote:

> For you know that it was not with perishable things such as silver or gold that you were redeemed from the empty way of life handed down to you from your forefathers, but with the precious blood of Christ, a lamb without blemish or defect. **He was chosen before the creation of the world, but was revealed in these last times for your sake.** (1 Peter 1:18–20, emphasis mine)

Look again, and you will see that before the world was, before people were, before the foundation of the world was set, God's Mission was our rescue. Before we had a problem, God had a solution to the problem He knew we would soon have. His Mission and plan included Him giving His life for us. By the way, Jesus still has this as His Mission today—to rescue those who bear His image.

God began the process of revealing His Mission when sin entered humanity through Adam and Eve, when they used their gift of free will to do to opposite of what God said. Below, check out the overview and chronology of God's rescue plan as revealed in the Bible.

The original mission from God …

- Began in the heart of God before the foundation of the world existed (Revelation 13:8).
- Promised by God to His image bearers after they sinned, and their sin brought death to all people. God said the woman's seed would crush the serpent's head (Genesis 3:15).
- Modeled when God saved humanity from itself by finding a friend named Noah and making him a partner in preserving humanity through the flood (Genesis 6).
- Initiated when God called Abram to follow Him and made a covenant with Him, creating a people through whom the rescuer would come into the world. Abram became Abraham, the father of many nations (Genesis 12).
- Preserved by God when Joseph was sold into slavery in Egypt. This act saved and preserved the people God had created as partners with Himself to bring the rescuer (Jesus) into the world (Genesis 40–50).
- Moved forward by God when Moses led the promised people from slavery in Egypt to the promised land (Exodus–Deuteronomy).
- Defined by God when God gave the Law and sacrificial system to His partners, His people (Exodus–Numbers).
- Developed by God when He gave the land He promised to His people of promise (Joshua–Judges).
- Illustrated again and again by God through the judges and God's patience with His promised people (Judges).
- Established by God as a lineage through which the rescuer would come, the tribe of Judah and King David (Genesis 38).
- Prophesied and predicted hundreds upon hundreds of times before the Rescuer entered the world, born of a virgin, just as promised by God to Adam and Eve (Isaiah 7–9).
- Given the perfect environment to be started during the 400 silent years between the Old Testament and the birth of Christ.

- Supernaturally announced by the angels to Mary and Joseph and the shepherds that Jesus was the One who would save His people from their sin, and He was now here on earth (Luke 1).
- Declared by John the Baptist and then by the Father Himself when Jesus was baptized (Matthew 3).
- Challenged by Satan in the wilderness temptations (Matthew 4).
- Begun as a movement when Jesus recruited and trained His disciples (Mark 5).
- Presented as true and then verified through Jesus's sinless life, His working of miracles, and His teaching about the Father and His Kingdom (the four Gospels).
- Fought for and won by Christ when He died on a cross, paying the penalty for all sin (Matthew 27, Mark 15, Luke 23, John 19).
- Sealed as true in Heaven and upon earth when Jesus rose from the dead, sealing forever God's satisfaction with His own standards of holiness and justice (Matthew 28, Mark 16, Luke 24, John 20).
- Commissioned by Jesus Himself—THE Mission of HIS Movement (Matthew 28:18–20).
- Established through the gift of the Holy Spirit and the launching of a movement called the Church (Acts 2).
- Lives today in the people who follow Jesus as King, Lord, and Savior (Ephesians 2:10).
- It will be established in God's final and forever chapter—eternity (Revelation 21).

Driven by a passion for His glory and WHO He is by nature, Jesus embarked on His Mission to rescue image bearers and destroy the work of Satan. "The reason the Son of God appeared was to destroy the devil's work" (1 John 3:8b). Jesus's motive? Love. Jesus paid it all for His glory because His very essence is LOVE.

The Mission of Jesus is much more than bullet points on a page or a system of theology; it is a true, living, and ongoing story of God's love. It's a mission where God has fought and won a battle that we had no chance to win ourselves. Eternal life and eternal death were and still are at stake.

When we read about Jesus in the Bible, we come across words that describe His victory stance. A victory stance is the position you take after winning. The Olympics have a platform for gold in the middle, the highest spot. The silver medalist stands on the right on a lower platform, and the bronze medalist stands on the left on the lowest platform. The Super Bowl has a stage in the middle of the field where the winning players and owners are awarded the Lombardi trophy.

As the victor, where does Jesus stand? The Bible says that Jesus is at the right hand of the Father, seated on a throne or sometimes depicted as standing. Paul actually gives us an amazing view of Jesus on His throne in the book of Ephesians.

> That power is the same as the mighty strength he exerted when he raised Christ from the dead and seated him at his right hand in the heavenly realms, far above all rule and authority, power and dominion, and every name that is invoked, not only in the present age but also in the one to come. And God placed all things under his feet and appointed him to be head over everything for the church, which is his body, the fullness of him who fills everything in every way. (Ephesians 1:19–23)

When Jesus sits or stands at the right hand of God, it is very important to know the fight He fought and won to be there. From the place where He stands, Jesus continues to accomplish what is impossible for you and me. Jesus earned His place. The work He did to get there could only have been done by Him. The work He does from there can also only be done by Him.

When Jesus left the throne of heaven, He set aside much of the benefit of divinity and became human. He then lived a sinless life in the face of opposition, injustice, temptation, and acclaim. The Bible says Jesus put on flesh and made His home with people (John 1:14). As He lived a human life, He stayed connected to His Father—perfectly—declaring that EVERYTHING He does is pleasing to the Father (John 8:29). Let me interrupt this God-sized declaration to say, WOW!

When the hostility of the religious leaders turned into hate, and the hate turned into action, Jesus was arrested. Upon His arrest, the people with power used it in the most brutal and mocking way. They beat Him nearly to death using whips, clubs, rods, a crown of thorns, fists, kicks, and slaps, destroying Him physically.

Just before these events, Jesus was in a conversation with His Father in heaven. In this conversation, Jesus asks Him if there is another way to accomplish the Mission. He asks the Father to let this cup pass from Him, meaning the cup of suffering and death. But Jesus submits to His Father, saying, "Yet not as I will, but as you will." You can read this conversation in Matthew 26:36–44.

Jesus knew what was coming, and with full knowledge, He submitted to the Father and the plan of rescue they shared before the foundation of the world. The Lamb was about to be slain. Standing before the various rulers, kings, governors, priests, and others, He was ridiculed and mocked. The friends Jesus had made betrayed and abandoned Him. Jesus then allowed His captors to rip the clothing off His beaten and battered body, causing His wounds to bleed all over again and exposing His naked body to public shame.

The Scriptures that Jesus knew proclaimed that everyone who hangs from a tree is cursed. I wonder if this thought was present when Jesus's hands were stretched out and nailed to the cross. What did Jesus think about as His feet were pierced with nails and He was lifted up for all to see? The Bible says that Jesus thought about those whose sins had so brutally hurt Him and destroyed everything He had created. At one point, He cried out from the cross for His Father to forgive them. Even as He hung in anguish, Jesus thought about you and me and how His death and resurrection would make us new.

Jesus's Father was also on His mind. I am again interrupting this God-sized declaration to say, WOW!

The story is not done. When Jesus died, His death was so powerful that for several hours in the midday, the sun stopped shining. The curtain in the temple that separated people from the most holy presence of God was torn from top to bottom. From the crowd, people shouted the identity of Jesus, saying that He really is the Son of God. People are usually not declared to be the Son of God upon their death, but Jesus was. On the cross, one of the criminals who was crucified next to Him asked to be remembered in eternity. This is a strange request to make of anyone about to die, but not if you are asking Jesus. This thief was given the very assurance of living in Paradise with Jesus. Once Jesus died, He was taken down from the cross, wrapped in about eighty pounds of spices, and then placed in a borrowed grave. At the entrance of His grave, a giant stone was placed, and elite soldiers from Rome were sent to guard it. What a "just in case" move this was. Ha! It didn't work.

The Bible tells us that during this time, while He was dead, Jesus took the good news of what He had just done to defeat sin to those who had died before Him. He preached to them and led a host of them into eternity with Him (Ephesians 4:7–10). After three days, Jesus rose from the dead, and His once vacant and dead body was filled with life again. Jesus left the tomb—alive!

The resurrected Jesus now begins to put the band back together, so to speak. His disciples had scattered. Some were leaving town, some were hiding in rooms for fear of being next, and others returned to their day jobs. In His own way, Jesus began to connect with them and unite them around His Mission to seek and save the lost and live a Jesus Mission Life. In His final appearance, He ascended back to heaven and took His place at the right hand of the Father, leaving us God the Holy Spirit.

I'd ask that you take a minute and read the last several paragraphs again. Jesus did all of this and more. He conquered every obstacle and roadblock that kept people from knowing Him. The work that Jesus did brought us from death to life, from darkness to light, from not being a people to becoming a people of God. The work Jesus did took down the wall that sin had created, which kept us from God. The death and resurrection of Jesus give all who receive Him into their lives and believe on His name the right to become children of God (John 1:12). Jesus opened the way for the image of God to be restored in each of us. The work Jesus did created a people of Mission. These people are made new by the grace and truth He spoke, embodied in His life, and proved at the cross and by the resurrection. There is nothing on the bulleted list on pages 54–55 that we can do for ourselves or anyone else, but Jesus can and did. It might be time for another one of these—WOW!

All of these words are about Jesus and His Mission. He came to seek and save the lost by giving His life as a ransom for many. Jesus made disciples, whose disciples made disciples, whose disciples also made disciples, and as a parting gift, Jesus handed His Mission to His friends, telling them the Holy Spirit would come and give them the power to live out the Jesus Mission Life to the very ends of the earth. His Mission drove everything He did—the very same Mission set before the foundation of the world.

Before I get too far, let me say with absolute clarity that Jesus was motivated to Mission by His love for His Father and people (us). Jesus was motivated by the glory of God. In fact, these two motives, His glory and His love, live in the heart of God and run throughout Genesis all the way through Revelation. God was motivated by His own glory and because He IS love. Jesus created us for His glory and because He is love; Jesus redeemed us for His glory and because He is love. His Mission shouts His glory and His love.

---

Side Note: The glory of God has two distinct meanings. First is beauty and reputation. God does what He does to display His beauty and reputation to people. The second is "full weight," meaning all who God is, seen and revealed in Christ.

---

As a follower of Jesus, the Bible clearly tells me to love others as Christ loves, and whatever I do, I do it all to the glory of God. It is impossible to bring glory to God and love others as Jesus did without living a Jesus Mission Life.

A Jesus Mission Life is one in which Jesus's disciples make disciples. In fact, so central to the Mission of Jesus is disciple-making that He declares this is exactly how He loved and glorified His Father (John 17). Let me finish this chapter by pointing to how Jesus finished when He was here.

> Then Jesus came to them and said, "All authority in heaven and on earth has been given to me. Therefore go and make disciples of all nations, baptizing them in the name of the Father and of the Son and of the Holy Spirit, and teaching them to obey everything I have commanded you. And surely I am with you always, to the very end of the age." (Matthew 28:18–20)

Jesus spoke these words when He was about to return to His Father. He had asked His disciples to meet Him on the mountain (v. 16). Since the mountain was not identified specifically, many scholars believe that the mountain was the very same place Jesus introduced the kingdom of God in the Sermon on the Mount. When they arrived, no small talk is recorded. Some worshipped, some believed, and some doubted (v. 17).[1]

Jesus grabbed their attention, declaring, "All power and authority in heaven and on earth are mine." Big, bold, authoritative, everyone was tuned in. It was not that long ago these guys saw Jesus die, and they were discouraged and hiding. Jesus began to appear to them, and in this final scene, He spoke with boldness, "I am large and in charge." (I might have embellished the words here.)

No one argued, no one raised an objection, and no one asked Him to repeat Himself. The risen and victorious Jesus, who predicted His own death and resurrection and then pulled it off, was speaking:

> ALL power and authority are mine. I have every bit of power to do what I have done and to help you do what I am about to tell you to do. There is nothing I do not have power over. There is no task too big, mountain too high, challenge too hard, obstacle too heavy. **All power is mine.** Oh, and did I mention that **I also have all authority?** Not some, not most, not the majority, I have it all. I earned it, and I have it. All authority. I have the final word. I have the top voice and the final vote. (paraphrase mine)

There is a lot of meaning wrapped up in these two declarations, but pay close attention to the range of His power and authority—ALL of it IN HEAVEN and ALL of it ON EARTH.

Jesus is boldly and confidently laying the groundwork for His next few words: "Go and make disciples." These four words could be translated as "as you go" or "everywhere you go" because, in this moment, the going was assumed. How do we know? Because … **everything** that was planned for Jesus to do by being the Lamb that was slain was ordained before the foundation of the world. **Everything** God did to get Jesus into this world, **everything** Jesus did while on earth, **everything** He accomplished on the cross, and **everything** that was won with the resurrection was to impact **all of humanity.** Then, it was all to be carried forward through the disciples, who Jesus trained to make disciples, whose disciples would also make disciples. This was Jesus's intention all along.

The covenant that God made with Abraham is being fulfilled through the Mission given to Jesus's disciples. Our mission is to take the New Covenant to all people through the Church that Jesus Himself is building, the Church that not even the very gates of hell can stop. The intention of God from beginning to end is His Mission to rescue people from their sin. Our part is for each of us to take His Mission everywhere we go by making disciples who also make disciples. This is Jesus Mission Living.

In 1989, I got married, and I remember every detail of the day. The songs, the dress Merrily wore, my suit, the crowd, the words of the preacher, our vows—I remember it all. The day itself was the culmination of all the love we shared and all that we were discovering and building together. Our wedding day is not just the day we became Lees; it is the day we launched the mission of being Lees. That day requires a lifelong response. The promises we made would be the expression of how we would live. When we left the church on the day that we had sealed our promise with a kiss and a prayer, Merrily and I began a life together. In public, we are married; in private, we are married; in the car, we are married; everywhere we go, we are married. There is no guessing, not for our friends, not for the people who meet us, not for our family, and definitely not for us—especially not for us. Honestly, my wife is my favorite person to talk about. "You may kiss the bride" was the great commissioning moment for our marriage.

Let's go back to the mountain again where the resurrected Jesus, the One with ALL power and ALL authority, told His disciples, with 100 percent clarity, the Mission: *make disciples.* Forgive the tongue-in-cheek, but duh. Of course make disciples! Jesus's marching orders have the obvious truth behind them as if He were saying, "I didn't do all of this, shape history, create a people, raise kings and judges and prophets, protect the people who would bring my final king into the world, give my life and then take it up again to have everything stop here on a mountain in Jerusalem. Everywhere you go, make disciples." What else could they do? How else could they respond? What else can WE do? How else can WE respond?

"As you go, teach those new disciples everything I have commanded." Jesus was not saying, "Hey guys, you have the curriculum we wrote in the upper room, teach that. Hey guys, you have the Bible studies we assembled while walking the roads from Capernaum to Bethany, go teach that." No, this is much bigger. This is about how He trained them, what He taught them about the kingdom, what He equipped them to go and do—"teach them **everything** I have commanded." They were not Bible study leaders or small group leaders; they were disciple-makers everywhere they went.

---

Side Note: We need to do the work it takes to become a disciple-maker, not simply a Bible study leader. One of these is transformation, and the other is a skill or task. Both matter but only one is the Great Commission.

---

Jesus continued by saying, "Baptize these disciples." Let me say a word about baptism. Baptism in the Bible is such a beautiful moment between God, His people, His community, and the world around us. Baptism is an act of obedience to God and paints a beautiful portrait of the work of the gospel in our lives. When we step into the water, a part of the portrait being painted is of our old life. We are placed under the water; this is a portrait of being buried with Christ, dying to our sin and self. Finally, when we come out of the water, it is a beautiful portrait of our resurrection in Christ, where we are risen to walk in a newness of life. The Bible puts it this way in Romans 6:

> Or don't you know that all of us who were baptized into Christ Jesus were baptized into his death? We were therefore buried with him through baptism into death in order that, just as Christ was raised from the dead through the glory of the Father, we too may live a new life. (Romans 6:3–4)

Others have described with this sentence, "Baptism is the outward sign of an inward faith." It identifies that Jesus is our Master. When we are baptized in the name of the Father, the Son, and the Holy Spirit, we are identifying who the Master of our lives is from this day forward. When I am baptized into Christ, I am also baptized into the community of people who are also in Christ.

Baptism is also the launchpad for the Mission of Jesus (Matthew 3:13–17). It is so much more than a hug from God, reminding us that we are His. Consider this: When Jesus was entering the water on His baptism, He told John, "This is the right thing to do. Without this, something is not fulfilled" (v. 15). When Jesus came out of the water, the Father in heaven ripped open the curtain of heaven and spoke, "This is my son, whom I love and with whom I am well pleased" (v. 17).

Everything in the life of Jesus flowed from this loving declaration from His Father when Jesus was baptized. In the wilderness, Satan came and challenged the very truth the Father declared. Satan challenged if Jesus was really the Son of God, if Jesus was really loved, and if Jesus was really loyal to the Father. Every challenge Jesus faced from people was a missile fired directly at the Father's affirmation. Every motive from Jesus came as a response to His Father's declaration. The baptism of Jesus launched Jesus's Mission as He was walking the earth.

Baptism was a launch pad for ministry for many other people in the Bible as well. The Ethiopian eunuch was baptized and then took the gospel to Africa. Paul was baptized and took the gospel to the uttermost parts of the world. The 3,000 on the day of Pentecost were baptized and took the gospel to Jerusalem and Judea and Samaria and the rest of the known world. The Philippian jailer was baptized and took the gospel to his family and to Philippi. It is a beautiful reality that the people who were baptized after the cross entered Jesus's Mission.

What would happen if every person who was baptized in our churches entered into training for mission? What would it be like for them to be well equipped to walk in the newness of life as mission, not limited to morality or a track to spiritual maturity? When 3,000 people met Christ on the day of Pentecost, they immediately entered into training (apostles' teaching, the breaking of bread, prayer, and the fellowship), and God added daily to the church.

Jesus has a Mission, and following Him means His Mission becomes ours. The aim of a Jesus Mission Life is to live our lives fully immersed in the Mission of Jesus. As you read this book, keep pressing into the truth that you are loved by God. The Mission of Jesus, while it can be a hard road to travel, is a privilege we have been given.

# *Stepping into Jesus's Mission*

## A prayer you can pray today:

*Dear Jesus,*

*Thank You that Your Mission to rescue people from their sin was also a Mission to rescue me. I ask You to widen my view of Your Mission. Help me know the love that brought You to earth. Help me to take Your Mission as my own. I am so grateful that You can actually do what Your Mission needs to be accomplished.*

*Amen*

## Some questions to move you forward:

What stood out to you as you traced the Mission of Jesus through the Bible?

Share anything in the story of rescue that was new or surprising to you.

Jesus has all power and authority and is standing at the right hand of the Father. How does this victory stance influence your understanding and appreciation of Jesus?

How does Jesus having ALL power and ALL authority shape how you see His instructions to make disciples?

Baptism is a beautiful declaration to those around us of the work Jesus did inside of us. How did you celebrate God's work in you when you were baptized? (Sometimes, it has been missed in the teaching about baptism that baptism is also the launch pad for Jesus Mission Living. Take a minute to commit to a Jesus Mission life.)

If you have not been baptized, how does seeing baptism as described in this chapter encourage you to get baptized to move toward a Jesus Mission Life? What are some of the obstacles that keep you from getting baptized soon?

## A step to take as you go:

Take time to learn the chronology of Jesus's Mission as written in this chapter. Don't just know the bullet points. Dive into the Scriptures and learn the story.

“The Church does not have a mission;
the Mission of God has a Church.”
—Christopher J. H. Wright

Chapter 

# Hey, Church, We Have a Mission from God!

The mission of every sports team is to win a championship. The mission of Disneyland is "to entertain, inform and inspire people around the globe through the power of unparalleled storytelling."[2] Chick-fil-A's mission is "to be America's best quick-service restaurant at winning and keeping customers."[3] Walmart says they started with a mission to save people money so they can live better.[4]

If you google any organization, business, or educational institution, you will most often find a mission statement. In fact, a careful look at organizations and their mission tells us that with every successful organization, there is clarity of mission and actions that align to that mission.

Mission is that thing that tells us what we are doing, how far we are willing to go to do it, and what we signed up for as a part of an organization. It provides an actual measuring stick for our practices and actions and anchors our efforts by giving them a direction that is specific. Mission is that road that rises to meet us when we meet, gather, plan, train, educate, and go. It is the catalyst of organizational identity.

When an organization loses its mission, it loses identity at best and, at worst, assumes a different identity or mission. The Church is no different, and I propose it has a single Mission. As you read this chapter, I encourage you to be open-minded. I am not asking you to agree with me 100 percent, for that would be crazy. I am, however, asking you not to miss something important because of the potential to say "yeah, but" through a bunch of sentences about mission and the Church.

For more than forty years, I have been serving in ministry, and more often than not, conversations about the Church and mission seem to bring out tensions and reveal our micro fractures. It is not my intention to do anything else but put forward a proposition that the Church has a single Mission. I think about this every day, a luxury many pastors and people do not have. The work of leading a church often dictates an already full schedule upon arrival. This is normal for any job, but when the expectations vary as much as the people who attend a church, additional layers complicate the role of the pastor. The expectations that Western Christianity puts on pastors today are very heavy, and quite frankly, a lot of these expectations are more a byproduct of culture than Scripture.

Jesus culminated His time on earth with what we commonly call the Great Commission. This commission itself has three distinct audiences. The first audience is the people who are present, the disciples who met with Jesus on the mountain. These disciples were commissioned to take the Mission of Jesus global. His emphasis was not on "going" but on "making disciples." Second, the community of faith that would spring from their disciple-making efforts. The commission of Jesus was and still is for the Church. Third, we, as Jesus's followers, are commissioned by Jesus to make disciples everywhere we go. The commission of Jesus is for me, you, and us as individuals. I'll write more about this third audience later.

When Jesus commissioned His disciples, there was an assumption that the global efforts were a part of the Mission. Every tribe, tongue, nation, people group, and person was within the global scope of the Mission God was handing the disciples. Then came Pentecost. Acts chapter 2 gives us the story.

## HOW THE CHURCH BEGAN (ACTS 2:1–41)

It had been ten days since Jesus told the 120 to wait for God the Holy Spirit to come (Acts 1). Jesus's followers invested much of their waiting in prayer. The amount of prayer is not really that remarkable; after all, it was a part of their culture to pray throughout the day. No, what was remarkable about this prayer was the One whom they were addressing. Jesus *and* the Father. No one had ever prayed like this before; it was indeed a new era of communicating with God. No high priest, no sacrifices, no rituals, just a new way of speaking directly with God. It was as if each prayer ended with a "We are ready."

On day ten, the room began to shake with a fierce wind. One person looked up, then another, and another. One hundred and twenty people tried to keep their balance by holding on to a wall, a chair, or each other. The small community realized they were all experiencing the sound and the force of the wind when God added something else to the moment—**fire**. Yes, fire, falling from heaven and a sound, like a wind that was blowing fiercely. In that moment, it is possible they remembered that Elijah experienced fire, shaking, and wind just before God spoke to him. Could it be God was going to speak again? Yes, He was, and oh, what a message it would be.

The disciples who were in the upper room ran outside and saw a gathering of Jews from all over the Roman world. These Jews had made the pilgrimage to Jerusalem for Pentecost, and they spoke different languages. Now, at Pentecost, traditionally the celebration of the harvest, the Holy Spirit was doing something brand new, and the people who had gathered would witness a miracle. Once outside, the disciples began to preach in the various languages of the people listening. The message? Jesus! His life, His death, His burial, and His resurrection were all part of God's plan for the rescue of people. Not only did God the Holy Spirit give the words and languages to the disciples, but He "cut into" the hearts of those listening, creating an open door for their response. After Peter preached, the people asked, "What do we need to do to be saved?" (v. 37). "Repent and get baptized," he said, which is what 3,000 of them did that morning, and that is how the Church began (vv. 38, 41).

How do you take the Mission of Jesus, which Jesus gave on a mountain, and share it with the first 3,000 people so that they would embrace Jesus? How do you accomplish this monumental task in a way that it also becomes their Mission? How do you create a community around a single Mission, to take the good news they had just experienced everywhere they would go? How do you commission people to make disciples when their languages are different, their homes are located in many countries, and their faith has now been interrupted by hope and grace and love? The 120 disciples, who had been waiting and praying just as Jesus instructed, knew what to do. They were armed with the Mission of Jesus and went to work. Acts 2 not only gives us the story but also lays out the process of how they helped the early Church thrive.

> They devoted themselves to the apostles' teaching and to fellowship, to the breaking of bread and to prayer. Everyone was filled with awe at the many wonders and signs performed by the apostles. All the believers were together and had everything in common. They sold property and possessions to give to anyone who had need. Every day they continued to meet together in the temple courts. They broke bread in their homes and ate together with glad and sincere hearts, praising God and enjoying the favor of all the people. And the Lord added to their number daily those who were being saved. (Acts 2:42–47)

Let's delve into each action to understand better what they were devoted to.

### The Apostles' Teaching

"They," meaning the 3,000 people who got saved, all started doing something with great devotion. They devoured the apostles' teaching. The apostles' teachings were the very words of Jesus they had received as they followed Him. The apostles taught and spoke these truths with the 120 and now to the 3,000, and I am sure to anyone else who would listen. The apostles' teachings were specifically the teaching, training, and the Mission of Jesus.

These gatherings, filled with the apostles' teachings, were much more than a small group or a Bible study for new believers. They were the training ground for the Mission of Jesus. The new disciples were immersed in the life and Mission of Jesus by the very teaching of those who had been trained and equipped by Jesus Himself.

The 3,000 new Jesus followers became experts in the life, death, burial, and resurrection (the Gospel), as well as the Mission of Jesus. How? Through the devotion of their hearts to be equipped and trained. New disciples were learning to take Jesus everywhere and to all people. Intuitively, these new Jesus followers understood that keeping Jesus to themselves was not an option. Wherever they went, they shared that Jesus Christ was the Messiah they had been waiting for. They told everyone that "Jesus has come, He has risen from the dead, He has rescued us, and He can rescue you too."

### The Breaking of Bread

With great devotion, the 3,000 anchored themselves to the Gospel by celebrating the death, burial, and resurrection of Jesus. When they gathered, they would pause to break bread and remember that Jesus's body was broken for them, that His blood made a New Covenant between God and all who come to Jesus by faith. To these new believers, the work of Jesus and the resurrection was not a theological construct with bullet points, slides, and music. For them, it was sitting with people who had seen and witnessed a risen Jesus. In my imagination, I can hear and see this kind of conversation a short time after Pentecost. (Jacob and Michael are fictional characters.)

JACOB: I cannot wait until sundown; I love our gatherings when we discover more and more about Jesus and His Mission.

MICHAEL: I love it too! Especially when we remember Jesus's death, burial, and resurrection through the bread and wine. I feel like I am made new all over again.

JACOB: Me too! I think about it all day long, and I finally see that the true meaning of the Passover lamb is the real Lamb of God.

MICHAEL: I never get tired of holding the bread in my hands and remembering Jesus, and I weep each time I take the cup, remembering His great love for me.

JACOB: When we finish with the commitment to do this until He comes, it reminds me that He is alive and coming back!

I don't know if these words were ever spoken, but the idea that they were devoted to the breaking of bread indicated it was deeply moving and spiritual to them. The breaking of bread anchored these believers to the reality of a victorious and risen Savior who will also come again. This celebration became a central part and practice within the community of faith as they met to be taught and equipped to live Jesus Mission Lives.

The mission of every Jesus follower is to introduce people to Jesus. This is the Jesus Mission Life, inviting others into a Christ-centered life, faith, community, and mission. Denying ourselves, taking up our crosses, and following Him is what Jesus said it means to be His disciples.

### Prayer

Their devotion overflowed to prayer. The Church was devoted to prayer, and their devotion sprang from three realities. First, the prayer life of Jesus was taught, trained, and modeled. Jesus's prayer life reflected deep love for the Father. Jesus's prayer life prompted total submission to the Father and the Father's Mission. Jesus's prayer life provided marching orders. Jesus's prayer life expressed and showed others the glory of God.

The second reality is that prayer was very much the relational side of following Jesus. At last, people could come with great confidence to God's throne of grace. Once there, they found mercy and grace in their time of need. Why? Because they understood they were talking to One who was tested like them in every way, and yet He was without sin. For these first-century Jesus people, this was a new and exciting way to pray. Prayer opened to door to direct access to the King and High Priest of their great salvation. Now, prayer was a personal conversation with the King of kings and Lord of lords, who sits at the right hand of the Father.

Third, these new believers in Christ understood prayer to be foundational to the Mission of Jesus and the birth of the Church. From prayer, Jesus resisted temptation, chose His friends, raised the dead, fed the masses, and healed the sick. Prayer gave Jesus the strength to bravely endure the cross and pay for sin. From the prayers of the 120 disciples in the upper room, God started a movement called the Church. The 3,000 who were the fruit of passionate and devoted prayer, in turn, devoted themselves to prayer. They believed prayer activated the work of God in building His Kingdom, also known as making disciples. They knew that no one lives a Jesus Mission Life without being devoted to prayer.

### The Fellowship

The fellowship is another landing place for their devotion. The word **fellowship** is defined as a **community** that **shares** something in **common with each other** as **partners and friends.**

One of my favorite illustrations of fellowship comes from J.R.R. Tolkien's *The Lord of the Rings.* In the movie version titled *The Fellowship of the Ring,* there is a scene where the leaders of men, dwarves, elves, and a few hobbits are gathered to decide the fate of the "One Ring of Power" that, if possessed by Sauron (the super bad guy), will destroy humanity forever, making those who survive slaves to fear and terror. During the gathering, there is a huge disagreement about what to do with this dangerous Ring of Power. Arguing, bravado, and accusing commence. "Let me have it; I will use its power for good," one guy says. "No one can handle its power; it must be destroyed," shouts another. "We must take it and destroy it in the fires of Mordor, from whence it was forged!" Taking the Ring of Power to Mordor would mean great risk and almost certain death. The tension rises, and the dwarf raises his axe to destroy the ring, but instead, the axe is shattered by the ring. More yelling, more tension, and in the midst of the tension, a few hear a soft voice, and a hush comes over the room.

Frodo, the small and gentle hobbit, speaks, "I will take the ring." From the smallest of those gathered, the courageous commitment to a mission is declared. Out of the silence, a response is given from one of the kings of men, "Then you have my sword." Next comes another commitment, "And my axe," and then another, "You have my bow." Soon, the entire circle of men, dwarves, and elves join together and in one voice enter into the mission to rescue people from the Ring of Power. With the commitment of their weapons and strength, we see the men rally and gather around the small and gentle hobbit. It is at this precise moment the voice of the narrator speaks, "And thus was born the FELLOWSHIP of the ring."[5]

The Fellowship of the Ring was a community of people dedicated to a single mission to which they brought their skills, tools, and weapons. This fellowship was created from mission and made up of people willing to give their very lives to accomplish that mission. How devoted are you to the Fellowship of Jesus and living out the Jesus Mission Life?

This scene gives me the most clear use of the word fellowship I have ever seen or heard. A community of people committed to sharing a common mission, working together for the benefit of others. This is the kind of fellowship that the first-century Jesus followers devoted themselves to. The fellowship of the King, His Mission, and His people were undivided because they all possessed the same marching orders given by the same King and Lord.

I see a much weaker use of the word fellowship in faith communities today. For many faith communities, fellowship is a noun to describe the gathering. We say we *are* the fellowship. Another use is as an adjective, describing a gathering of people to eat food, sing songs, and celebrate a moment of connection. Fellowship is when we sit in a circle and study, pray, or, as we like to say, "do life together." Still another use of the word fellowship is a mutual relationship with other Jesus people. I rarely, if ever, hear the word fellowship defined as "a unified group of people, unified around Jesus's single Mission."

Online grocery shopping has become quite popular. Grab your computer, get your basics and a few preferences, and then, at your convenience, drive to the store where your groceries are delivered and loaded into your car. Today, many people treat the fellowship like online grocery shopping. We look to get a few basic needs met and satisfy our preferences, and we certainly hope it is convenient.

For those who were meeting together in Acts 2, the fellowship held a different meaning and, thus, a different purpose. Their commitment to the fellowship, a Jesus Mission Life, expresses itself in three words, "They devoted themselves." Together, as the fellowship, they became disciple-makers wherever they went. The result? God added daily to the Church.

The lesson I get from *The Fellowship of the Ring* is that authentic fellowship centers on a shared mission for a common good for all. Statistics about what makes a devoted Jesus follower abound, but they all have to do with attending church and giving a percentage of time and money. The alarming reality is that, according to several different resources, the average Jesus follower in the USA attends church about 60 percent of the time, gives less than 2.5 percent of their resources to the Mission of Jesus, and does not attend any form of small group. This is not being devoted.

The "order a few basics and get your preferences" model of

fellowship is not compelling enough to make us change our lives into Jesus Mission Lives. Yes, we are *for* the Mission of Jesus, but are we devoted enough to pursue being equipped, trained, and commissioned to Jesus's Mission? The biblical idea of fellowship is a devoted commitment to mission and each other because we are united by Christ. This biblical kind of fellowship deems Christ and His Mission worth everything and produces Jesus Mission People living Jesus Mission Lives everywhere they go.

Two words describe this kind of devotion: ALL IN! Because of their devotion, they rearranged their schedules, finances, priorities, possessions, connections, and commitments, and they were all in. No one had needs; the joy of Christ filled their hearts, and people saw them as amazing in temple courts, in homes, in worship, and in generosity. God's response to this devotion? He added daily to those who were being saved.

Today, in the twenty-first century, 2,000 years after Pentecost, we use Acts 2:42 as a dream version of what we want the Church to be. We say how great it would be if God would visit us like this again. We declare as revival worship services on the steps of the capitol or spontaneous gatherings of worship. We hunger for change, but often we fear transformation into this kind of believer. We desire God to move in this world but lack the devotion needed for God to move. *We want the Mission of Jesus without the devotion to Jesus and His Mission.*

Often, we model our services on Sunday after Acts 2:42, but let me suggest that Acts 2:42 is much less a description of how they did church and much more a description of how they trained disciples, who, by the way, made disciples whose disciples also made disciples. This is why the church multiplied each day—well-trained disciples made disciples whose disciples also made disciples—Jesus Mission Living.

Let me connect two thoughts here.

First, you cannot separate mission from the training it requires.

When we separate mission and training, mission almost always goes away because all we have left are untrained people. Untrained people believe in Jesus's Mission but rarely live Jesus Mission Lives. Poorly trained people choose mission by comfort and not the command of God. If we, the Church, do not train our people in such a way as to transform them into disciple-makers, we will never see what God did at Pentecost. Where there is no training, there is no mission. Guess what? Where there is no mission, there is no revival. Revival is not the mission; revival is the result of well-trained people living Jesus Mission Lives. Revival is not the mission; revival is the result of a people and Church on Mission.

Jesus left 120 well-trained disciples who were ready for Pentecost. Three thousand people got saved because the 120 were trained and knew what to do. New believers were added daily to the Church, and none of them were left to wonder what their commitment meant. Those who were trained and discipled by the 120, and eventually the 3,000, were all commissioned to live a Jesus Mission Life everywhere they went. Today, I believe we in the Church have hearts that want to be ready but are radically under-trained, completely untrained, or, in the worst case scenario, we have been trained for a different mission than Jesus's Mission.

Second, the training Jesus did was specifically for His Mission to seek and save the lost. His brilliant strategy was to train a small army of people really well. Then Jesus commissioned that army to live Jesus Mission Lives everywhere they went. That is exactly what happened in Jerusalem, Judea, Samaria, and across the world. The Mission of our Savior, the strategy of our Savior, and the fruit of His training are beautiful. It is to this Mission that God gave His Church.

---

Side Note: Make sure your prayer and discussion today aim fully at loving your church and your pastors. Do this by seeking how YOU can add to the Mission of Jesus at your church. God is not honored when we bash the church, and He is dishonored when we bash pastors.

---

# Stepping into Jesus's Mission

## A prayer you can pray today:

*Dear Jesus,*

*Thank You for Your Church and for the Mission You have given her. I am asking for this Mission to become clear in every part of Your Church across the world. Help me take my place, and may the word "devoted" perfectly define my commitment to You, Your Mission, and Your Church. I am grateful to be a part of Your Church.*

*Amen*

## Some questions to move you forward:

What is something that stood out to you in this chapter?

What is your understanding of the word devoted?

Compare and contrast our twenty-first-century understanding of a devoted Christian with what you have just read about the devotion of a first-century Christian.

"They devoted themselves" describes the first church's passionate approach and dedication to a Jesus Mission Life. What words would you use to describe your desire to live a Jesus Mission Life?

The apostles' teaching specifically referred to what Jesus taught and trained His disciples to do. The breaking of bread was specifically how they anchored themselves to the life, death, and resurrection of Jesus. Prayer is the commitment to be a people of prayer. The Fellowship is the connection and unity the people had around the Mission of Jesus. Share any areas of growth these descriptions encourage in you.

## A step you can take as you go:

Take a spiritual assessment of your life this week by asking, "What would those who know me best say I am devoted to?" If you feel brave, ask those who know you best to answer for you. Use what you discover or the answers you receive to reveal how to grow in your devotion to living a Jesus Mission Life. A great starting place in the discovery process is to read the Gospel of John.

# Chapter 5

## Unity—How Mission Makes Us One

In October 1987, in Midland, Texas, an eighteen-month-old toddler, although barely stable and able to walk, was roaming her aunt's backyard when she stumbled and fell into a well. The opening was about eight inches wide, and she was twenty-two feet down. One leg was trapped, folded forward over her body, and when word got out, people from all over the entire community spent the next fifty-six hours pulling together as one, united around one purpose: to rescue Baby Jessica.

Baby Jessica's story captured the attention of an entire nation. People held prayer vigils and gave over a million dollars to her rescue, and before 24/7 news reports were a thing, there were 24/7 news reports that kept the nation aware of the progress. President Reagan said the entire nation became big brothers and sisters, aunts and uncles, grandpas and grandmas. I remember praying for her rescue myself.

The medical community unified and provided fifteen surgeries to care for this baby, who, in the end, only lost a toe to the tragedy. Construction crews, oil rig drillers, paramedics, engineers, and other experts united to rescue Baby Jessica. Food and water were donated to keep the people helping or reporting fed. In 2007, *USA Today* ranked the Baby Jessica story number 22 out of 25 on its list of "lives of indelible impact."

I remember telling some of the students I was working with at the time how the mission to rescue Baby Jessica created a strong bond of unity in her community and across the entire country.

I was in a Central American country training pastors and leaders when I asked the following question, "What is the mission of the Church?" Out of sixty pastors, we had forty-seven different missions. The next day, I was invited to share at a pastors' prayer gathering. The day began with some relational connections, breakfast, a few announcements, and some prayer. It was a pretty good morning; most of the pastors stayed through the prayer time.

When I asked the pastors who had gathered that morning, "What is the purpose behind today's meeting?" they answered, "We want unity in our churches and in our city." We talked about the fruit of unity, and many great comments were shared: "We do not fight anymore." "We share pulpits twice a year." "We help the police by working with kids and gangs." "We love each other and pray for each other." These were really good answers.

As our discussion continued, I asked the pastors if I could read some of Jesus's prayer recorded in John:

> My prayer is not for them alone. I pray also for those who will believe in me through their message, that all of them may be one, Father, just as you are in me and I am in you. May they also be in us so that the world may believe that you have sent me. (John 17:20–21)

For the next hour, we discussed how unity is defined and achieved. Our conclusion was that unity is "the supernatural work of God's Spirit in the community of God's people who are united around God's Mission, operating in God's strategy and values together." That is an important sentence; go back and read it again.

Jesus's words tell us **the fruit of Mission is unity.** The Mission is to make Jesus known, and unity does just that—it makes Jesus known.

Unity is how those around us come to believe that Jesus really was sent—on Mission—by the Father.

## TRAGEDY AND MISSION

Over my lifetime, I have seen very few things truly bring the unity we defined above. The truth is that love doesn't always keep us together. Being more pointed, I have found only two true unifiers—tragedy and mission.

When people groups experience tragedy, they often unite. Like Baby Jessica, people unified for her rescue. History shows that disasters, wars, and calamities can bring people together. The kind of unity that comes from tragedy can be very powerful, but it actually has a short shelf life. Pearl Harbor, the Oklahoma City bombing, Hurricane Katrina, and the attacks on September 11, 2001, of the NYC Twin Towers, the Pentagon, and Flight 93 are all examples of tragedies that created unity.

The problem is that when tragedy is the unifier, the unity produced is fragile. It begins to break down whenever the problem is solved or when politics enters. When the solution to a problem becomes disagreeable, unity dissipates. Sometimes, unity is crushed under the cost of solving a problem or the next problem that comes along.

Mission unites us for a while, too, because mission often comes from calamity. We are one—until we're not. The multitude of competing missions, the ease at which we change missions in the middle, and our tendency to drift from our main mission has a devastating impact on unity.

I sat in a room and listened to a presentation inviting me to help stop illiteracy in a developing part of the world. The presenter provided statistics and examples of success. The slides showed smiling kids who could now read, get an education, find employment, feed their families, and feel better about themselves. It was all very hopeful, and I truly believed in what they did.

But I did not give or jump in to help, and I left the presentation wondering if I was a little hard-hearted. I did agree with their mission; I am for kids reading and finding hope. But the reality is that with so many missions in this world, I only have space for a few. The way we do missions in the church today causes mission groups to compete with each other for volunteers, finances, and visibility. My travels allow me to cross paths with people doing amazing work around the world—digging wells, providing undergarments and hygiene for adolescent teen girls, rescuing kids from trafficking, feeding people and providing medicines for the vulnerable, educating entrepreneurs for business, and so much more.

I was flying to a Central American country to train pastors and leaders, and through conversations and the enormous number of printed t-shirts being worn, I could see that more than 60 percent of our plane was filled with mission teams. One mission group asked me for all my contacts and stated they do a better job than I do. It struck me that these people did not seem excited about each other's work; they were rather competitive and eager to tell why they were unique in their mission. Of the people I spoke to, only one stated that they were there because of the Gospel of Jesus. Because of the abundance of missions, there is not an abundance of unity around the Mission of Jesus.

Did you know that according to the National Association of Nonprofit Organizations & Executives (NANOE) there are more than 1.5 million nonprofits in the USA? That means there is one nonprofit for about every 235 people.[6] A lot of people are starting a lot of organizations with a lot of missions in mind. The best storytellers, the best resourced, are the ones that rise to the top of the mission list, not necessarily the ones with the most focused Jesus Mission. How wonderful it would be if every one of these nonprofit organizations were driven by the one Mission that brought Jesus to earth for which He died. How wonderful if we, the body of Christ, chose His Mission as our Mission.

Side Note: I am for as many people finding ways to serve others in the name of Jesus. People who hear from God and act are some of the most courageous, faith-filled people I know.

The truth is that when the mission changes, unity is fractured, and people are hurt. I was having a conversation with a younger gentleman who was sitting next to me on my flight home from Paris. When we began to discuss Christians and Christianity, he turned to me and said, "Let me ask you a question. Don't you all work for the same guy?" (meaning Jesus). I started to answer when he asked a second question, "I mean, if you all have the same boss, and that boss is Jesus, wouldn't you all get along better?" It seemed as if this question had been on his mind for some time.

"Sir, I am only guessing, but do you have some faith history?" I asked.

"Yes, I do," he responded. Over the next few minutes, I heard a sad but familiar story of a person who left the faith, deconstructed their own faith, and now practiced no faith. The reason given was a lack of credibility of those who practiced Christianity. This loss of credibility was not about our morality or theology; it was about our lack of unity. This man told me a story about his church fighting, splitting and dividing, and making villains out of other Christians. "How can I believe in a God who is not big enough to keep His own kids from fighting?"

I listened and shared with him how sorry I was for his experiences in his faith history. As I sat next to him, I felt like any explanation I offered was too small or just an excuse. He was still facing me as if he were pleading for an answer that would give him permission to return to Jesus, so I said, "You are right. We should get along better, but more than get along; we should be united around the same mission." I asked if he had siblings, and he said there were four kids in his family. I asked if they had ever fought growing up. The answer was a smiling yes. Looking up and making more than glancing eye contact, I said, "Sir, families do not fracture because they squabble; they fracture when their mission changes."

Now we were really talking, not just venting reasons for deconstructing faith. I asked him, "How old were you when your parents divorced?"

"How did you know my parents were divorced?" he blurted, half with surprise and half feeling like I had some creepy superpower.

"Your face gave you up when I said families do not fracture because they squabble; they fracture when their mission changes. Somewhere along the way, you experienced fracture in your family because the mission of your parents changed." I explained that his faith experience suffered from the same basic problem as his family's. His faith community either had too small a mission so it changed too often, or it had too many missions and could not create or sustain unity. Our conversation ended with my strong encouragement that he was indeed loved by God. I invited him to embrace Jesus and His Mission, one he would never outgrow, and then to find some people who share this same Mission.

This is the unfortunate result of disunity. Yes, unity reveals Jesus, but make no mistake, disunity wrecks the faith of many people who get caught in quarrels, fights, and missions that change. Quite often, I speak with people who, like the man sitting next to me on the flight, have deconstructed their faith because the mission they thought they were embracing changed, and they were caught in the disunity of their mentors, church, or leaders. These people have either lost any sense of mission or embraced too small of a mission. This is why unity is so important to Jesus and His Mission.

## JESUS AND UNITY

When Jesus was on the earth, His Mission was to seek and save the lost. When He died and rose again, and the penalty for sin was paid, Jesus handed the Mission to His disciples to share the good news of what He accomplished on the cross everywhere they went. For the disciples of Jesus, this Mission never changed. I am convinced that a survey of sixty first-century pastors and churches on the Mission of the Church would not have yielded forty-seven missions.

In John 17, we have a written record of the conversation Jesus had with His Father the night He was arrested and beaten. I will not dissect the entire chapter, but I will say unity and Mission are center stage. This theme comes through in the way Jesus describes how in-step He and the Father were. They were one. In fact, in most of John 17, the relationship between Jesus and the Father is defined by their actions and the unity they share. I will paraphrase much of the words of Jesus in this chapter, but you can look up the exact words in your Bible.

What was important to Jesus was that the Father and His plans were known and that the Father was glorified. "I have made you known." "I have glorified you," Jesus says. Jesus is praying, "Father, what you wanted done, I did it, and that is how I glorified you." This is unity. What did Jesus say was the very thing the Father wanted done? Make disciples who would make disciples whose disciples would also make disciples. Jesus says, "The ones you gave me, I still have them (except Judas, who was bad from the beginning). They know you, and they are ready to go, so when I leave, can you take over protection duty?" (again, unity) (John 17:1–12, paraphrase mine). As Jesus continues to pray, He shifts His focus to the disciples of the disciples. In this section, He asks for unity again.

Let me add my perspective on this prayer. I think Jesus understands mission drift. Mission drift is when a person or organization begins to drift off mission. Subtly or overtly, organizations suffer mission drift. Often, with no intention or malice, mission drift enters, and for Jesus people and churches, this drift is a unity killer. Every church I have ever attended, served, led, or planted has had to fight mission drift.

I think Jesus saw mission drift time and time again with the three (Peter, James, and John), the twelve disciples, the seventy (those He trained and sent on a mission), and the 120 (those who gathered in the upper room to pray after Jesus ascended back to heaven). Mission drift destroys unity, so Jesus prays for unity. Jesus prays His Church and His people would have the kind of unity that He and the Father have. Theirs is a unity with *zero mission drift.* Jesus and the Father have a unity perfectly anchored in the loving and gracious Mission of multiplying disciples who make disciples, whose disciples also make disciples. So Jesus prays, "Father, make them one as we are one; this is how people will really come to know me and you" (John 17:21, paraphrase mine).

Jesus is saying, "When these people have the same mission, the one we have, and they are unified around that Mission, the good news will travel, and people will tell others about me, and the world will know that I am the guy" (paraphrase mine). It is also within the parameters of this Mission and this unity that the disciples of the disciples will know the Father and know the love of God.

When a community lacks Jesus's Mission, it will always lack the kind of unity that reveals Jesus and the Father and His love. It is the Father and His love that sent Jesus into this world to seek and save the lost. It is the Father and His love that told Jesus there is no other way to rescue people from their sin and from death. It is the Father and His love that strengthened Jesus for the Mission that began before the foundation of the world. Jesus and the Father are ONE and in 100 percent unity.

Let me wrap up this section with a piece of my heart. Pastors, leaders, and Jesus followers, God has given me such a deep love for you. I believe in you so deeply that I have given my whole life to serve Jesus by serving you. I pray every day for you, and here are three of my concerns.

First, I am not convinced that, corporately and personally, we have the same mission as Jesus. My experience in ministry is that the meeting has become the mission. What we do on a Sunday or in a group has become the church's mission. The GATHERING of people has eclipsed the SENDING of people. Almost all our energy and finance goes into a weekend gathering, and by comparison, very little goes to the Great Commission of Jesus. There is very little alignment of our activities, budgets, and programs to the Mission of Jesus. *I am concerned we have mission drift.*

Second, we have work to do. With eight billion people in the world, only a billion might be fully committed to Christ. Did you know that 98 percent of all our resources go to people who are already surrounded by the Church, and nearly three billion people with no gospel witness at all get the final 2 percent of the resources given to and through the Church? *I am concerned we have mission drift.*

Third, as a nation and across the world, people are paying the high cost of mission drift. Remember, the singular Mission of the Church is disciples making disciples whose disciples also make disciples. This mission drift has cost this country a culture; we are seriously a post-Christian culture in America. This mission drift has cost the Church generations as the exodus from churches gets greater with every generation. This mission drift has opened the door to abusive sexuality, making porn commonplace in the majority of lives. This mission drift is why we cannot solve problems of racial injustice, violence, divorce, family decline, and more. We have made converts, not disciples. We have made converts and told them that a good Christian goes to church more often than not, sits in a circle once a week, gives a percentage of time and money, does a few minutes of reading and prayer in the morning, and is in a rotation to serve when they can. I cannot imagine this standard was the fuel that led the early church to deny itself and take up a cross, and then literally lay down their lives to follow Jesus. *I am concerned we have mission drift.*

# Stepping into Jesus's Mission

## A prayer you can pray today:

*Dear Jesus,*

*Thank You for the Mission You have given us that can make us one. Will You ignite my heart with Your Mission? May I never settle for anything less than disciples making disciples? Use me in whatever way You choose in the mission of my local church. I love that Your Mission is bigger than my distractions.*

*Amen*

## Some questions to move you forward:

Tragedy or mission: Describe a time that either one of these created a sense of unity in you with others.

Share your response to this definition of unity: "Unity is the supernatural work of God's Spirit who unites us with Jesus in His Mission. The Spirit unites the community of God's people around God's Mission, operating in God's strategy and values together."

What are you discovering about Jesus's and the Father's unity through how Jesus prayed in John 17?

What are you discovering about the unity Jesus wants for us through the way Jesus prayed in John 17?

Mission drift occurs when we lose focus or attention on the mission, causing us to drift away from it. For the Jesus follower, the Mission given to us by Jesus Himself is to make disciples who make disciples. Give an example of mission drift in your own life when it comes to Jesus's Mission.

When it comes to living a Jesus Mission Life, what factors positively or negatively influence mission drift?

What is something you do or can begin to do to stop mission drift?

## A step you can take as you go:

The Mission of Jesus is to seek and save the lost, and our expression of a Jesus Mission Life is to make disciples who make disciples. We will all experience mission drift. Take a few minutes to examine what causes Jesus's Mission to drift in your own life. Begin to build a plan to stay (or get) on Mission and share this with someone who can help, pray, or join you.

# Chapter 6

## Mission and Purpose

There is a well-meaning and constant challenge given to Jesus followers in faith communities across the world: "You have a purpose." The instruction that follows is, "Find your purpose." In a camp, a church service, a small group, or other places where Jesus followers gather, how many thousands upon thousands of people have been encouraged to find their purpose?

When it comes to the idea that we have a purpose and that we are to find our purpose, I want to challenge you to replace two words with two different words. I believe if we take this challenge, Jesus Mission Living will become a description of our lives.

The first word I want you to replace is *purpose*. Purpose, by definition, means motivation. My purpose equals my motivation—what drives me. I'd like you to replace the word purpose with mission. *Mission*, by definition, means an assignment. My mission is the assignment I have been given. For Christ-followers, the mission (assignment) we have been given is Jesus's Mission—to rescue people by making disciples who make disciples.

The second word I want you to replace is "find." Find suggests a search for something elusive or missing and thus ongoing. Replace the word "find" with "choose." Choose is a word that suggests an act of the will, a decision made.

This is so much more than semantics because it drastically impacts how we live and practice a Jesus Mission Life. When I am encouraged to find my purpose without first understanding the assignment given to me by Jesus, my mission, I am backward in my approach, and satisfaction eludes me. What would happen if we all lived with the focus of *choosing Jesus's Mission?*

About now, there are a lot of "wait-a-minute," "yeah, but," and "I-am-not-so-sure" thoughts running through heads. Why? Because what I have written goes against our cultural approach to purpose. Today, in the faith world, the way we use the idea of purpose is individual and often driven by our own wiring and personality. Finding your purpose puts way too much emphasis on the word *your*, and this always gets in the way of the mission (2 Corinthians 4:7). A much more biblical approach would be to say, choose HIS Mission. Embrace HIS Mission as your own. When you have made this choice, then let the love (2 Corinthians 5:14) and glory (1 Corinthians 10:31) of God become the motivation of your heart and life, your purpose. The mission we have is driven by Jesus's Mission, and it is the assignment we have because we follow Him. We actually have an assignment (mission) that never changes, regardless of how my seasons of life shape my motivation (purpose).

Purpose, because it is about motivation, will always be linked with "motivation to a task." When I get up in the morning and feel hungry, my purpose is to get food. When I am tired at the end of the day, my purpose is to get some sleep. When my car says three miles before my tank is empty, my purpose is to get fuel. The way purpose is actually lived out changes my purpose with each task. The urgency of the task dictates the passion of my purpose. That is why our purpose changes with age, the status of life, health, pain, and the baggage we carry. Motivation that is linked to a task allows personal urgency, changes in life, spiritual development, or the lack thereof, to decide our mission. At the end of the day, purpose is dependent upon me.

Our mission was and is decided when we began our friendship with Jesus. Our mission never changes from the moment we meet Christ to our last breath. "For me to live is Christ" (Philippians 1:21). Each of us has been crucified with Christ, and it is no longer we who live but Christ who lives in us (Galatians 2:20). Our mission IS 100 percent the same as Jesus's Mission to seek and save the lost. This is our assignment from Jesus Himself—"Make disciples wherever you go" (Matthew 28:18–20). "You will be my witnesses in Jerusalem, Judea, Samaria and to the ends of the word" (Acts 1:8). "As the Father has sent me, I am sending you" (John 20:21).

In one very real sense, because of the image of Jesus in us, when we follow Jesus, we step into the Mission we were made for. Jesus Mission Living is much more about our choice to live out our design than a purpose we go find.

Throughout my faith journey, I can remember hearing these words about having, finding, and living my purpose. In my heart, I said, "Yes, I want to find my purpose." But I soon realized I didn't quite know what I was looking for, where to look, and what to do if I actually did find my purpose. Does this in any way sound familiar to you? Here is my own story of when I chose mission over trying to find purpose.

I met Jesus at a Vacation Bible School. At that time, I asked Jesus to come into my life and forgive my sins, promising to follow Him forever. I was three years old.

I knew at a very young age that I would end up in ministry. Life has a way of sending us detours, and mine has been no exception. Just a few months before I met Jesus, my birth father tried to kill my mother, and my grandfather stopped him. My birth father abandoned our family, and a few years later, he took his life. My amazing mom somehow managed to deal with her pain and still love three kids. It was also during this time my grandparents showed up for me and my siblings in huge ways. My mother remarried a truly great man whom I call my dad.

Shortly after meeting Jesus, I remember experiencing my first form of sexual abuse. It happened again a year later and then again, more severely after that. Back then, you just didn't talk about stuff like that.

In school, after being tested in reading, I was sent to what was called a remedial reading class. It was not so much that I couldn't read, but something in my head couldn't retain much of anything I read, especially if it was not immediately useful to me. I memorized Scripture like crazy and knew every story in the Bible, but I couldn't process or retain the words in most books. By now, the abuse in my life was creating havoc in my soul, and if you remember, we just didn't talk about stuff like that. All the while, I really loved Jesus and wanted to know Him, follow Him, and serve Him. There was an epic war going on inside of me. With each twist and turn in my life, the Mission of Jesus was pushed aside. Pain and sin have a way of blurring the Mission we were made for, Jesus's Mission.

At thirteen and a half, I found myself with no way or place to process what was done to me when I was a kid. I felt broken, afraid, and ashamed. I hated this part of my life, but I also deeply loved Jesus at the very same time. I very much wanted to serve Him and know Him. But, inside the soul and mind of thirteen-and-a-half-year-old Leonard, there was a battle being waged. One night, weary of the fight, the Holy Spirit spoke gently to me. Not an audible voice; no, this one was even more clear. This is what I heard:

"Leonard, I love you, and you are no accident! I made you on purpose. Don't let your pain choose your road; let me give you My Mission. It will become your life mission, too."

I sat in my room and prayed and cried and prayed some more. I felt a new sense of hope, and I felt deeply loved by God. The very next day, a youth pastor I knew saw me and said these very familiar words: "Leonard, you have a purpose; go find your purpose." Our conversation ended in a dare. This youth pastor dared me to read my Bible for sixty minutes a day for 365 days, one whole year. I did it, and God used His Word to heal so many of my deepest wounds. He still uses His Word to make me whole, by the way. Looking back, I am so grateful for God's perfect timing in my life. But in all honesty, at the end of a year—even with the healing and love God gave me—I was still searching for purpose.

When I was a freshman in high school, on our winter retreat, the speaker told us his story. He said he went to jail and nearly ruined his life because he didn't know his purpose. This made me perk up; after all, I didn't want to go to jail. When he found his purpose, he got a good wife, a good ministry, good kids, and lived a better life. He defined purpose as that special thing only I could do because I was fearfully and wonderfully made by God on purpose and with purpose. I wanted all of that, so finding my purpose gave me more of an incentive than ever before. What I never understood is that I was looking for a motivation (purpose) without a mission or too small a mission.

But again, when I got home, I was still short, not skinny, struggling in school, afraid people would find out my secrets, and wishing the cute girl liked me (she didn't). I didn't feel at all special or wonderfully made. When I asked various leaders about not feeling special and not knowing what the thing was God had for me to do that only I could do, I received this advice. I was told that I was a leader, I was funny, and I could do anything I put my mind to. Then I was instructed:

*"Do more devotions; you will find your purpose."*

*"Find your spiritual gifts; this will help you find your purpose."*

*"Serve in a ministry; that is how you will find your purpose."*

*"Pray more; that is how you will find your purpose."*

*"Be more serious at church (I was fourteen), and that is how you will find your purpose."*

*"Trust God more; that is how you will find your purpose."*

I took all of this advice and tried, with a sincere heart, to do it all. Guess what? I still didn't feel like God made me all that special. After all, special people don't have the war going on inside of them like I did at this age. My internal struggles made my purpose change with every mission I had. I wanted to be liked and loved, feel better inside, serve Jesus, be a good Christian, keep my secrets, and be good at sports. For the next year, I searched for my purpose; after all, I was told I had one that only I could do, and I should find it. But, because my mission was as clear as mud, my purpose switched with the hundreds of missions rushing around inside my soul. This search for what made me special yielded very little except frustration.

At fifteen and a half, I was literally cornered by the camp speaker on the first day before I even got my bunk. (I cannot remember his exact words, but I do remember what I heard him say.) "Leonard, stop thinking you have a purpose and stop looking for your purpose!" Not the message I was accustomed to hearing. He continued, "Leonard Lee, God is not asking you to find anything. He is asking you to embrace Jesus's Mission, to live a Jesus Mission Life. Only when you decide to give your life to His Mission, and only when you choose a Jesus Mission Life, will you really have a purpose. Then and only then will you become who He made you to be." And just like that, he walked away. I stood there, completely stunned. The speaker wasn't a bully but actually a family friend. He was my pastor for the first nine years of my life, and he also baptized me. He walked our family through much trauma when I was young, so I listened.

That night in the evening session, the speaker spoke, people sang, and I surrendered to letting the single Mission of God become my single mission in life. I accepted the assignment given to me by God. I committed the rest of my life to building and living a Jesus Mission Life. This commitment moved me from the Christian school and transferred me to a public high school where I was determined to share the good news of Jesus with every person I could. Over the next three years, about one hundred of my friends met Jesus and were given Bibles. They were also taught to read them, pray, be in church, and share their stories.

Looking back, it was the power of this preacher's words that propelled me to give my life to the Mission of Jesus. Now, more than four decades later, the Mission of Jesus has protected me, driven me, strengthened me, and healed me. The Mission of Jesus has lifted me when I was down and provided direction and guidance for every life decision. The Mission of Jesus has introduced me to some amazing people, taken me across the world, put me in rooms where I did not belong, and stretched me in countless ways. The Mission of Jesus has filled my heart with joy and meaning. I have lived nearly every day since I was fifteen and a half, captured by the love of God and the Mission of God. This is what it means to live a Jesus Mission Life.

Here is the catch: it is not my mission; it is Jesus's Mission. My life is not driven by something I was told I had or something I was challenged to find. My life is driven by something much greater—the very Mission of God established before the foundation of the world. I quit looking for a motivation and accepted an assignment. The more I love Jesus and the deeper my friendship with Jesus goes, the more I understand that Jesus's Mission is truly an amazing gift. Jesus's Mission demands my life and my all. I now have a better understanding of one of the more difficult teachings of Jesus: "If you want to be my disciple, deny yourself and take up your cross and follow me. Take up My Mission!"

Constantly, Jesus teaches us that His Mission is so important that it is worth everything. Jesus's parable, the Pearl of Great Price (Matthew 13:46-45), tells us that once we find God's Kingdom and His Mission, we have found the one thing worth everything we have. His Mission and Kingdom are the Pearl of Great Price. In the Kingdom of God, God requires our love for Him to eclipse all other loves. The Mission of Jesus is for those in His Kingdom to make disciples who make disciples whose disciples also make disciples. This is the Jesus Mission Life, and this Mission is lived out as a citizen of His Kingdom. His Mission is the gift Jesus gives to all Kingdom citizens, everyone who will love God with all their heart, soul, mind, and strength, and their neighbors as themselves (Mark 12:30).

"Semantics, Leonard, just semantics." This was the response of a trusted friend as we talked about purpose and mission. I don't think so and let me tell you why. I meet people all over the world who love Jesus and believe they have found their purpose but never actually embrace the Jesus Mission Life—they never become a disciple who makes a disciple. Remember, purpose is motivation; mission is an assignment.

I believe with my whole heart that our uniqueness expresses itself best as we live out the Jesus Mission Life. Jesus's commission to His disciples was not to find their purpose but to live out His Mission by making disciples everywhere they went. There is a reason it is called the Great Commission and not the Great Co-purpose. Look at the following graph and see the comparisons.

| FIND MY PURPOSE | A JESUS MISSION LIFE |
|---|---|
| A motivation based on desire or need. | An assignment from Jesus. |
| I have to go looking for it. | I do not have to look for it; it's already given to me, and I receive it as a gift. |
| Changes with age, life, and responsibilities. | Remains the same, expressed through different ages, life, and responsibilities. |
| Mysterious or often hard to find. | Plain and found in the Scriptures. |
| Trial and error to find it. | Embrace it and become skilled. |
| Skill or desire-based expressions. | Expressed within all my life. |
| Only so many places to express it. | Expressed as I go, everywhere I go. |

This is not semantics. Each of our lives must be driven to live out and fulfill the Mission of the Father, Son, and Holy Spirit. The Mission of God supersedes everything because it is THE MISSION OF GOD! It is the Mission of God before the foundation of the world. It is the Mission of God, as God's response to sin. It is the Mission of God throughout the entire Bible, from Genesis to Revelation. It is the Mission of God today. Right now, it is still the Mission of God. Receive this assignment, this Mission, as a gift from God, and I guarantee nothing will ever be the same.

The point of my story is that instead of searching for our own unique purpose, I believe we must embrace a mission that already exists and has existed before the foundation of the world. This gift is God's Mission and is being given to each of us by Jesus Himself. Are you willing to take hold of His Mission and make it your own? Are you willing to build a Jesus Mission Life? Once you do, then God will empower your own unique design to live out His Mission everywhere you go for as long as you go.

The disciples embraced the Mission of God as their mission. The commission Jesus gave as He left earth, the make-disciples-everywhere-you-go commission, tells us that God's Mission was the life mission for these men and women. In Acts 1:8, Jesus told His disciples that when the Holy Spirit comes with power, that power is to be used to tell people in Jerusalem, Judea, Samaria, and the rest of the world about Jesus.

The Mission of Jesus is given to the disciples when Jesus says to His friends, "As the Father has sent me, I am sending you" (John 20:21). The Mission of Jesus is expressed after He sat with a Samaritan woman and then told His disciples that the field is ripe and ready to be harvested (John 4:35). The harvest was full when the entire village came to meet Jesus, and just like the Samaritan women, everyone who met Jesus received a new mission and story to tell.

The way Jesus moved about, spoke, loved, preached, and trained disciples all revealed how central the Mission of God was to every moment of His life. Jesus did not leave heaven to find His Mission; His Mission brought Him from heaven, and He embraced the Mission that belonged to His Father. This Mission was His purpose (motivation) for everything He did, everywhere He went. His Mission is what brings us to every person and place and moment.

Following Jesus means we are destined to live out His Mission, not find our purpose. Jesus's gift of His Mission is not about stretching our comfort zones where we talk to strangers about the cross of Christ; it is about each of us fulfilling our God-given design.

Jesus knew that purpose changes with life, but HIS Mission is expressed in every season of life because it never changes, not since before the foundation of the world. There are many things we do that are right and noble, but they are not meant to be our purpose but a place where a Jesus Mission Life is lived. Parenting, marriage, work, and earning money are the arenas in which a Jesus Mission Life is so potent.

I didn't write this chapter to say your life has no purpose but rather to invite you into building your life around Jesus's Mission to seek and save the lost. These words are about taking the **coMISSION** of Jesus to make disciples who make disciples as your mission. The Mission of Jesus is what Jesus Himself commanded us to give our entire life to, and when we do, His Mission becomes our purpose. This is a Jesus Mission life.

Jesus knows that without His Mission, we will make relationships, talents, abilities, and vocations our smaller missions, and our purposes will change with each one. These are not our mission—these are the arenas in which we live His Mission. Mission is how we live when life is hard, relationships change, money is good, or money is scarce. Jesus Mission Living is Jesus-centered, not results-centered.

Have you ever experienced your purpose changing with your situation and circumstances in life? I cannot recount the number of people I know who approached an arena of life designed for mission and claimed this arena as their life purpose. When this arena changed with grown children, a job change, health situations, or other circumstances, these people lamented being lost and feeling like they needed to find another purpose again. Purpose is too generic. Mission, especially the Jesus Mission Life, is specific and comes from a higher source than just ourselves. Jesus Mission Living, by nature, involves a larger picture than our life or accomplishments. People do not find enough strength in having their own purpose. The strength we need is found only in His Mission.

# Stepping into Jesus's Mission

## A prayer you can pray today:

*Dear Jesus,*

*Thank You for gifting me Your Mission. Will You help all the motivation of my life, the exercise of purpose, be directed to only Your Mission? I am asking You to make Your Mission clear in every arena of my life—in my family, friends, work, school, leisure, and everywhere I go. I am grateful that Your Mission never changes. Amen*

## Some questions to move you forward:

What were the things in this chapter that stood out to you?

By definition, purpose is a motivation, and mission is an assignment. Take a few minutes and think about these differences.

Purpose is about being fulfilled in life, and mission is about fulfilling the assignment being given to us by God. Take a few minutes to think about these differences.

Read Matthew 28:18–20. What is the Mission Jesus handed to His disciples? What has He handed to us?

How does the perspective of finding your purpose vs. embracing God's Mission as your assignment encourage or challenge you?

What is the potential impact in the arenas of your life when you embrace God's Mission as your assignment?

Mission is a gift, not a burden. Where do you struggle to see the Mission of Jesus as a gift? Why?

We see mission as a gift when we see the bigger picture of what God is doing and wants done. In what arenas of your life do you need to see God's bigger picture?

## A step to take as you go:

Write down on a 3" x 5" card one or two statements from this chapter that will help you live a Jesus Mission Life. If you have not yet memorized Matthew 28:18–20, write it out and memorize it today.

# Chapter 7

## Choose Jesus's Mission *(It's Good for You)*

Standing before a thousand students, I shared with them that only two things can ruin their lives, and only two things can make their lives count—their environments and their choices. Bad environments and bad choices make life miserable. Good environments and good choices make life better. As I spoke, I explained how the only way to overcome a bad environment is a good choice. With a few illustrations about environments and choices, I presented the good news that Jesus Christ is the best choice we can make regardless of our environment. Our choices matter.

In September 2021, Merrily and I moved 2,250 miles from our home in California to Tennessee. When we were looking for a house in Tennessee, I had my list, and Merrily had hers. My list included several acres with space to build a garage/meeting place for me and the ministry. I wanted the space to put a couple of small homes (forget that I had no money) so people could stay, and then I wanted to enjoy wide open spaces where I could write, study, and spend time with God. If there was enough property, maybe I could also hunt and fish. Having huge campfires with friends (never mind, we did not know a soul where we were moving) would make life grand.

After I texted Merrily the umpteenth house listing that met my wants, she finally said, "Leonard, you have a calling and a mission on your life, and it does not involve lawn care, property management, building projects, and the upkeep of several acres of land. If we choose any of these properties you have sent me, you will sidetrack your mission for something you do not really like—yard work." I now live in a van down by the river.

Okay, I don't really live in a van down by the river, but because I married a woman who understands the ripple effect our choices make so well, I do live in a home that I love in an area I love. Our choices matter.

A Jesus Mission Life is the choice we make and the life we are commissioned into when we first meet Christ. A Jesus Mission Life is not a next-level kind of faith; it is the faith we see throughout the entire New Testament. The struggle today is not whether we are supposed to live a Jesus Mission Life; the struggle is how we can live a Jesus Mission Life in the twenty-first century, which gets back to what I told the students, that the answer to those struggles is found in our choices and our environments.

For the next few pages, I want to challenge you to choose a fully engaged Jesus Mission Life. You might be pushed, nudged, encouraged, or even frustrated as we come to the crossroads of choosing a Jesus Mission Life. This is not a sales pitch; Jesus doesn't need one, He is God. This will not be a life improvement chapter where we say that your life will get easier and less complicated and that the words "smooth sailing" will define the rest of your life. There will be no promises of prosperity, no guarantees that your relationships will mend, all your wounds will heal, and your finances will improve. Choose Jesus's Mission for your own. Build a Jesus Mission Life—that is it. Why? *Because Jesus is worth everything.*

In Spring 2023, I trained a group of leaders in West Africa to live a Jesus Mission Life by making disciples who make disciples. Many said, "If we do this, it will cost us our lives." When we finished, we commissioned them, and they began to pray, "Jesus, where can we take this good news?" Over the next several months of prayer, as they were honing their training, they made a choice: "We will go across the river, share the good news of Jesus in Muslim villages where there is no church or Christian witness."

In November 2023, with a plan in place, about fifty of the trained disciple makers got into boats, crossed the fast-moving river, and set off to various villages. After a few days with seeds sown for future ministry, they came back to the boat to return home. Divided into two boats, they crossed the river. One boat, carrying about forty of our disciples who chose to be disciple-makers, hit something in the river. The boat capsized, and they all drowned. (In some countries, the safety standards we are accustomed to do not exist.) When I got word that evening, I felt sick to my stomach. I wanted to question God. I wanted to catch a flight and go to them and their families. I wanted to understand what was so far beyond my understanding, but all I could do was pray and cry.

We were able to provide the burial linens, hire people to dig graves, and provide food for the families whose unexplainable loss brought both confusion and grief. Of all the truths these families wanted to share in the midst of their grief and loss, they wanted people to know that living a Jesus Mission Life is worth it.

Before we lose the point, let's go back to our choices and our environments. We mostly make choices by weighing out the value returned for an investment deposited. If the cost is not equal to the reward, we choose no. We make choices by the effort required to make the choice. Is being healthy worth the cost of exercise? We make choices by the potential of reward or payoff. Will the cost now be worth the payoff later? My friends in West Africa made a choice based on two heartfelt convictions and beliefs. First, Jesus is worth it. Second, Muslims across the river who had never heard of Jesus were worth it.

We also make choices out of our histories, wirings, and environments. Here are just a few examples:

- The choice to fight or the choice for peace.
- The choice to change and grow or the choice to stay the same.
- The choice to learn or the choice to keep the knowledge we have.
- The choice to forgive or the choice to hold the wound and grudge.

How we handle and resolve conflict, how we organize our lives, how we view money, and how we engage our neighbors are all choices that come from our environments. Who we marry and how we raise our kids, both in what we choose to do or what we choose not to do with our kids, are influenced by our environments. Did you know that most addictions begin before someone turns sixteen years of age? Choices and environments matter.

So, doesn't it make sense that when it comes to building and living a Jesus Mission Life (living our lives as disciples who make disciples), our choices and environments matter?

Several years back, I was meeting with a group of about eight or nine guys, and we were focused on building a Jesus Mission Life. All of these guys were nineteen to twenty-two years old, loved Jesus, and were willing and ready to choose a Jesus Mission Life. As we sat in the apartment of a couple of these guys, I asked the question: "What is Jesus worth to you?" Answers came like microwave popcorn, you know—heat, pop, pop, pop, poppoppoppop … I sat, listening and trying to compile a list of their answers. "Everything" was the first answer. My time, my sleep, my money, my thought life, my attitude. We made a list of more than twenty-five things that were impacted by the worth of Jesus in our lives. It was a lot of fun, and since I had been discipling these guys both in the group and individually, I followed up with a challenge: "Prove it. Prove to me that Jesus is worth everything to you. I do not doubt the answer is true in your heart, but how does 'Jesus is worth everything' translate to your daily life?" It was already after 10:00 p.m., but we talked for another hour. For weeks, each individual meeting I had with these guys centered around the topic of how much Jesus was worth to them.

How would you answer the question, "What is Jesus worth to me?" Just writing it on these pages, I can feel the weight of the answers in my own heart and life. "What is Jesus worth to me?" is a point-in-time question, one we answer when we decide to follow Jesus. "What is Jesus worth to me?" is also a daily question, often a moment-by-moment question. The follow-up question is, "How will I show His worth through my CHOICES?" Here are three Jesus Mission Life choices we can make every day.

### ONE—CHOOSE THE JESUS MISSION LIFE FOR YOUR OWN LIFE

One year, I was speaking at a summer camp when the team competition moved to the Tug-O-War contest. For those who never had the chance to play, Tug-O-War is a game where a giant rope is laid out on a field. A ribbon is tied to the center of the rope, and two teams grab the rope, one at each end. When GO is sounded, each team pulls as hard as they can until the ribbon in the middle has been moved to their side. There are three important positions in gripping the Tug-O-War rope.

**The Anchor.** This is the person in the back who holds the line, shouts the command to pull, and refuses to give ground to the other team. Often the rope is wrapped around the Anchor's waist.

**The Point.** The Point is the person in the front whose strength and quickness give the momentum-building first pull, hopefully giving the advantage to their team.

**The Pack.** The Pack is the group of people in the middle. Their job is to pull in rhythm with the Anchor and the Point.

I have seen Tug-O-War contests won without a strong Point or a beast of an Anchor, but never without a Pack who does their part well.

In the Mission of God, we tend to focus on the Point and the Anchor as the real Jesus Mission Living people, but the truth is, the Mission is not accomplished without the Pack doing their part, pulling in unison. In other words, we all have to grab the rope and pull.

Most of us reading this book identify with one of these three places—Anchor, Point, or Pack. In the Jesus Mission Life, understanding the importance of the Pack is vital.

The Pack are the people whose prayers just never seem to stop. The Pack are the people whose giving supports missions all over the world, in their communities, and in their churches. The Pack are the people whose hands and feet pull the rope every day. Let me introduce you to a few Pack members who pull with all their might.

#### Lois Dietz Pulled the Rope Through Prayer and Sacrificial Giving

Lois never traveled anywhere I did. She never spoke any language other than the "Southern" she learned as a girl growing up in Missouri. She didn't finish school much past seventh grade, nor did she have a driver's license. But, wow, did she understand the Jesus Mission Life! Widowed in 1973, Lois found a way to live by making dolls, quilts, knitting, and sewing. When I would visit her, I always took a peek at her Bible, and I was always impressed by how worn it was. Her prayer life consisted of a constant flow of prayers for others, her family, and her love for Jesus. Her fixed income was not much, so imagine my surprise when Lois approached me to say, "I am going to support your ministry for $25 a month." This was indeed the Widow's Mite (Mark 12:42). Lois's eternal impact will need the space of heaven to be measured because from her sewing machine, her chair, and all the places in her home where prayers were sent to the throne of God, Lois chose Jesus's Mission as her highest life. I always told Lois that whenever I am on a campus telling students about Jesus, traveling to Africa or India or any other country, her knees touched the ground long before my feet ever did.

### Jeffrey Pulled the Rope by Sharing the Love and Kindness of God

Jeffery was born with Down syndrome, and he really, really loved Jesus. I met him when I was in high school, and over the several years I knew Jeffery, he told everyone he met that Jesus indeed loved them and that they could know God's love. He always had a small gospel tract that had the story of Jesus on it and handed those out with such joy. He did this until he passed. Jeffery lived a Jesus Mission Life, and it started with a choice to love others with Jesus's love.

### The Woman at the Well Pulled the Rope by Sharing her Jesus Story with Her Community

Approaching the well to draw water was a morning practice for the women in her village. The fact she did it at noon speaks to her reputation. Her choices had damaged it in a way that made her an outcast to her entire city. Feeling the sting of rejection from her community, on this day, there was a stranger (Jesus) at the well. The conversation begins with Jesus asking for water and ends with her embracing Jesus and a Jesus Mission Life. Immediately after her time with Jesus, she went to the very people who had pushed her out, telling them that she had indeed met the One who God had promised would come and save them, the Messiah. Her entire village came and met Jesus. She lived a Jesus Mission Life, and it started with a choice to tell her village. You can read her story in John 4.

### My New Friend in North India Pulled the Rope by Faithfully Praying for Me

She was one of the illiterate women in North India. When I met her, her first words to me were, "I am nothing; I am a nobody." She said this sentence to me five or six times before she paused. I said, "Tell me your name," and she looked up. For the first time, we made eye contact. "I only do what Jesus tells me to do, and six months ago, Jesus told me to pray every day, for long hours pray. I pray for a person who has a strange name." I smiled and said, "Jai Masiki," which means "praise the Lord" in Hindi. She continued, "I am nothing; I am nobody," and then said, "I never hear of this name before. I thought, who names child this name? It is a strange name." I smiled again, and she continued,

"Tonight they introduce you to speak. Pastor Singh said, 'This is friend from America, and his name is Leonard Lee.' I looked up and began to cry because this is the name I have been praying for every day for the last six months."

This woman lives a Jesus Mission Life. For more than two decades now, as an answer to this woman's prayers, we have been serving in India. We have seen thousands of pastors trained, tens of thousands of people fed and provided for with medicines, given blankets to people who spend their winters at 15,000 feet elevation, led kids programs, launched medical clinics, funded sewing centers for battered women, and much more. It all started with a choice to pray for a guy with a strange name. This is a Jesus Mission Life.

*Choices make a difference.* Do not focus on your spot on the rope in the Tug-O-War contest; focus on the mission and pull together. I say this because my job often causes people to act as if I play a more important role in the Mission of Jesus than they do. I don't. There is nothing I do that can be done without other people living their Jesus Mission Lives. Praying, giving, helping with administration, connecting me to other people, and traveling with me are just some of the countless ways in which people choose to live Jesus Mission Lives. Billy Graham once said, "The world is filled with much better preachers and leaders than I; I am just the most prayed for." We all pull the same rope together.

Choosing the Jesus Mission Life as your own is not about preaching, traveling, writing, or training pastors. Choosing the Jesus Mission Life is each of us choosing to take our spot along the Tug-O-War rope and pulling with all our might for the Mission of Jesus: to seek and save the lost. When we do, something that cannot happen by ourselves happens—Jesus's Mission.

Jesus Mission Lives are not one-size-fits-all; they are built around the ways in which God has made each of us. You may never lead a team to Brazil, but you can offer the same hope you found in Jesus to your neighbor. *Grab the rope and pull.* You might never sing and lead worship, but you can be the song of hope to a kid in a troubling situation as a big brother or sister. *Grab the rope and pull.*

The wisdom of God is that He perfectly combines who He made us to be with His Mission to seek and save the lost. The Jesus Mission Life is the life that combines His Mission with His wisdom in making you the way He made you. But this is more than design; it is also how our stories are written. When we grab the rope and pull, God takes our brokenness and our sinfulness that has now been redeemed by God and makes it useful in His Mission as well.

I can write about my friend Jeff, whose freedom from alcohol addiction has become a story of hope. Countless people have found freedom from their hurts, habits, and hang-ups. He is a disciple-maker, and his Jesus Mission Life is a reflection of the ways God has set him free. God has redeemed his sinful mess and now uses it to help others find the freedom that only comes through Jesus.

I can write about my friend Heidi, whose life is invested in those who need a family because the one they were born with is gone or unable to provide the needed love and care. She lives a Jesus Mission Life by serving the vulnerable and creating a network of churches and businesses that all grab the rope and pull together. Her personal life is one of a disciple-maker.

My friend Deborah, a woman whose whole family was murdered by rebels and, as a young girl, was trapped in a refugee camp. Upon meeting Jesus, she vowed to bring the hope of Jesus to girls in West Africa. She lives a Jesus Mission Life.

My friends Rebecca, Miala, Unwango, Andrew, Michael, Justin, and Scott all live Jesus Mission Lives as teachers, pastors, businessmen, retirees, students, office workers, project managers, single moms, widows, divorcees, cancer patients, and survivors of violence and abuse. Jesus Mission Lives are beautiful stories that God is writing, and you are the parchment upon which this story is being penned. Each page is filled with your personality, your wiring, your pain, and your joy, and what makes these stories so beautiful is your choice to make a Jesus Mission Life your own. But we must make the choice to grab the rope and pull, to make Jesus's Mission our own mission too.

## TWO—CHOOSE TO USE WHAT YOU HAVE FOR OTHERS

My second-grade teacher, Mrs. Jones, was about a thousand years old when she was teaching my class. She was not a large person, quite the opposite. One day, we came into the classroom and saw all the books stacked on one end of her desk. There were a couple of bricks and rocks, too. One by one, we were invited to lift the heavy end of the desk. To a classroom of seven-year-old boys, the challenge was fun, but we couldn't budge it.

Then Mrs. Jones told us that she would lift the desk and only use one hand. We laughed, said no way, and even dared her to try. In an instant, Mrs. Jones grabbed a small red brick and a three-foot metal pry bar flattened on one end. Putting the brick on the ground next to the desk, she wedged the pry bar's flat end under the bottom edge of the desk and used the small red brick as a pivot point, called a fulcrum, and with one hand, she lifted the heavy end of the desk by applying pressure to the other end of the metal pry bar. "This is leverage, class," she said.

When I got home, I grabbed a rock from the yard and my dad's metal pry bar and I lifted the refrigerator, bookshelves, tables, beds, desks, and anything else that wasn't nailed to the floor. I had discovered a power beyond my strength—*leverage.*

Choosing a Jesus Mission Life is about leverage, using a power beyond your strength. Often, when in conversations about a Jesus Mission Life, we tend to give attention to what we lack. "We do not have the gifts, the talent, the money, the connections, the knowledge, the skills, the confidence," and the list goes on and on. I find very few people who think the Mission of God is not important. Very few people disagree with our need to grab the rope and pull with all our might. But many of us struggle to see how we can grab the rope and pull because, with such an important mission, we are often distracted by what we do not have.

One of the training sessions I do is called "Leverage: Finding the Power Beyond Our Strength." And just like little old Mrs. Jones, who impressed an entire class of second-grade boys by lifting a heavy desk with only one arm, we need to use leverage to live a Jesus Mission Life.

My travels around the world have put me in places where poverty is at its worst. A while back, I was in West Africa speaking to a group of pastors and leaders who, by every standard in every part of the world, are extremely poor. Economic, food, medical, and shelter are all in scarcity. I visited their homes with dirt floors and patchwork walls and roofs that will need to be redone after the next big rain. As a guest, I slept on a thin mat made of thatch leaves, and in the morning, I realized I had more food in my backpack than they did in the house.

When we gathered that morning, I asked them to tell me about the obstacles Christians face in choosing a Jesus Mission Life. Poverty was the first, second, and third answer. "We have nothing, our opportunities to get anything are limited, and the resources we need to do the work are just not here. We believe in the Mission of Jesus; we just do not feel like we have anything to offer to this mission." Wanting to give proper respect to the pain in their voices and on their faces, I listened carefully and spoke softly.

I wish that the feelings of not having much to offer to the Mission of Jesus were isolated, but they are not. Yes, poverty most certainly writes in **BOLD** letters that you have no place on the rope. Poverty might not be the cause, but you, too, could be struggling to see that you indeed do have a place on the rope. Your struggle could be in knowing how to grab the rope and pull with all your might. The thinking that we have little or nothing to offer to the Mission of Jesus is false thinking, and nothing could be further from the truth.

We talked for a while when I asked them, "How much of what you lack will God hold you accountable for?"

"None," they responded.

"So our task today is not to focus on what we lack but rather to give our energy to discovering and using what we have," I explained. "Let's state the obvious: You have Jesus, God the Holy Spirit, and a Father in heaven who loves you beyond measure. You have the Gospel, which is the power of God, the Word of God, and the people of God. You have 2,000 years of history to learn from. We know we have all of this, and that is a lot, and we know that when you say you lack, it is not Jesus you lack. But what if you discovered a power beyond the strength you currently have? What if you discovered you have more than you think, more than you know, and that you have an enormous power beyond your strength?" This was the question I wanted them to answer. It is this question that sets the table for us to leverage our entire lives for the Mission of Jesus. I told them about Mrs. Jones, and for the next three days, we walked through the life-changing training on leverage.

If you wonder what this has to do with you, the answer is *everything*. We desire that people find and then follow Jesus. We want people to find the hope and joy we have found in Christ. We want people to know they are forgiven and loved by the One who made them. But when we actually work to align ourselves with these heartfelt desires, it quite often seems beyond our reach, beyond what we think we have. That's where leverage comes in. **There are five areas of our lives we can leverage to find the power beyond our strength.** Let's go through these now.

### We Leverage What We Know

I asked my friends in Africa to take out a piece of paper and make a list of everything they knew how to do. Do you know how to read? Do you know how to farm? Do you know how to fix meals? Do you know how to repair roofs? Do you know how to write? Do you know numbers? Do you know how to teach, tutor, sing, or play an instrument? What do you know? It took a couple of hours to fully exhaust this question, but with the help of the Holy Spirit, every person in the room had a couple of pages dedicated to what they knew.

Next I said, "Circle anything on your list that someone else might also need to know." This took some time, but in the end, there were a lot of circles. I continued, "Put a star next to anything you circled if you know someone personally who needs Jesus who might also need to know that specific thing you know." After a few minutes, their papers had dozens of circles and stars. Finally, I instructed, "Write the name of that person next to your circle and star." When they finished, we broke into groups and began to pray for each name, asking Jesus for an opportunity to use what we know to love others and meet needs.

### We Leverage Who We Know

Next, I instructed the pastors and leaders to take out another piece of paper and begin making a list of people they knew. On the list were the names of teachers, pastors, people who sang, people who were great cooks, business owners, car repair specialists, coffin builders, farmers, athletes and footballers (soccer), seamstresses, artists, political leaders, soldiers, officers of the law, and craftsmen. Every person in the room had nearly two pages of names of people who they already knew.

"Circle any name of a person who is a phone call away," meaning they could contact them and it would not seem strange. I instructed them to put a star next to anyone who knows something they know, too, who they would be willing to talk with about following Jesus or helping them help others follow Jesus. "Pray for that person."

At the end of this session, I asked them to put on their list between five to ten names of people they need to know.

### We Leverage What We Have

As our training continued, I asked them to make a list of everything they had, from a pot to cook in, to a plot of land to farm. From a roof over their heads, to a goat that gives milk. From a phone to connect, to a chicken that gives eggs. When we were done, these dear people had pages and pages, listing what they had right then and there.

"Circle anything you have that can be used to love someone else in the Name of Jesus." They took several minutes to circle items they had that they could use to love others in the Name of Jesus. By now, they were catching on. I then gave instructions to put the name of someone next to what they had circled. "In groups, share the items you circled and the name of the person you can love, and begin to pray for them."

Each time they got in a group, they added more to their lists of what they knew, who they knew, and what they had because, together, they were seeing with new eyes. Every person in the room had more than a dozen names on their lists of people to pray for.

### We Leverage Our Obstacles as Opportunities

Our next step in discovering a power beyond our strength was to make two columns on a sheet of paper. On the top of one column, we wrote the word "Obstacles." On top of the other column, we wrote the word "Opportunities." We spent the next few hours asking two questions. First, "What obstacles do we face?" Words like religion, time, money, education, skills, and food were written. These are very real obstacles that can be quite paralyzing.

"In the next column, write the opportunity these obstacles provide you in loving someone else." This was the most difficult part of the training we did because it required each of them to shift their focus. "Now, take your list of people from the 'What you know,' 'Who you know,' and 'What you have' lists, and see if they have any ability to turn an obstacle into an opportunity."

This step surfaced people who had the ability to provide food, medicine, education, and skills to others in the Name of Jesus. By now, the room was buzzing; people were sensing they indeed had a power beyond their strength. I saw people in the room reveal that another person in the very same room was on their list and a collaboration that had never even been thought of began. I saw people connect needs they knew about to other people's strengths, opening the door for opportunities that had never been seen. The growing list of what to leverage made the room electric with excitement and energy.

### We Leverage Our Culture

Our final worksheet was about the culture in which they lived. "What are some built-in cultural expectations you can use?" Some cultures cannot say no to the hungry. Some cultures value work ethic. Some cultures value generosity. "Make a list of your cultural expectations. What does your culture celebrate and why? What does your culture punish and why? What does your culture expect from men, women, children, and young people? When does someone become an adult in your culture? What are the religious practices of your culture?"

We answered these questions. With each answer, I asked, "What can you leverage from this expectation or value?"

When we finished this training, one pastor said to me that he never felt this strong or rich. I asked him what had changed because he still had no money and I had not added to his resources. He answered, "I have found a power beyond my strength because I stopped looking at what was missing to do God's Mission; now I look at God's Mission and ask, 'What do I have that I can leverage?' I am rich beyond what I ever knew before."

This lesson applies to you and me, not just to poor people in Africa or another part of the world. God gave you your personality, knows your skills, and understands the way you are hard-wired; after all, He made you. He did not make some of us able to grab the rope and some of us unable to grab the rope. We all have the same mission, but we do not all do the same thing on the same mission. If you are willing, **I have included the leverage training worksheets in the appendix at the back of the book.** Take some time and use this process to discover a power beyond your strength and see what God has given you to leverage for His Mission. *The choice is yours.*

## THREE—CHOOSE A LIFE OF SACRIFICE

Sacrifice is also a huge part of Jesus Mission Living. Sacrifice is the giving up of one thing for something we hold more important. I love pocket knives, but I do not love cheap pocket knives. I am willing to give up more of my money to have a better knife. I love the classic flat-window Ford Bronco from 1966–1977, but I am unwilling to give up more of my money to get one of these.

Jesus Mission Living requires sacrifice. The sacrifice of self. The sacrifice of our own personal mission. The sacrifice of time. The sacrifice of our resources. The book of Philippians speaks to these kinds of sacrifices, so let's check them out.

### Sacrifice of Self (Philippians 2:1-11)

When I say sacrifice of self, it can sound pretty ominous. The call Jesus gave us to deny ourselves certainly does. Sacrificing self means we are willing to put others first. Paul the Apostle, in the book of Philippians, describes what it looks like to deny self better than anyone I know.

> Therefore if you have any encouragement from being united with Christ, if any comfort from his love, if any common sharing in the Spirit, if any tenderness and compassion, then make my joy complete by being like-minded, having the same love, being one in spirit and of one mind. Do nothing out of selfish ambition or vain conceit. Rather, in humility value others above yourselves, not looking to your own interests but each of you to the interests of the others.

> In your relationships with one another, have the same mindset as Christ Jesus: Who, being in very nature God, did not consider equality with God something to be used to his own advantage; rather, he made himself nothing by taking the very nature of a servant, being made in human likeness. And being found in appearance as a man, he humbled himself by becoming obedient to death—even death on a cross! Therefore God exalted him to the highest place and gave him the name that is above every name, that at the name of Jesus every knee should bow, in heaven and on earth and under the earth, and every tongue acknowledge that Jesus Christ is Lord, to the glory of God the Father. (Philippians 2:1–11)

In these eleven verses, Paul describes Jesus and how He approached His Mission. He denied Himself to the point of leaving heaven and dying on a cross. Paul also says to let Jesus's denial of self become our example. In other words, we are to have the same mind as Jesus—put others first like Jesus did. Remember, it was the Mission of God that brought Jesus to earth.

### Sacrifice of Personal Mission (Philippians 3:4-16)

What does it mean to give up our personal mission, or missions, to focus on the Jesus Mission Life? Paul, again in Philippians, gives us some insight. Look at the way he explains his life and focus:

> Though I myself have reasons for such confidence. If someone else thinks they have reasons to put confidence in the flesh, I have more: circumcised on the eighth day, of the people of Israel, of the tribe of Benjamin, a Hebrew of Hebrews; in regard to the law, a Pharisee; as for zeal, persecuting the church; as for righteousness based on the law, faultless. (Philippians 3:4–6)

In the words above, Paul tells the Philippian readers that his mission was to be the best Jewish leader possible. He also says he was succeeding. He had embraced his mission at the highest level, and his success was moving him up the ranks of the religious elite.

But then, Paul met Jesus, and his Mission changed (Acts 9). Jesus gave him a new Mission. The same is true for you and me. It might not look the same as Paul's, but it is the same Mission. Paul was the Point person on the rope. Once Paul met Christ, he was changed, and in the change, Paul sacrificed his mission for Jesus's Mission.

> But whatever were gains to me I now consider loss for the sake of Christ. What is more, I consider everything a loss because of the surpassing worth of knowing Christ Jesus my Lord, for whose sake I have lost all things. I consider them garbage, that I may gain Christ and be found in him, not having a righteousness of my own that comes from the law, but that which is through faith in Christ—the righteousness that comes from God on the basis of faith. I want to know Christ—yes, to know the power of his resurrection and participation in his sufferings, becoming like him in his death, and so, somehow, attaining to the resurrection from the dead. Not that I have already obtained all this, or have already arrived at my goal, but I press on to take hold of that for which Christ Jesus took hold of me. Brothers and sisters, I do not consider myself yet to have taken hold of it. But one thing I do: Forgetting what is behind and straining toward what is ahead, I press on toward the goal to win the prize for which God has called me heavenward in Christ Jesus. (Philippians 3:7–14)

What Paul is communicating to the Philippian readers is that his new Mission caused him to consider everything he had as loss. He now considers anything other than the Mission and calling in Christ to be rubbish. He might have said it this way: "Because of my new friendship with Christ, I have a new mission, and this is all I want to know—Jesus and His Mission."

When we follow Jesus, we must sacrifice our mission for His. This is what it means to follow Jesus. If you'll remember, Jesus's Mission is to seek and save the lost, and a Jesus Mission Life is one that makes disciples who make disciples. I love how Paul speaks to those who find it difficult to embrace this mission or to find their place on the rope.

> All of us, then, who are mature should take such a view of things. And if on some point you think differently, that too God will make clear to you. Only let us live up to what we have already attained. (Philippians 3:15–16)

Let me paraphrase these words. Paul is saying, "Mature Jesus followers know that they have to sacrifice their mission for Jesus's Mission. They grab the rope and take their place in God's Mission. If you do not agree, listen to God and He will tell you. So let's go live Jesus Mission Lives because we are Jesus Rescued People."

### Sacrifice of Time (Philippians 1:20–26)

Time is a treasure we hold on to. For almost every choice I make in my life, time is a factor in my decision. A Jesus Mission Life requires the sacrifice of our time. Today, the average Jesus follower in the USA attends church three out of five Sundays. Less than half are involved in any form of ministry, in or out of the church. Just over 43 percent of church-going people participate in a small group, including Sunday school, down almost 7 percent in the last decade. Apart from faith activities, our time has a lot of demands placed upon it.

When Paul talks about his time, he does so in two ways. *First, he understands that where he gave his time, sacrifice was required.* His words that tell of his desire to depart, to have finished the race, are strong. Paul knows that eternity with Christ is better, but to be here and live a Jesus Mission Life is a better sacrifice.

> I eagerly expect and hope that I will in no way be ashamed, but will have sufficient courage so that now as always Christ will be exalted in my body, whether by life or by death. For to me, to live is Christ and to die is gain. If I am to go on living in the body, this will mean fruitful labor for me. Yet what shall I choose? I do not know! I am torn between the two: I desire to depart and be with Christ, which is better by far; but it is more necessary for you that I remain in

> the body. Convinced of this, I know that I will remain, and I will continue with all of you for your progress and joy in the faith, so that through my being with you again your boasting in Christ Jesus will abound on account of me. (Philippians 1:20–26)

Paul's declaration is that in every way, the way he chooses to use his time and the way he lives every day means that Christ and His Mission will happen. "In my life and until my death, all of my time is mission-focused. In jail, on the road, with you, or apart from you, I will use my time here for God's Mission" (paraphrase mine).

A Jesus Mission Life requires sacrifice. To live a Jesus Mission Life means you and I will sacrifice our time. It takes time to love others like Jesus, using what you have or know to build bridges of friendship and hope. It takes time to make disciples who make disciples. The commitment is much greater than seventy-five minutes on a Sunday and ninety minutes during the week to sit in a circle. Jesus Mission Living is 24/7–365.

Jesus Mission Living requires time with Jesus. In Part Two, you will read about two indispensable investments of time with Jesus, without which it becomes impossible to sustain a Jesus Mission Life. It takes time to become equipped and trained to become a disciple-maker. Our fast-paced culture wants to have a seminar, a class, and be on our way. My experience is that when I hold training on becoming a disciple-maker in the way of Jesus, less than 5 percent of a church's people attend. If it is more than half a day, that drops to 2 percent.

It takes time to disciple someone. A weekly meeting, a few times a week with a person, text, phone, email all require prioritized time. Make room for prep time for yourself so you can effectively disciple someone. Faithfully equipping your disciple well so that they can eventually make a disciple takes time. Then there is life with a disciple, pointing them to the Scriptures so they can keep their eyes on Jesus in every season of life. It takes time.

I often invite people to enter into a disciple-making role with someone where they are discipling another person. Over 95 percent of the no's I hear fall into two categories. First, they say, "I do not know how." Second, they say, "I do not have time." It is never an issue of believing in God's Mission; it is an issue of not sacrificing something else that fills their time, either to become skilled or to invest in another disciple.

We cannot build a Jesus Mission Life without choosing to sacrifice our time to make space to be trained and then disciple someone else.

*A second aspect of sacrificing time is expressed in making the most of the time you have.* Finding time is difficult, but we are already in places where we can impact lives. Sidelines at games, carpools, cooking an extra meal for someone, a conversation in line at the store or restaurant. Sometimes, the extroverted Leonard, when he goes out to eat, says to his server, "Before I eat, I always try to say thank you to God for the people who made my food and the people who brought it. Is there anything I can pray for you?" The answers are incredible. Once, the server was waiting for a green card, and he sat down at the table; we grabbed hands and prayed together; we almost had church right there. Another time, the server began to cry and said, "I need Jesus. Can you help?" Rarely does anyone say, "No, I am good." If I am to make disciples wherever I go, then I work to start conversations, make invitations, and be salt and light.

I believe that God is good and He loves us; this is not a hard story to tell. The door has opened to the good news of Jesus in so many ways when I am making the most of every opportunity. Making the most of your time might not look the same as what I do. Paul told his disciple Timothy "to be instant in every season" (2 Timothy 4:2). Peter tells us to "always be ready to make a defense of our hope" (1 Peter 3:15). Again, Paul instructs us to "make the most of every opportunity (season) (Ephesians 5:16). Here is a great prayer to pray before you leave the house.

> *"Jesus, point me to any person that I can be salt and light to. Will You give me the eyes to see and the courage to speak grace and truth to anyone You bring across my path? You promised that Your Spirit would give me words when I need them. Will You do that today?"*

Praying a prayer like this prayer opens my eyes to see God at work.

### Sacrificial Mission Giving (Philippians 4:14-20)

Lastly, I believe our sacrifice is financial. I am writing a book on mission, not a book on giving. But after more than four decades of mission living, I know that sacrificial mission giving is very important. That is why I love what happened between the Jesus followers in Philippi and the apostle Paul.

> Yet it was good of you to share in my troubles. Moreover, as you Philippians know, in the early days of your acquaintance with the gospel, when I set out from Macedonia, not one church shared with me in the matter of giving and receiving, except you only; for even when I was in Thessalonica, you sent me aid more than once when I was in need. Not that I desire your gifts; what I desire is that more be credited to your account. I have received full payment and have more than enough. I am amply supplied, now that I have received from Epaphroditus the gifts you sent. They are a fragrant offering, an acceptable sacrifice, pleasing to God. And my God will meet all your needs according to the riches of his glory in Christ Jesus. To our God and Father be glory for ever and ever. Amen. (Philippians 4:14–20)

These dear people encouraged and blessed Paul through giving. They funded the work of Jesus through giving. They sacrificed and sent money. Their sacrifice enabled Paul to continue his Jesus Mission Life. In the end, they understood that a part of building a Jesus Mission Life is generously and sacrificially funding the kingdom work of God.

The Philippians had experienced a life-transforming friendship with Jesus. Philippi served as a Roman outpost and a popular trade route; the population was about 13,000 people. This was fairly large for a city in the first century. The people there were predominantly poor, and a large portion of the population was made up of slaves. There was no Jewish synagogue in Philippi. When Paul entered the city, he met a few people who began to follow Jesus, but troublemakers from outside the city got Paul arrested. Paul was miraculously freed by God, and the jailer, along with his whole household, met Christ. (The household would entail family, slaves, workers, and servants.) Paul says that the people in Philippi gave several times to assist in the work of spreading the gospel.

Here are a few observations about the sacrificial mission of giving.

**Sacrificial mission giving is just that—giving to resource the spread of the Gospel of Jesus to others.** Paul supported himself through his own work, but traveling, caring for his disciples, starting churches, and living on mission required extra help. The Philippians helped several times.

**Sacrificial mission giving connects Jesus Mission People in one place to Jesus Mission People in another place.** Paul used the giving of the Philippian Christians to care for believers who were persecuted in other places, helping with food and other needs, too. The generous support Paul received encouraged the persecuted believers in Thessalonica, implying they were not alone in their suffering.

**Sacrificial mission giving encourages the ministry.** Paul was deeply moved by their gifts and generosity. Paul knew that for these people to give was sacrificial; they were mostly poor. He knew that their giving accompanied prayer for him and his disciples. He knew that their giving showed they were grateful for his ministry to them.

**Sacrificial mission giving blesses the giver.** Paul told them that what brought the most joy was what their giving would do for the people in Philippi. God uses our sacrificial mission giving to encourage the giver. When we give to the kingdom work of disciples making disciples, our giving supports the initial start of the ministry. It also contributes to another generation of disciples making disciples. There is such spiritual contentment when we give confidently and know that what we give makes a life-long and life-changing difference.

**Sacrificial mission giving matters to God.** Paul called it a sweet aroma, an offering that makes God happy. This kind of giving brings joy to Jesus, because this kind of giving uniquely supports the Mission of Jesus to seek and save the lost.

For all of the ministry years God has graciously given Merrily and me, we have survived on sacrificial mission giving. God uses hundreds of people throughout the year who give gifts of $10 to $20,000; every gift causes a profound sense of gratitude in us. In turn, Merrily and I are both committed to sacrificial mission giving with what God generously shares with us. We use the following questions to decide where we will give:

1. Does the ministry we support verbally and practically proclaim the Gospel? We know there are places where people do amazing work with vulnerable people; we only partner with those whose work also makes Jesus known to the vulnerable in word and deed.
2. Does the ministry we support multiply? This means that unless we are specifically moved to give, we do not give to events, and as hard as this might sound, we only give to compassion-type needs when the gift solves a problem over just meeting a need. We want to rescue people caught in trafficking, but more than that, we give to ministries that both rescue and aim to stop trafficking. We want to help plant a farm more than buy a ration of food. We want our gift to go places where it multiplies, where people are developing people and disciples are making disciples.
3. Does the ministry we support deliver on its promises? A friend raised funds for a vehicle, saying this vehicle would bring life-

changing help to people in remote regions. But after examination, a different vehicle was purchased, and the help never arrived in those remote regions. We want the mission and the people we support to deliver on their mission.

4. Is the ministry we support biblically strong? Please understand that I am not saying I must agree with all their theology; rather, I want the ministry to have a foundation that is biblical and clear. Our funding never goes to support the prosperity gospel ministries I see around the world. I was asked to give money and time to a massive outreach in a different country. The people sponsoring the event claimed that sickness was a lack of faith and that God wanted these tens of thousands of people to become rich. If we would come and give to the event, they were quite sure God would multiply a hundred-fold back to us our gift. We said no, and the head of the event immediately called his security team to usher me out of the building.
5. Will my giving impact people? While giving is personal, it is not optional. We want our giving to go where it impacts the most people with the Gospel. We have given to hospitals that serve HIV patients because they also present the good news of Jesus in word and deed. We have given to support rescuing people from slavery when the rescue includes a plan to share Jesus. We have provided emergency food for people whose lives have been tragically uprooted by flooding or persecution, but we only partner with ministries that speak grace and truth to people. We do not give to animal rescue places, not because we do not care—we love animals, but we want our giving to impact people who bear the image of God. Jesus came to seek and save lost people.

As you build a Jesus Mission Life, it will take sacrifice—of self, personal mission, time, and resources. That is a conversation between you and Jesus. Have it, and you won't regret it.

# Stepping into Jesus's Mission

## A prayer you can pray today:

*Dear Jesus,*

*Thank You that You have a place on the rope for me to pull. I am asking You to move me past any sense that what I need to live a Jesus Mission Life is beyond my grasp. Will You show me what sacrifice is needed if I am to live a Jesus Mission Life? I am so grateful that You sacrificed Yourself for me.*

*Amen*

## Some questions to move you forward:

From this chapter, what is something that stood out to you? Why?

The title of this chapter is "Choose Jesus's Mission." What are some ways you see people choosing a Jesus Mission Life?

Using the picture of a Tug-O-War, where do you see yourself on the rope and why? Anchor? Point? Pack?

Regardless of where we are on the rope, we must pull with all our might. Personally, what do you think it means to pull with all your might?

A Jesus Mission Life can sometimes feel larger than our strength to live and seem beyond our own abilities and capacity. What do you do when you feel like a Jesus Mission Life is beyond your ability or capacity?

The Laws of Leverage provide us a power beyond our strength—what we know, what we have, who we know, turning obstacles into opportunities, and our culture. Of these five, where do you find yourself most successful in finding a power beyond your strength? Where do you find the biggest difficulty?

Sacrifice is to give up one thing we love for something we love more. Sacrifice in a Jesus Mission Life is to see Jesus and His Mission as worth everything. Take some time to interact with these four areas of sacrifice: Sacrifice of Self, Sacrifice of Personal Mission, Sacrifice of Time, Sacrifice of Resources.

About which of these four areas of sacrifice is God speaking most to you? What will you do with His voice concerning sacrifice?

## A step to take as you go:

Using the four areas of sacrifice and the book of Philippians, read Paul's letter each day this week and make note of a way to choose sacrificial Jesus Mission Living. Share with a friend what you are learning.

I do believe; help me overcome my unbelief! (Mark 9:24)

# Chapter 8

## You're Gonna Need a Bigger Faith

I used to love playing in the ocean until I watched the movie *JAWS*. This movie forever changed how I see the ocean. The movie industry has added anxiety to me "playing in the ocean," and Shark Week doesn't help. In the movie *JAWS*, there is this one scene where Sheriff Brody, Matt Hopper, and Captain Quint hunt the shark. As they are out on the ocean, the shark flashes its giant head and teeth next to the boat and startles Sheriff Brody. Seeing the size of the shark, he backs into Captain Quint's cabin and says, **"You're gonna need a bigger boat."**[7]

This scene paints for me a picture of how our hearts and minds interact with the idea of living out a Jesus Mission Life. We read words from Jesus that we are to make disciples wherever we go. We read words from Jesus that we are to imitate Him, love like Him, and share His thoughts and teaching, and all of these words flash their teeth. At that moment, we hear, **"You're gonna need a bigger faith."**

Growing a bigger faith, the kind that lives Jesus's Mission everywhere, requires us to understand faith better. So, what is faith? Often, it is much easier to understand faith by describing what faith does rather than attempting to define what faith is. In the rest of this chapter, I hope to provide clarity about faith by pointing out what faith does in six specific ways—faith grants us access to the Father Himself; faith allows the finite to relate to the infinite; faith trusts God; faith believes God; faith acts on God's truth; and faith lives wisely.

Let's take a look at all the things faith does for us and our Jesus Mission Life.

## FAITH GRANTS US ACCESS TO THE FATHER

Faith is such an amazing gift from God because it allows us access to Him. Years back, I was helping lead a city-wide event for students. My responsibilities made it necessary for me to have access to every part of the venue—backstage, the catwalks above, the security room, and all across the floor. I was also given a headset that gave me access to real-time conversations with people who were all working in unison to make this event happen. Faith is our "All Access Pass," providing us with real-time entrance into the presence of God, giving us direct access to Him—His wisdom, His love, His strength, and a greater understanding of living out a Jesus Mission Life.

God has a plan for us, and it is not small; it is an eternity-shaping, earth-shaking, life-changing plan, and we gain access to this plan through a deep and abiding friendship with Jesus. From this friendship, we live out our Jesus Mission Lives in partnership with Jesus. All that God has planned for you and me is accessed by our faith. Our faith gives us an all-access pass to everything God has planned for us.

But to live out this all-access pass that we have been given, we need to see what faith does. It is in the doing of our faith that we discover the substance of what faith actually is. If I am to live out the Jesus Mission Life God has gifted to me, I am going to need a bigger faith. My faith grows when I understand what it actually does—it grants me direct access to the Father Himself.

*"Faith gives us access to God and the life He has planned for us to live."*
*—Leonard Lee*

## FAITH ALLOWS THE FINITE TO BECOME FRIENDS WITH THE INFINITE

In the Bible, the word *faith* has a singular focus and multiple ways of expressing itself. The singular focus is how we relate to and interact with God. God has no other avenue for people to relate to Him other than faith. The Bible puts it this way: "Without faith it is impossible to please God" (Hebrews 1:6). Apart from faith, there is nothing we do that makes it into God's throne room.

God is not like us. We are limited, He is not. We are sinful, He is not. We can only see in part, He sees everything. We only know a tiny small piece, He knows everything. The vastness of the space between God and people cannot be measured by human measurements. The altogether difference between who God is and who we are cannot be bridged by any human effort.

Faith and trust have always been the bridge between God and people. Adam and Eve had to trust God's design for the world, to lean into Him by faith that what He assigned them was perfectly suited to them. These first two people had to trust God's vision for them to fill the earth with their kind and rule this sphere. Without this trust, they could not properly steward God's generous image within them or what God had created for them. Adam and Eve had to have faith that the trees in the middle of the Garden were not for them and that God's command to not eat of them was a good and loving command. Even in a perfect world, it took faith in God.

Sin made it worse for Adam and Eve and each of us, too. Trusting God and living a life of faith has the greatest urgency because eternity hangs in the balance for us and others. In one very real sense, faith is how we build a friendship with God. Much more than the access point of how we know God, it is the operating system, too.

Faith is for the finite, the limited. God is infinite and has all knowledge; therefore, He has no need for faith. He is limitless in knowledge, holiness, perfection, power, and unchangeability. This makes God the only acceptable object of faith. One of God's many qualities that makes Him worthy of our faith is that He is faithful. He is trustworthy.

As we describe faith, our description gains practical insight when we understand that faith is how we live in friendship with God. Faith accesses every promise from God and drives all of our obedience and movement toward God.

*"Faith is how finite people build a friendship with an infinite God."*
*—Leonard Lee*

## FAITH TRUSTS GOD

One of the primary expressions of faith is a growing trust in the object of our faith. Since 1989, Merrily has been able to share any critique of me and offer suggestions for growth because I have faith in her, both as a Daughter of the Most High God and as a friend and partner in the life we are building together. This faith in Merrily expresses itself in trusting her heart, her thinking, her wisdom, and her words. I have faith that she wants the best for us, for me, our family, and the ministry, so I trust her and the places from where her words come.

It is very important to know that trust is primarily a process of our thinking and a byproduct of our thought processes. When I have faith in God, it means I trust God. Before we go further on this, my thinking does not mean my understanding of Him. Finite (people) cannot have a full understanding of the infinite (God). But we can and must know that our faith in Christ is actually reasonable, meaning not without reason. We can examine "The Faith," our set of beliefs that form Christianity. When we do, we can intellectually know that the Bible is reliable, the resurrection really happened, Jesus really lived and died, and God is true and real. We can know that God created just as He said He did and that we have a reliable and true account of Jesus's life and the early church.

At the end of this chapter, I will give a list of go-to resources if you want to see how reliable "The Faith" we possess actually is.

I was in North India training pastors, and as we gathered, all the seats in the room were flimsy plastic chairs. I am not built for these chairs. Standing and staring at my chair, I took a look at me and then at the chair and then at me and then at the chair. My pastor friends began to laugh as I was clearly saying that I did not trust the chair to hold my weight.

In our session, we talked about trust being the decision to place the full weight of my life upon what I knew about God. The chair was a great example of not trusting something to hold my full weight, so I only put a part of my weight on the chair. Building a Jesus Mission Life requires a growing faith, as expressed in a growing ability and desire to place more and more of the weight of our lives on Jesus. This is trust. (By the way, the next session, they brought me a couch to sit on.)

When I trust God, I live by faith. I take what I know about God, His faithfulness, His power, His wisdom, His grace, and His purpose and Mission, and place the weight of my life upon Him in an act of submission and obedience to Him.

Trusting God means that He has earned enough credibility for me to not require full understanding and knowledge in every detail. Hebrews 11 is filled with people who are commended for trusting God (faith) even though they did not have all the information. These people placed the weight of their lives upon what they did know about God. Moses trusted God and went back to Egypt, where he was a wanted man and a fugitive, to lead more than a million slaves out of bondage to the edge of the promised land. Abraham trusted God to leave his home, traditions, and religion to go to a place he did not know.

A Jesus Mission Life is trusting God to become a disciple-maker based on who He is. A Jesus Mission Life is trusting God because He is asking us. I love the sentence from the Bible, "For we live by faith, not by sight" (2 Corinthians 5:7). Sight is always trying to talk me out of trusting God. When it comes to a Jesus Mission Life, sight throws up more objections than we realize. When it comes to a Jesus Mission Life, culture sends messages from every angle that you are not enough and that you are not adequately informed. This message is in direct opposition to the promise of God the Holy Spirit who will come and will testify and will remind us and will give us words.

We live in an anxious tension that people will hate us and reject us if we talk about Jesus and that we might offend. Yet, we are told that we need to love others just like Jesus did. Every day, we are tempted to live by sight over faith. Materialism is sight over faith. Misplaced or misaligned priorities are sight over faith. Legalism is sight over faith. Fear is sight over faith. Needing full understanding before acting is sight over faith. Seeking first the kingdom of men is sight over faith. In all honesty, writing these words and this chapter has given me pause to examine again just how much of my faith journey is sight over faith. Every bit of my disobedience to God and distraction from His Mission is a case of sight over faith.

Here is the crazy part of sight over faith. God has proven more reliable than my sight. He is more faithful and demonstrates His patient faithfulness to me every day. But too often, when push comes to shove, sight shoves faith out of the way. Jesus has proven trustworthy in every season and part of my life, but sight still seems to wield a lot of strength against my faith. My biggest struggle and victories in living out a Jesus Mission Life seem to come down to the battle of faith and sight.

*"Faith allows us to trust God, putting the weight of our lives upon Him."*
*—Leonard Lee*

## FAITH BELIEVES GOD

In the Bible, a common word used to describe the followers of Jesus is the word believer. In the culture of the early Church, this term was used to define how they lived out their beliefs more than a statement of faith they adhered to. They were called believers because they lived like they believed something was true.

A constant struggle in the Christian world is the alignment of belief and action. We live as actual believers in Christ when our beliefs and actions align. A simple example: I believe in gravity, so I do not jump out of tall trees or anything high off the ground. My decision is not about fear but rather the use of wisdom. I believe in gravity, and my belief provides wisdom from Jesus through the Holy Spirit of God.

A believer, by biblical definition, is someone who has integrated what they believe to be true of God (biblical truth, not opinion) with their heads, hearts, hands, and feet. The head believes something is true. The heart accepts as true what you believe. Hands are the ways you live out what is in your head and heart to those around you. Finally, feet are taking this truth and sharing it with others. Faith is believing, and biblical believing moves God's truth into action. True belief can only be fully realized in a Jesus Mission Life.

**BEWARE: Don't betray what is in your heart!**

We sometimes act in ways that are not consistent with what we believe in our hearts. When it comes to a Jesus Mission Life, there is a lot we believe. We believe that God is not willing that any should perish (2 Peter 3:9). We believe that God loves people (John 3:16). We believe that people need Jesus (Acts 4:12). We believe the Gospel is true (Romans 1:16). We believe Jesus is the only way to the Father (John 14:6). We believe that the resurrection of Jesus matters to everyone (1 Corinthians 15:14). We believe that we are to take this good news of Jesus to the ends of the earth (Matthew 28:18–20). We believe Christ makes us new (2 Corinthians 5:17). WE ARE BELIEVERS!

These are just a few of the truths we hold to as believers in Christ. These are also life and world-changing beliefs. In almost all of my conversations with Jesus people, the vast majority of them agree 100 percent with everything I just wrote. In addition to agreeing 100 percent, these are people who love Jesus and long for His work to be done on earth like it is in heaven. But somewhere inside so many of us, there is a disconnect between what we believe and actually living a Jesus Mission Life, and we end up betraying our hearts by how we live.

Did you know that less than 4 percent of Jesus followers in the U.S. have yet to experience inviting someone to follow Jesus and then disciple that person? Yet, we believe Jesus's Mission is important. What is in our hearts, what we believe, is betrayed by how we act and live.

Theology matters, and our doctrine matters. But, having great theology or wonderful doctrine is not enough if it only informs our heads and never leaves our minds. Until our theology and doctrine have made their way from our heads to our hearts to our hands and our feet, they lack their intended potency in living a Jesus Mission Life. The doctrine or theology that Jesus is God remains powerless in my life unless I live under His authority as God. The doctrine or theology that God is love is impotent in my life until I live as one who is deeply loved by God.

When I sincerely believe a doctrinal or a theological truth but fail to live by faith under the authority of that truth, I betray my own heart. People matter to God, but if I believe this with all my heart yet live a life of unforgiveness and gossip, I betray my heart. We have a Mission from Jesus Himself, but unless I submit to Jesus by building a Jesus Mission Life, I will walk by sight, betray my own heart, and miss the life that God has planned for me. My theology, my doctrine, must make its way past my head to my heart, hands, and feet. This happens when what I believe is aligned by faith with how I live. This kind of faith amazes Jesus.

Jesus was amazed by the faith of the centurion. Only twice do we see in Scripture that Jesus was amazed at someone's faith.

> When Jesus had entered Capernaum, a centurion came to him, asking for help. "Lord," he said, "my servant lies at home paralyzed, suffering terribly." Jesus said to him, "Shall I come and heal him?" The centurion replied, "Lord, I do not deserve to have you come under my roof. But just say the word, and my servant will be healed. For I myself am a man under authority, with soldiers under me. I tell this one, 'Go,' and he goes; and that one, 'Come,' and he comes. I say to my servant, 'Do this,' and he does it." When Jesus heard this, he was amazed and said to those following him, "Truly I tell you, I have not found anyone in Israel with such great faith." (Matthew 8:5–10, emphasis mine)

Jesus was amazed because the centurion placed his life under the authority of God through faith. In fact, there was nothing in the centurion's doctrine or theology that was correct, but he got faith right, and Jesus was amazed and acted in grace. Jesus recognized this man's understanding of the way that faith puts itself under the authority of the one it is trusting. The faith that amazes Jesus acts in line with its beliefs. "I believe you can speak the word and heal my servant; just say the word, Jesus." Living a Jesus Mission Life takes faith.

The question we need to answer is, "Do we live our lives as if everything we believe is true?" If not, we do not have all our doctrines and theological truths in proper alignment. (We don't; none of us do.) Here is a great faith and action alignment assessment for each of us. Write in the left column a sincere and actual truth or doctrine that you hold with sincerity. Use an "I believe" statement. In the right column, answer the question, "How will I live today as if this is 100% true?" When you give an honest answer, make a prayerful commitment to move this answer from your head, to your heart, to your hands, and then to your feet. I got you started with the first one.

| AN ACTUAL TRUTH I BELIEVE IN MY HEART ABOUT JESUS: | HOW WILL I LIVE TODAY AS IF THIS IS 100% TRUE? |
|---|---|
| I believe Jesus loves me. | I will live with confidence that I am loved. |
| | |
| | |
| | |
| | |
| | |

*"Faith aligns belief with how to live. We now live under the leadership and authority of God in all ways." —Leonard Lee*

## FAITH ACTS UPON GOD'S TRUTH

Somehow, in much of Western culture, we have made faith all about our theological agreement with the Bible. I have faith because I believe these truths. I believe in grace but struggle to live in God's grace. I believe in love but struggle to love others. I believe in the Bible but struggle to read it much or often. I believe in Jesus but do not live out His Mission. I believe in the Gospel but might not be able to explain it to you. I believe in forgiveness but have a list of people whom I have not forgiven. I believe in compassion and helping others but rarely find time to help others. I believe in giving but I spend far more dollars on my own smaller missions or myself than Jesus's Mission.

Do you want to know why this list above is so difficult to read? Because it is true. Acting upon our beliefs is what a Jesus Mission Life does. Jesus said we need to be people who "do" what He says, not just "hear" what He says. Faith is action.

Demons tremble at God because of what they know to be true about God. Demons also tremble at Jesus-followers because of what happens within us when our faith is activated, our actions align with our beliefs, and we live Jesus Mission Lives. He trembles at the power of the Church when the faith and beliefs of the community of God's people are connected to Jesus Mission Churches. Our faith is action.

*"Faith acts in such a way as to move beliefs from head to heart, from heart to hands, from hands to feet." —Leonard Lee*

## FAITH LIVES WISELY

Today, churches are filled with genuine believers in Christ who have struggled to connect their beliefs to a Jesus Mission Life. Faith is the bridge.

James, the brother of Jesus, began to follow Jesus after the resurrection. Prior to Jesus rising from the dead, he thought the words and life of Jesus amounted to a bunch of crazy talk and, at one point, wanted to have Jesus put away. Then, the resurrection of Jesus happened, and James was changed; his brother became his Savior. Fast forward about twelve to fifteen years after the resurrection, and James writes a letter to Christians; this is the New Testament's book of James.

In this letter, James writes to Christians who are scattered because of persecution and are now living around the region of Judea and Samaria. These scattered Jesus-followers were trying to live out a Jesus Mission Life. The entire theme of his letter could be summed up in this sentence: "Make sure you are connecting what you truly believe with how you live your Jesus Mission Life" (paraphrase mine). Throughout his letter, James connects our faith and wise living. Look at a few sentences from the first chapter of James:

> If any of you lacks wisdom, you should ask God, who gives generously to all without finding fault, and it will be given to you. But when you ask, you must believe and not doubt, because the one who doubts is like a wave of the sea, blown and tossed by the wind. That person should not expect to receive anything from the Lord. Such a person is double-minded and unstable in all they do. (James 1:5–8)

*So, what is the diagnosis of our disconnect?* James goes straight to the heart of the matter: "If any of you lack wisdom." Because we all lack wisdom, this is a really long line of people. James could have been looking back at his own life, spending years and years next to Jesus and missing who Jesus was. James, when using his own wisdom about Jesus and His Mission, concluded that Jesus must be crazy. He saw Jesus as having crossed the lines of their culture, the Jewish faith, and rational thought. When James wrote, "If any of you lack wisdom," he was putting himself first in line in the "lack wisdom" category—a life where his genuine belief was disconnected from action because he was using his own wisdom.

The apostle Paul addresses this very disconnect in 2 Corinthians 5:16 when he says that his own wisdom, his worldly point of view, made him get Jesus wrong: "So from now on we regard no one from a worldly point of view. Though we once regarded Christ in this way, we do so no longer."

*What is the solution to our disconnect?* We ask God for the wisdom needed to live fully connected in our beliefs and actions, to live a Jesus Mission Life. James writes that God's wisdom is as far away from us as a simple question. "Can I have your wisdom?" Ask God. If you are finding yourself in this disconnect between being a true believer and living a fully engaged Jesus Mission Life, ask God for the wisdom to build that bridge from belief to action.

Again, in my mind, I imagine James and Jesus's conversation after the resurrection. They stand face to face, and James begins to weep. His brother is alive again; his brother is the Messiah. His brother was not crazy after all, but rather, his brother was right. His brother is the Son of God, and with each realization, James's body crumbles to the ground. Now, kneeling in front of Jesus, through sobs and groans, James makes a simple confession and a request. "My Lord, I believe. Can I still follow you?"

Of course, God says YES!

I love that James's letter speaks of a different wisdom. If it were a story, he might say these words: "When I lacked wisdom, I asked, and God said YES! Now with God's wisdom, I see Jesus more clearly." If you lack the wisdom to connect and build the bridge from what you believe to how you live, ask Jesus for His wisdom. No one ever lived a more perfectly connected life than Jesus. His belief in the Father was directly connected to His Mission. Our belief in Jesus is also directly connected to our mission. Ask Jesus. He says yes and never finds fault with our desire to seek His wisdom.

But, there is a condition to the yes. You have to ask in faith. In fact, James is so adamant about this condition of asking in faith that he says without this faith, you will receive no wisdom from Jesus. He then describes the person who asks God without faith as double-minded, unstable in all their ways, and easily tossed around by every wind. Ouch.

What is James really getting at? I think his own story tells us. James, at one point in his life, believed that his own wisdom was better than Jesus's wisdom. James thought, "Jesus has lost his mind; he speaks words that are fighting words; he keeps breaking the Sabbath rules; he makes statements that indicate he believes he is God." How sad for Jesus it must have felt for His family to form these thoughts about Him. James lacked God's wisdom to follow Jesus because he thought his wisdom was better.

The faith I need and the faith you need to receive God's wisdom is not about believing harder; that if I ask Jesus, He will give me wisdom. The faith each of us needs is to believe that the wisdom Jesus gives is better than the wisdom we have at the moment. Without faith that embraces God's wisdom over mine, I will bounce back and forth between my wisdom and God's wisdom. I will be unstable in all of my ways. When I choose my wisdom over God's wisdom, it is because my faith lacks the strength to truly believe and act in faith. I actually have faith in my wisdom over God's wisdom. For me to constantly connect what I believe to what I do, I need to ask God for wisdom and ask in faith.

This is James's story. He started from a "my wisdom" diagnosis of Jesus and thought Jesus was crazy. After the resurrection of Christ, James began to diagnose Jesus from the perspective of God's wisdom and Mission. When he finally did, James was transformed, and he gave the rest of his life to building a Jesus Mission Life. By the way, his entire letter is about how our belief is connected to our actions and Jesus Mission Living. James gives us the insight that the connection is faith. Jesus Mission Living is when we choose in faith to believe that God's wisdom is better than our own wisdom.

Let me add a final thought on our view of wisdom. We must understand that wisdom is more than wise words. Jesus connected for us that wisdom is proven wise by our lives and the fruit of our lives, not simply our words: "But wisdom is proved right by all her children" (Luke 7:35). In this chapter of Luke's Gospel, Jesus is speaking to people who measured wisdom in the currency of words. Jesus said that wisdom is proven real by the connection of wise words and wise living.

In the twenty-first century, we tend to ascribe the most wisdom to people by the standard of how much we agree with their words. People get elected by their words more than their actions. People justify bad actions with wise-sounding words, obscuring the truth of Jesus that God's wisdom is proven to be the best wisdom based on how He acted. Friends, this is the crossroads of faith and Mission.

The wisdom of God seems foolish until I let go of my own wisdom and, in an act of faith, believing it to be better than my own wisdom, leave it behind so I can choose the wisdom of the One whose Mission began before the foundation of the world.

*"Faith receives God's superior wisdom to build and live a Jesus Mission Life."*
*—Leonard Lee*

## ENTERING THE HALL OF FAITH

Every major sport has a Hall of Fame. This is a place where those who have been outstanding in their sport are elected as the best of the best. Several years back, I visited the Pro Football Hall of Fame in Canton, Ohio. Walking through the rooms and seeing the bronze busts of these players was really a great experience for this sports-loving guy. I read their stories, heard their games and exploits being recounted by first-hand witnesses, and in some ways, I even relived my own history as a kid, having watched so many of these guys. It was truly an awesome day.

After I left and had time to reflect on my experience, I felt prompted to make my way to Hebrews 11. It is in Hebrews 11 we read about people God recognized as heroes. These people's lives were shaped by seeing God through the eyes of faith; they lived by faith and not by sight. This life of faith connected their beliefs with their actions, and when their faith was put into action, God used them in powerful and practical ways to further His Mission. Hebrews 11 introduces us to people who, when confronted with conventional and human wisdom, chose God's wisdom. They believed that God's wisdom was better than what they had or what existed. Their process of faith led to building lives that were used by God to advance His Mission. Their lives paved the way for Jesus to enter into this world and are an example of what it means to live a Jesus Mission Life today, right now.

If a Jesus Mission Life seems too big or outside the grasp of what you know about you and your life, then you are **going to need a bigger faith.** Let me wrap up this chapter and part one of this book with two Jesus moments from the Gospels: Mark 9:14–27 and Matthew 17:14–21. I encourage you to get your Bible and read these accounts now; they are great, and they are true stories!

In Mark's Gospel, a crowd comes to the disciples of Jesus. Jesus, Peter, James, and John were just arriving from a different assignment (Mark 9). As Jesus approached, He saw the discussion was a bit heated and asked His disciples what was going on. What you read below is my paraphrase of the story, taken from both Matthew 17 and Mark 9. "A man brought his son who was demon possessed and we could not cast out the demon and the religious elite were challenging us about this."

---

Side Note: What started as a mission of compassion quickly changed to a mission of theology. We need to pay attention to this change of mission in us and in our faith communities.

---

As Jesus arrived, the crowd's attention shifted to Jesus. The father of the boy stepped forward in an honest and desperate moment. "My son is possessed and the demon is trying to kill him. Nothing, not even your disciples were able to help." After a short conversation and a brief rebuke of the faith of the crowd, the dad spoke to Jesus. "If you can," he said to Jesus. "Will you help?"

Jesus replied, "IF I can?" Jesus had been doing miracles and teaching extraordinary truth with divine authority, and instead of a fully engaged and awakened faith, people were looking for a sign to see if Jesus could deliver. "IF I can. If you believe, anything is possible." Jesus was working toward a moment of truth with this dad and the crowd and also with His disciples. These words make for an authentic moment between Jesus and a desperate dad. "Lord, I believe but help me with my unbelief."

Could any story in the entire Bible better summarize our struggle to connect our faith to a Jesus Mission Life? Reading *A Jesus Mission Life,* you might think, "I believe but do not know how to get there. I know the Jesus Mission Life is what you want for me; I believe you, Jesus." The words "help me with my unbelief" are just as faith-filled and beautiful to Jesus as the words "I believe."

Inside of me is a voice that whispers, shouts, invites other voices, and fuels my unbelief. "Leonard Lee, you are not that good." "Leonard Lee, you are too old and slow and lack the needed fire to live this Jesus Mission Life." "Leonard Lee, people do not care." "Leonard Lee, the world is gone to hell in a handbasket; it is too late now." "Leonard Lee, culture is where your fight is, and you have no voice." Do any of these doubts sound familiar? What do your own doubt-fueling voices tell you?

This dad's honest confession led Jesus to act. This honest confession moved Jesus to free the young man and restore him to life and his family. Daily, often more than once or twice or twenty times a day, I need to confess in honest faith, "Jesus, I believe, help me with my unbelief."

In Matthew's Gospel, we see the words in chapter 17 are the same story as recorded in Mark 9 but from a different angle. I will focus on the disciples and Jesus. Jesus was finalizing His training for His disciples and revealing His death to them. We know from His words that His expectation was that these disciples would take Jesus's Mission as their own. Jesus was training them in the faith needed to live a Jesus Mission Life.

"Why could we not do this miracle?" asked the disciples. In a blunt and honest answer, Jesus said, "Your faith is too little." Then Jesus gave some of the most faith-building and hope-giving encouragement to those of us who need help with too little faith.

> He replied, "Because you have so little faith. Truly I tell you, if you have faith as small as a mustard seed, you can say to this mountain, 'Move from here to there,' and it will move. Nothing will be impossible for you." (Matthew 17:20)

Jesus gives us hope in three ways. **First, He gives hope by saying that big faith is not all that big.** A mustard seed, smaller than the seed inside a pepper, is all the size you need. A mustard seed, from a few feet away, you cannot even see it. A mustard seed, if it drops on the ground, is so small you cannot find it. A mustard seed, unimpressive and tiny, is all the size of faith you need. We can find that! We can get that much faith if we want to. Jesus is saying that the faith you need is not far away.

**Second, mustard seeds grow huge.** They do not just become a small plant; they become a huge tree. A mustard tree can be as tall as twenty to thirty feet and grow twenty feet wide. All from this tiny seed, when planted and tended to, grows a giant, reproducing tree. Jesus is encouraging His friends that their faith, when planted well, can have a great impact. This is an encouragement to plant and water seeds of faith. I am not referring to the prosperity gospel teaching that says, "Got a need, plant a seed." I am saying that if you want to build a Jesus Mission Life, you can. You can start with a small seed planted in Jesus and end up with a giant faith tree that produces more faith for others.

**Third, you don't have to wait. Mustard-seed faith is not weak.** The tiniest of seeds can move a mountain. Jesus is telling His disciples that even the smallest amount of faith is powerful and matters greatly when it is placed in the right person. You are not the right person, and neither am I. Sometimes our faith seems weak because it is planted in the wrong person. "Leonard, believe in yourself!" Well-meaning and sometimes helpful words, but not the message of Jesus for building a Jesus Mission Life. Believe in Jesus! Why? For all we have stated in this book so far, and because only HE knows how to take a mustard-seed-sized faith and move a mountain with it.

Let's be honest. There is nothing that is the size of a mustard seed that moves me or changes my life. Strength the size of a mustard seed is not enough to bolster my courage, get me to change, or transform me. Banking investments the size of a mustard seed is not a strategy for building finances. Love the size of a mustard seed is not enough to build a thriving marriage. Self-talk or counsel the size of a mustard seed is not enough to spark hope for healing, for overcoming wounds, or for forgiving others. Mustard seeds are tiny, but *faith* the size of a mustard seed is more than enough.

Jesus is breathing hope into a faith that is filled with doubt, that often sees the task or life we are called to do and live as too big. Jesus is reminding us that faith is different because faith, as you remember, is how we access and interact with God. Placed in Jesus, faith the size of a mustard seed is all we need. In the wisdom of God, it is more than enough to move mountains and change the world. Embrace the Mission of Jesus as your own and build a Jesus Mission Life! Take that mustard-seed faith and place it in Jesus, having the faith that His wisdom is better than yours. Take your mustard-seed-sized faith and get started; you do not have to wait for it to grow to make it powerful.

What are you waiting for?

I have one final thought before we launch into Part Two. Holding the mustard seed of faith in your hand, seeing how small it is, and then beating yourself up spiritually is not what Jesus has in mind for you. He is inviting you to plant that seed of faith in Him, tend to that seed of faith, and water that seed of faith. When we do, we will celebrate the tree that will come as a part of planting that seed of faith in Jesus. Take a step of faith and say YES! to a Jesus Mission Life; you will never regret it.

# Stepping into Jesus's Mission

## A prayer you can pray today:

*Dear Jesus,*

*Thank You for giving me the faith I need to live a Jesus Mission Life. Will You help me plant my mustard-seed faith in You? Will You grow it to its fullest for Your honor and glory? Will You help me with my unbelief? Will You help me build a Jesus Mission Life? I am grateful that You will say yes to each of these requests. Amen*

## Some questions to move you forward:

What is something you discovered in this chapter about faith?

What does it mean to trust God?

To be a believer is to have alignment in what we truly believe about God and how we live. Where is a place you have alignment, and where is a place you need alignment?

Think of a time when you had to choose between your wisdom and God's wisdom, and share it.

When we ask God for wisdom, we must have the faith to believe His wisdom is better than our own. What makes believing this a struggle for so many people?

What is a place in your life where you might need the prayer, "Help my unbelief!"?

From the three hope-giving thoughts about having mustard-seed faith, which ones speak to you most, and why?

How do you plant your faith in Jesus?

As you begin Part Two of *A Jesus Mission Life*, what do you hope and pray God does in and through you?

## A step to take as you go:

Take some time this week to write down five things you truly believe about Jesus, and then write how you want those beliefs to shape your life. Take some time to pray over this list.

## PART TWO

# HOW DO WE BUILD A JESUS MISSION LIFE IN THE TWENTY-FIRST CENTURY?

Greater love has no one than this: to lay down one’s life for one’s friends.
(John 15:13)

# Chapter 9

## Two Words: "ALL IN"

By now, I hope you have felt moved in your heart and mind enough to be drawn towards Jesus and a Jesus Mission Life. I know from experience many of you reading this book may also be asking this question: "How do I build this life?" This is what we'll cover here in Part Two. We will break down how to embrace and be embraced by Jesus and His Mission.

Often, when I ask people how they are doing, the same two words appear in almost every answer. *Busy* and *tired.* I get why. The number of everyday responsibilities we have fills our schedule to the top, sometimes over the top. With the weight of work, school, commuting, family, sports, making meals, homework, and our own needs, it is no wonder some people want to lock themselves behind a door or get far away from all the noise. Busy and tired.

Can I make a confession? I like being busy, and I really don't mind being tired. I have a lot of fun with all the things I do to keep the words "busy and tired" as some of my most true adjectives when describing my life. I think most reading these words could also say that there are some really enjoyable moments of busyness and that you get tired doing some really fun things with people you love. No judgment here; in fact, when I hear these words used, I almost always say, "I hope you had fun getting tired."

What can make life feel super chaotic and frustrating is when we add something to an already full life. You know how it is; you worked a full day, and about ten minutes before you leave, your boss says, "Can you get me that report before you go home?" Or you get that text from a loving family member who says, "Can you stop by the store on the way home for ..." and the list of just a few things feels like a full shop with a couple of extras, too. Your teacher adds an unexpected assignment just before the bell, and what is manageably busy now feels overwhelming.

Imagine how it feels showing up at church, finding your parking spot, hustling the kids into their classes, finding your seat, and then the announcements include three more events, a campaign for extra funds, a couple of really important "opportunities" to serve, and don't forget to read your Bible and pray, get in a small group because we all need community, and did we mention bring a friend? We actually do not need to imagine how this feels, do we? Here is what we all have in common: there is nothing in this paragraph we are against.

To the busy people reading this book, the folks who work hard to care for your families and make a future for yourself and those you love, well done! To the person longing to give their kids experiences they never had or maybe did have that were life-shaping in so many good ways, well done! To the student, the intern, the new guy, well done for starting something new. To the parents, employer, and employee reading these words whose life is on what feels like a twenty-four-hour spin cycle, squeezing all the space from your life, you are doing things that matter; well done!

Let's not forget the person just barely hangin' on, the single mom or dad, trying to make ends meet. To the recovering addict, who is taking sobriety one day at a time, I want to say, well done! Busy and tired are not words to describe sin; they are words to describe us as we live.

I was talking to a group of men about embracing and building a Jesus Mission Life when one of the guys spoke up and said, "I don't know about all this mission stuff, pastor; I sure wish I had known this was a part of the commitment before I decided to follow Jesus." We all laughed together, and then the laugh got muffled by the reality of the comment. This amazing gentleman felt like he had started one kind of

Jesus journey but was told later that the journey is really much more intense.

My friend was saying, "I want Jesus, but all of the mission stuff is really hard for me to fit into my life. I didn't know I would have to work the family business for Him. I don't have time for the extra stuff you are now telling me I need to do." He was feeling some spiritual bait and switch. Maybe you do too at times when you hear a great speaker, see how busy your church invites you to be, read an inspirational book, or hear a podcast, and suddenly there is somehow a new pressure or more pressure on you.

Following Jesus is not a "choose a commitment level" friendship. "I'll take Package B. Three weekends a month, a percentage of time, a percentage of money, devotions a few days a week, and add a small group two times a month." "I'll take Package C. Two weekends a month, but I get to choose them. If I can, some time and money, no small groups, and I'll do devotions if I remember." No, friend, following Jesus is ALL IN!

Okay, you already knew that, but why is it so hard to live an ALL-IN Jesus Mission Life? The commitment we make to Christ is for Him to be our Savior, the One whose life, death, and resurrection frees us from death and the weight of our sin, making us God's own kids. The same commitment is also to make Christ Lord of our lives. It is a commitment to submit and surrender our lives to Jesus, to obey Him, to follow Him, and to be transformed by Him in the process. Following Jesus is an ALL-IN commitment. When you met Jesus, you most likely responded to His love with similar words of commitment. "Jesus, I ask you to come into my life, forgive my sin, be my Lord and Savior."

One reason being "ALL IN" is so difficult for us is that we actually don't know what being "ALL IN" means. "ALL IN" has the potential to reveal itself in hundreds of ways as we navigate our days. This is not a we-are-dumb statement; it is a we-are-limited statement. When I got married, I made some promises that were about being all in—for better or worse, in sickness and health; whether rich or poor, I am here, ALL IN. When we said these words way back in 1989, we were saying that, because of love, we were willing to sign a blank check and let life fill in the total.

To be ALL IN, our faith is much like the blank check people write when they get married. We are telling Jesus we want you to be the center of everything. We know that "Top Billing" is the only place for someone who holds the title of King of kings and Lord of lords. The throne of the One who was dead and now lives, who is the Alpha and Omega, should be "At The Center." The One who never changes, never slumbers, and never sleeps deserves to be "First Place" in our lives. It just makes sense the spot for the One who is always present, always right, always knows, always loves, always gives, always forgives, and always stays is "Above All Else." Jesus says this is the spot He deserves in our lives.

Can you imagine Jesus saying, "Just make a little space for me; I can wait."? Of course, you can't. But sometimes, the way we prioritize our lives shows we are more "partly in" than ALL IN. I believe you want more than this, and we all know Jesus wants more than this. But how do we get there? He tells us in John 15.

### THE TRUE VINE

The words Jesus spoke as He made His way to the cross provide a great framework to understand what it means to be ALL IN. On Jesus's final evening before His arrest, I imagine the conversation might have gone something like this. John 14 ends with Jesus saying, "Let's get going." The disciples stand and stretch their legs. Some might be looking at their newly washed feet and feeling a range of emotions. The intensity in Jesus is palpable; in fact, the Bible says His soul was heavy, and I am sure that this heaviness created uneasiness in each of the disciples. As they walked to Gethsemane, where Jesus would soon be betrayed, they passed by the temple. On one entrance to the temple were beautiful and ornate golden vines. It is likely that this image was in their view or mind as Jesus walked and shared these words found in John 15.

> I am the true vine, and my Father is the gardener. He cuts off every branch in me that bears no fruit, while every branch that does bear fruit he prunes so that it will be even more fruitful. You are already clean because of the word I have spoken to you. Remain in me, as I also remain in you. No branch can bear fruit by itself; it must remain in the vine. Neither can you bear fruit unless you remain in me. I am the vine; you are the branches. If you remain in me and I in you, you will bear much fruit; apart from me you can do nothing. If you do not remain in me, you are like a branch that is thrown away and withers; such branches are picked up, thrown into the fire and burned. If you remain in me and my words remain in you, ask whatever you wish, and it will be done for you. This is to my Father's glory, that you bear much fruit, showing yourselves to be my disciples. (John 15:1–8)

The words Jesus spoke are best seen through the lens of Jesus's Mission. The preparation of His disciples for His Mission was in 100 percent full swing. Jesus said with boldness, "I am the true vine." In Jesus's time, some people taught that God's vineyard was the people of God; here, Jesus says without the vine, there is no vineyard. "I am the TRUE vine."

The word *true* used in John 15 paints this picture for us. Jesus not only looks like the vine, but He also possesses every function of a vine. Jesus was saying, "I am the vine that looks and acts like a vine, in every way; there is no other vine." Jesus's words revealed to His friends the reality that there are fake vines, too. Every day, people are connected to a vine that does not function like Jesus.

Many of the people passing by the ornate golden vines on the temple most likely would say that the Law is the true vine or the Temple is the true vine, and the gardeners are the priests. Jesus was saying that no other vine looks and acts like He does. He is the True Vine, and branches cannot bear His fruit when they are attached to other vines.

Other vines might have the look but cannot deliver the fruit; Jesus is the TRUE Vine.

Jesus's declaration, "I am the true vine and the gardener is my Father," is a source-of-mission-and-strength statement. He was saying, "I have a Mission different from the temple and an authority different from the Law and priests, and when you abide in me, you bear Mission fruit" (paraphrase mine). What a contrast, what a revelation! This matters to us today because, like the people then, we have some vines that are not true vines. Buildings, religion, ministries, special and favorite teachers, specific authors, our own religious practices, our families or careers, our nationalism, politics, or causes can act as a vine that is not true, but a vine nonetheless. Because these vines are not the TRUE Vine, they cannot lead us to the lasting Kingdom fruit Jesus wants.

It is impossible for our education, pain, money, abilities, talents, and schedules that make us both busy and tired to be true vines. The American Dream, possessions, or our addiction to the habits of being in pursuit of more in every aspect of life all act as vines that do not match up to the title of being true. Only Jesus, the True Vine, lets the branches produce the eternal fruit from the Father's Garden.

The Gardner is the *Father*. He is the One who tends the garden, plants the garden, and decides what will grow in the garden—it is His garden. Again, we sometimes act as if it is our garden, our life, our rights, our decisions—again, our garden. When we act as if the garden is ours, guess who becomes the gardener? If you said, "We do," advance to Go and collect two hundred fake vines.

As Jesus and the disciples continued toward Gethsemane, it was very important for His friends know that He was still the TRUE Vine and they could trust Him. Over the next twelve hours, Jesus would be arrested, tried, beaten, and marched towards His executioners' cross. At that moment, Jesus would look like He lost, like He was just another vine, not the TRUE VINE. Everything they had learned and placed their hope in would be challenged. They would need to remember

Jesus's words, "I am the true vine, and my Father is the gardener. No matter what it looks like, stay with me, abide in me."

Let me interrupt this story with a refocus. The single mission of the Church is Jesus's Mission, disciples making disciples. The single mission of the Jesus follower is a Jesus Mission Life. When He tells His disciples that it is the Father's Garden and He Himself is the True Vine, He is saying that the goal of the Vine is to sustain branches so they will bear fruit. Jesus's DNA, as the True Vine, is now the DNA of the branches. In one sense, Jesus was saying, "What you are going to experience the next few days is a part of My Mission, My plan to rescue the world. STAY with Me; I am the TRUE Vine. Rome, who will condemn me; the Temple where I will be tried and beaten; the priests and council who are terrified of Me—all of them are fake vines. Me, I am the True Vine, and we are actually in My Father's Garden."

Take note that it was in the Father's Garden that Jesus was arrested, beaten, tried, and executed. But because it was the Father's Garden, and the Father is the Gardener, and Jesus is the TRUE Vine, everything that happened was used to fulfill Jesus's Mission. All of this is such a consistent message from Jesus. "I was sent by My Father to sustain the purpose of My Father's vineyard, to bear much fruit."

---

Side Note: It might be worth noting here as well that fruit here is not the Fruit of the Spirit Paul spoke of in Galatians 5, but the fruit that is the reproduction of kind after kind. In context, it is disciples making disciples. Now, back to the story.

---

Jesus continued, "Remain in me." Another translation uses the word abide. *Remain,* or *abide,* has such a round and full meaning for us. It means to stay, to go the distance, to wait, holding fast to Jesus. To abide is everything the words ALL IN carry and even more. Then, amazingly, Jesus added, "Abide in me and I in you." Hold the phone; Jesus said, "Be ALL IN on Me because I am ALL IN on you, and the result of this kind of commitment is fruit!" Our commitment is not one way; it is all the way in both directions.

Christian missionary Jim Elliott once said, "He is no fool who gives up what he can't keep to gain what he cannot lose." It was not long after this statement that Jim, at the age of twenty-eight, was killed by the Huaorani people of Ecuador, the people he and his friends were trying to reach with the gospel. (This story is told in the movie *The End of the Spear* and is well worth watching.) What Jim was saying is that Jesus, the True Vine, is worthy of our being ALL IN. The Father, the owner of the Garden, tends the Garden with precision, intention, and care and is worthy of our being ALL IN. The people who are only named as "fruit to be made" are worth you and I being ALL IN. And YOU are worth it, too; Jesus and His Father are ALL IN on you. Dang, that is good to know.

As we continue in John 15, Jesus said many remarkable words. He spoke of the care the Father gives the Garden, using words like trimming, pruning, lifting, and clearing away what gets in the way of fruit-bearing and what does not bear fruit. The Father planted this Garden to bear fruit, and the intentionality He demonstrates in caring for it shows His focused commitment to its Mission—to bear fruit.

The Father never needs to prune the vine because Jesus is the True Vine, but the branches need His care. I love the tender partnership between Jesus and the Father. Jesus, the True Vine, sustains and nurtures each branch for maximum fruitfulness, while the Father, the Gardner, cares for and tends to each branch for maximum fruitfulness.

Often, people feel uncomfortable reading John 15, especially when Jesus said that every branch that does not bear fruit is cut off and burned. Dozens of times, I have been asked by a worried Jesus follower about these sentences because they are afraid that they are the branches that will be cut off and disposed of by the Father. This kind of worry is not the intended response. Jesus's intention was to show the Father's care for the vine and branches. The Father cuts off fruitless branches, also known as sucker branches, that can only take nutrition from the vine and cannot bear fruit. This is not you! If you know Jesus, you can bear fruit because HE makes it possible for you to bear fruit. The Father will prune you so you can.

Jesus's use of the vine and branches shows us that the Mission, plan, and intention of every believer is to bear fruit. A great question for us to wrestle with is, "Is it my intention to bear fruit for Christ by abiding in Him?"

Remember, Jesus was on the way to Gethsemane, where He would be arrested, assaulted, insulted, and tortured, all for the purpose that there could be even more branches in the future. Jesus continued, "Apart from me, there is no fruit." There is no ability for a branch to bear TRUE fruit apart from abiding in Jesus the TRUE Vine. To bear the kind of fruit Jesus and the Father have planned, we must abide in Jesus. Jesus was telling His friends that without Him, the last three years were a waste, and no matter what it looks like in the future, He will still be the True Vine.

How do I sustain the fruitful Mission-of-Jesus lifestyle? How can I build a Jesus Mission Life? The answer is to get close to Jesus but with the Mission of Jesus in mind. Jesus makes two statements here about His words: they make us clean, and they can take root in us. For the disciples, this was not a Bible study; the words were the actual words of Jesus, the ones they heard and we are hearing now. Thank God we have so many of these words recorded for us in Matthew, Mark, Luke, and John; we must read them over and over.

Jesus also said that not only do His words make us clean, but they align our hearts and requests in prayer to God the Father and the Kingdom Mission. When we abide in Him, when His words abide in us, we hear Him, and He hears us, and He answers us. I am going to make a confession here. I have asked a lot of things from God that did not come from a posture of abiding. Are you sometimes struggling to believe God is listening? "Abide in me, let my words abide in you, and then ask."

John 15 is filled with love, grace, and ALL IN commitment from Jesus and our Father, but keep reading and see who else is here.

> When the Advocate comes, whom I will send to you from the Father—the Spirit of truth who goes out from the Father—He will testify about me. And you also must testify, for you have been with me from the beginning. (John 15:26–27)

Just hours before His arrest and crucifixion, Jesus said to His friends, "I am sending My Holy Spirit, and He will increase your understanding and knowledge of Me so you can tell My story; this has been our plan from the beginning." So amazing is the truth of the Gospel, the Mission of Jesus, that the entire Godhead is involved in the Father's Garden. God is working to anchor us to Jesus, the only True Vine, and then empowers us through God the Holy Spirit so we can bear lasting fruit.

John 15 is all about how the Godhead makes our lives fruitful and fruit-filled. How? ABIDE in the TRUE Vine. Submit to the pruning of the Father. Live in step with God the Holy Spirit as you share the good news of Jesus with others. When we do, our lives bear fruit, kind after kind, disciples making disciples. I have a choice when I hear or read these words. I can ask some hard questions and use the answers to move me deeper into the process of being ALL IN, or I can accept Options B or C and miss out on the beautiful connection to the Father, Son, and Holy Spirit. (Options B and C are not offered by Jesus.)

Here are the hard questions we can ask ourselves: Am I bearing fruit (disciples making disciples)? Am I abiding in the TRUE Vine? Am I willing for the Father to prune my life so I can bear more fruit? Am I listening to God the Holy Spirit? If you answered no to any of these questions, welcome to being a person-in-process. Keep reading; there is more. In the middle of John 15, these words stand out. Read them out loud if you dare.

> My command is this: Love each other as I have loved you. Greater love has no one than this: to lay down one's life for one's friends.

> You are my friends if you do what I command. I no longer call you servants, because a servant does not know his master's business. Instead, I have called you friends, for everything that I learned from my Father I have made known to you. You did not choose me, but I chose you and appointed you so that you might go and bear fruit—fruit that will last—and so that whatever you ask in my name the Father will give you. This is my command: Love each other. (John 15:12–17)

In the context of the passage, Jesus was saying, "Here is how you are going to get this done. You are going to love each other like I have loved you." That is no small sentence. "Like I have loved you. You are the fruit of My love for you, and now I want you to use the same love to bear more fruit. The greatest form of love is to lay down your lives for each other." (Can you say, ALL IN?) "This is what friends do (I am about to show you how), and I am changing the dynamic of our relationship from servant to friend. You see, servants do not know the inside scoop, and you know the full Mission, the full plan, the full connection because what the Father told Me, I have made this known to you" (paraphrase mine).

Jesus told His friends, "You did not choose me, but I chose you; I chose you for my Mission, to bear fruit. I want that fruit to last, to remain and reproduce." Did you know the only fruit that remains is fruit that reproduces? These words are not mechanical; they are personal and loving. These words are organic in the sense of life giving birth to new life. It is as if Jesus was saying, "I handpicked you guys to abide in Me so you can bear fruit. You are made for My Mission; this truth and reality rests in My image, the image I gave you in the beginning when I created you. I want this for you so bad. I want you to live fully into what I made you for, to bear fruit, to live out My Mission as friends and partners."

If John 15 were condensed, Jesus would be saying, "My Father and I have been working on this Mission, the one to rescue the world. It is this Mission that makes the Garden His and Him the Gardener. I am the only way this Mission can be accomplished, so I am the one and TRUE Vine. You are My plan to execute the Mission that Me and My Father have had since before the foundation of the world. You are branches intended to bear fruit. My Spirit? He activates My story in you and Our story in the world. We, Father, Son, and Holy Spirit, are working together to create a movement where every branch bears fruit and that fruit bears more fruit and more fruit. I am calling you My friends because only friends have this kind of access to My Father's plans and Mission. When My words are alive in you, they clean you, prepare you, and give you a direct line to Me to answer your prayers. So, let's be ALL IN on each other."

## THE WIN IN ALL IN

A word about ALL IN. If any of the previous words in this chapter or book encourage or challenge your heart and mind, it could be that God the Holy Spirit is speaking to you. Instead of guilt, shame, or anger, can I invite you into the process our loving Father, our beautiful Savior, Jesus, and the indwelling presence of God the Holy Spirit have already invited you to? The Bible word is *sanctification.*

Sanctification is a word that means to be set apart for a beautiful reason. Being sanctified includes being holy and set apart for God's purpose and plan. By definition, sanctification always includes the Mission of God for the glory of God. But sanctification is both a place where we stand and a process in which we live.

We are justified by faith, we have peace with God, we have access to God, and we stand in grace (Romans 5:1–2). This is what the True Vine gives us by faith. But we are also in the process of learning to follow, learning to trust, choosing to love, choosing to imitate, and bearing fruit. This is the lifelong process of sanctification—to be set apart for a purpose, a reason—and that reason is to live in friendship with Jesus by abiding in Him and partnering as friends in His Mission to bear fruit.

What a generous and beautiful Jesus we have! He lifts us from death to life and then works His might in us to join us to His purpose and Mission. Ephesians 1 records a prayer that Paul prayed for the Jesus-followers in and around the city of Ephesus:

> For this reason, ever since I heard about your faith in the Lord Jesus and your love for all God's people, I have not stopped giving thanks for you, remembering you in my prayers. I keep asking that the God of our Lord Jesus Christ, the glorious Father, may give you the Spirit of wisdom and revelation, so that you may know Him better. I pray that the eyes of your heart may be enlightened in order that you may know the hope to which He has called you, the riches of His glorious inheritance in His holy people, and His incomparably great power for us who believe. That power is the same as the mighty strength He exerted when he raised Christ from the dead and seated Him at his right hand in the heavenly realms, far above all rule and authority, power and dominion, and every name that is invoked, not only in the present age but also in the one to come. And God placed all things under His feet and appointed Him to be head over everything for the church, which is his body, the fullness of Him who fills everything in every way. (Ephesians 1:15–23)

In short, Paul prayed for us to see that the same power that accomplished the work of salvation by raising Jesus from the dead is at work in us. It is the very same power that exalted the living Christ above everything, where He is on Mission through His Church, to bring the beautiful reign of Jesus to everyone, everywhere.

Connect these words to Ephesians 2, and you will see that the power that raised Jesus also raises us. When we were dead in sin, now, because of faith in Christ, we are alive, saved by grace.

> As for you, you were dead in your transgressions and sins, in which you used to live when you followed the ways of this world and of the ruler of the kingdom of the air, the spirit who is now at work in those who are disobedient. All of us also lived among them at one time, gratifying the cravings of our flesh and following its

desires and thoughts. Like the rest, we were by nature deserving of wrath. But because of his great love for us, God, who is rich in mercy, made us alive with Christ even when we were dead in transgressions—it is by grace you have been saved. And God raised us up with Christ and seated us with him in the heavenly realms in Christ Jesus, in order that in the coming ages he might show the incomparable riches of his grace, expressed in his kindness to us in Christ Jesus. For it is by grace you have been saved, through faith—and this is not from yourselves, it is the gift of God—not by works, so that no one can boast. **For we are God's handiwork, created in Christ Jesus to do good works, which God prepared in advance for us to do.** (Ephesians 2:1–10, emphasis mine)

In verse 10, the connection to the prayer in chapter 1 comes alive in chapter 2 with the beauty of God's love for you and His amazing gift of mission—His Mission. Look at verse 10, broken down. It is so great!

**For** (because this is true)

**We are His handiwork** (His beautifully written poem)

**Created in Christ Jesus** (the Gospel)

**To do good works** (we have a mission)

**Which He has planned in advance for us to do** (what He was already doing and wants us to join Him in).

*Handiwork* is a word that means "poem." God is writing a beautiful poem with our lives; each word and sentence and rhyme and cadence all come from His creation, the new creation in Christ (2 Corinthians 5:17). His purpose in writing such beauty in our lives? So that we can take our place in the work He is already doing (think Mission).

We are to be intentional with the process. Embrace the Mission of Jesus and let the poet of your soul write the most beautiful poem in you, an eternity-shaping poem with your life. This is the WIN in being ALL IN.

# Stepping into Jesus's Mission

## A prayer you can pray today:

*Dear Jesus,*

*Thank You that You are ALL IN on me. I am asking for the eyes to see what it means to be ALL IN with You. Show me how to abide in the Vine. Show me the ways in which the Father will tend to the branches so I can see His work in my life. I am so grateful for You, Holy Spirit, as You show me Jesus and how to speak about Jesus.*

*Amen*

## Some questions to move you forward:

What are some All IN commitments people make today?

Jesus said He is the TRUE Vine. What do you think that means for Jesus-followers?

Jesus said His Father is the Gardener, who prunes and cares for us, the branches. What do you think that means for Jesus-followers?

God the Holy Spirit teaches us about Jesus so we can tell others. How does this truth encourage or challenge you as you build a Jesus Mission Life?

Read John 15:16 and put it in your own words. Remember that the fruit here in John 15 is disciples making disciples, not the fruit of the Spirit.

Abiding or remaining in Christ, being ALL IN, is essential for fruitful living. What are some abiding or remaining disciplines you practice now or think would be important to start practicing?

## A step to take as you go:

Take time to begin and build a list of abiding or remaining disciplines. Use this list as a tool for conversations with other Jesus Mission Life friends to be a mutual encouragement and accountability with each other.

Then Jesus said to his disciples, "Whoever wants to be my disciple must deny themselves and take up their cross and follow me." (Matthew 16:24)

# Chapter 

## Training

When I played baseball in college, I could not hit a curveball. Throw me a fastball, and I could at least close my eyes and swing. Throw a curve, and I was flinching, dropping out of the box, and swinging and missing so badly that people wondered if the boy holding the bat was even on the team.

ME: Coach, I can't hit a curve. What do I do about that?

COACH: If you want to hit a curve, you have to take more swings.

Following my coach's input, I got into the batting cage and had more curveballs thrown at me in an hour than I would see in an entire season. I would hit toss-ups to learn to keep my eye on the ball. A toss-up is when someone tosses the ball in the air, and you need to hit it. We would say hit it on the way up, hit it on the way down—all to train me to keep my eye on the ball. Then I would go back to the batting cage, where I would hit again and again, followed by live pitching from our pitchers in practice until I was game-ready.

Guess what? The coach was right. With training and practice, everything about standing in the batter's box during a game changed. Instead of thinking, "Don't throw me a curve, I cannot hit those," I thought, "Throw what you want, I am practiced and ready."

When it comes to building a Jesus Mission Life, reading these words is like standing at the plate, hoping the pitcher does not throw a curve.

*Don't make me talk about Jesus at work. Don't make me share Jesus with my neighbor or classmate. Don't let someone ask me a hard question about the Bible or church. Don't throw me a curve.* But if we are going to build a life of mission, we gotta take our swings.

For me, taking my swings has been a life lesson for nearly everything I have wanted to build into my life. If you want to be a musician, you gotta take your swings, learn music, and practice your instrument. If you want to build a life of fitness, you gotta take your swings and commit to doing the exercises. If you want to be a better leader, you gotta take your swings by studying leadership skills and practicing leading. Likewise, taking our swings for the Jesus Mission Life is about training, study, preparation, perspective, and clarity.

For the next several chapters, we will focus on taking our swings to see if we can discern life-transforming principles in building a life of Mission. As you read, will you pause to pray and ask God to speak to you?

We'll begin with *training*—our first swing, if you will. The meaning of training is *a specific and repeated series of actions or activities designed to bring about a specific outcome.* I am an idea person, sometimes a crazy idea person. In my lifetime, I have wanted to do a full marathon and a century bike ride in Death Valley. I have also wanted to hike the Pacific Crest Trail, all 2,650 miles, and along the way climb Half Dome in Yosemite National Park. I have wanted to be on the TV show *Survivor*, and I wanted to be on *The Amazing Race.* I still want to be on a cooking show and a singing show. I want to write a best-selling book, too. (If any of you want to buy 25,000 copies of this book, feel free.) When I say I have wanted to do these things, I mean I have actually researched how to make them happen and maybe even took notes. Sure, some of these "wants" are far beyond any possibility for me. Some require more talent than I have, and some require a dedication of time I do not have or am just unwilling to give. Some of these ideas have timed out, and only a younger version of myself with better knees and back could do the work. The truth is that the ideas that I call crazy could not compete with what I believe has been a different mission for my life.

What do all of these ideas have in common? Completing them would take training, practice, time, and more training. Look again at the definition of training—*a specific and repeated series of actions or activities designed to bring about a specific outcome.* Without training, there's no possibility of making any of these happen.

A while back I was watching a boxing video of heavyweight fighter Mike Tyson. It was presented on a split screen. On one side of the screen was how Mike Tyson trained and sparred, and on the other how he fought. One side showed him hitting the heavy bag, the speed bag, shadow boxing, and sparring. The other side showed several of Mike's actual fights, revealing the way Mike Tyson's training was actually expressed when he was in a real boxing match. I sat mesmerized at the correlation between his "repeated series of actions" in training and the absolute precision these actions created in the ring when they were deployed against another fighter. Tyson's strength, speed, skill, and stamina were all honed to perfection through training. Because of his training, when his fighting skills were unleashed on an opponent, they were devastating.

YouTube provides countless information videos. Want to know how to use a chef's knife? There is a video for that. Want to know how to play the guitar? There is a video for that. Want to know how to read faster? There is a video for that. Pick a topic you want to learn, go to YouTube, and you will find there is a video for that. But let's face it. Watching a video on YouTube might show you how to assemble a BBQ or change a filter in your refrigerator, but when you want to develop a new skill, watching a video will never make you a great chef or a great musician—only training does that. Only a "repeated series of actions or activities designed to bring about a specific outcome" will do that.

Anyone seeking to build a Jesus Mission Life, someone who becomes a disciple who makes disciples, needs to know that only training can bring this about. Amazing biblical sermons can point you in the right direction, inspire you, motivate you, and even be a catalyst for the mission, but they do not train you. Theology and membership classes can educate you, give you much-needed foundational truth, and grow your faith IQ, but they do not train you. Beautiful worship services invite you uniquely into the presence of God, ignite passion in you, bring healing in you, and become a centering force in your life, but they do not train you. Only training trains you. Our lives cannot become Jesus Mission Lives without training.

In the twenty-first century, how does one train to become a disciple-maker? Not many churches or universities offer much, if any, training in the specific Mission of Jesus, disciples making disciples. What is offered, in place of training, is a system that includes a form of membership and a covenant of commitment and morality. Circles, where we sit together and talk about Jesus and life. We sometimes use a series of beginner Bible studies to help new or young believers grow in Christ. Many churches have people-moving classes we call Next Steps or 101, designed to move people through a process of faith and maturity.

Let me stop for a second. ***I am for everything I just listed!*** I have led and written materials for each of these processes. But nothing I just listed is actual training; nothing is a "repeated series of actions or activities designed to bring about a specific outcome." Here is what we know: where there is no training, mission suffers greatly, and often there is no mission. So, how does one train to become a disciple-maker? I'm glad you asked. Let's dive into this now.

## THE JESUS PROCESS

True disciples make disciples, and for us to live out the Mission of Jesus by making disciples, we must first become one ourselves. I was in a Bible study with some guys, and the question came up, "What is a disciple?" It was a fun discussion, and we were all seeking some kind of understanding. One of the guys in the Bible study said that he always thought a disciple was the most serious kind of Christian. You are a follower, then a believer, then a good Christian, and then you become a disciple. I had the chance to say that those words are all supposed to mean the same thing. It was funny to hear one of the guys, proudly declared as he was leaving, "I thought I was just a Christian, but I am a disciple of Jesus."

I wonder how many of us might not be quite clear about what a disciple is or how to become one. We become a disciple of Jesus when we trust the work of Jesus Christ to forgive our sins through His life, death, and resurrection. Our trust/faith in Jesus is where we are made right by God (the biblical word is justified), and we become a disciple of Jesus. Here are some other words that define what we become when we place our trust in Christ: follower, believer, Christian, son/daughter. All of these words hold the same value of commitment to Christ; they are words that make us ALL IN. But since we have used the word "disciple," let's define that word here.

The New Testament was written in Greek, and in the ancient Greek language, there are three basic meanings for the word *disciple* that can give us a better understanding of what the Bible means when it is used. Jesus used this word twice in Matthew 16:24, "Then Jesus said to his *disciples*, 'Whoever wants to be my **disciple** must deny themselves and take up their cross and follow me'" (emphases mine). Three basic implications of the word disciple can help us build a more complete picture of what Jesus meant.

**First, a disciple is a student or apprentice who has a master/teacher.** In the days of Jesus, a student would choose a master/teacher and then submit themselves to this master/teacher. For His Mission, Jesus chose His disciples. In doing so, Jesus became their master/teacher, and they became His students. His disciples called Him Rabbi, which means teacher. To be a disciple, we need a master/teacher. I am a disciple of Jesus, so Jesus is my master and teacher. Paul told others to follow him as he followed Christ. We are apprentices of Jesus through a discipler, and when we disciple others, they are apprentices of Jesus too.

**Second, a disciple pursues excellence in their learning.** The idea that we can be a disciple and only commit part way was foreign to Jesus. "Then Jesus said to his disciples, 'Whoever wants to be my disciple must deny themselves and take up their cross and follow me'" (Matthew 16:24). The plan of every master/teacher was that their disciple would get the life, skills, knowledge, and learning from them and that the student, the disciple, would seek excellence in learning from their master.

**Third, a disciple is a student who, in pursuit of excellence, becomes a practitioner of the way of their master/teacher.** It is not enough that the disciple gathers information, gathers knowledge, gathers some skills along the way—we call this an education. No, the disciple was expected to become the next generation of master/teacher, passing along in life and practicing what their own master/teacher gave them.

As a disciple and disciple-maker, my training regimen is centered on a process I call The Jesus Process. I am going to give the short version here, but soon, this resource will also be available in book form. Until then, you can get a more detailed look now if you want to check out my podcast, "Say Yes & Become," wherever podcasts are provided. Check out episodes 85–90 specifically. The Jesus Process is a simple way of discipling and training disciples to make disciples the way Jesus did.

### Follow

For every person who would be a disciple, the process begins with the choice to **follow**. Following is taking steps in the direction of Jesus until your footsteps match His footprints. You are prayerfully stepping in the direction of Jesus to become a **follower** of Jesus. Following Jesus is always about what we see and what we hear, specifically seeing and hearing Jesus. Training someone to see and hear Jesus is to equip them to become an expert in Jesus's love, His life, His Mission, His strategies, and His relationship with His Father.

You begin the process of training (repeated specific actions intended for specific results) by immersion into the Gospels. After all these decades of following Jesus, I still read the Gospels (Matthew, Mark, Luke, and John) several times a year. Repeatedly reading the Gospels will change you by connecting you to Jesus's life while He was on the earth. I see Him and hear Him when I am repeatedly immersed in the Gospels. As a principle of life, we cannot follow someone we cannot see or hear.

### Trust

The natural byproduct of following is trust. **Trust** is a thinking and mind process. Sure, emotions play a part in shaping our thoughts, but trust primarily comes from our thinking. In training to be a disciple or disciple-maker, the mind must be renewed. When I am in training or training others, we take time to examine how to renew our thinking. Renewing my thinking involves three disciplines.

1. **I need to examine my thinking.** As a kid, whenever I got in trouble, my stepdad would ask me, "What were you thinking?" My response was most often "I don't know" or "I wasn't really thinking." Over time, his question became a powerful tool in my life, and now I also ask, "What am I thinking?" These questions, when honestly asked and prayerfully answered in partnership with God the Holy Spirit, have revealed so much to me. My secrets, pains, sinful habits, actions of self-preservation, fears, unforgiven people, expectations of self and others, disappointments, and more have been exposed by these questions. These questions have also revealed love, friends, places of growth and healing, and progress that can only be seen

when answering these two questions with honesty. "What was I thinking?" helps me look backward to examine a pattern of thought. "What am I thinking?" helps me examine my thoughts at a specific moment in the here and now. I need both of these questions if I am going to discover my freedom in Christ and move toward a Jesus Mission Life.

2. **I need to renew my thinking.** Ephesians 4, Romans 12, and several other places in the Bible point to my need to change the way I think by renewing it with God's thinking. God's thinking is always right because He has a full view of everything, knows everything, and is always wise. So when the Bible tells me to put on the mind of Christ, it is not saying to make a slight adjustment in my thinking; it is saying take off the old thoughts and put on new ones, Jesus ones, that make my mind new. His thoughts are not mine. His thoughts are not similar to mine. His thoughts are not even in the same neighborhood as mine. They are better, immeasurably better, and altogether different from mine. Scripture says that His thoughts are as far above the heavens and the earth (we cannot measure this distance), so much better than my thoughts (Isaiah 55:8–9). And guess what? He shares these thoughts with His friends!

3. **I need to bring all my thoughts captive to obey Christ.** Second Corinthians 10:5 tells me to bring every thought I have and make it captive to obey Jesus. I don't know about you, but I have a habit of talking myself out of trusting Jesus. If I am going to trust Jesus in a way that I **do not** talk myself out of, I need to stop the uprising of non-Jesus thinking that happens every day. I need to take these thoughts captive to obey Him. How do I do this? Paul tells us how in Philippians:

    > Finally, brothers and sisters, whatever is true, whatever is noble, whatever is right, whatever is pure, whatever is lovely, whatever is admirable—if anything is excellent or

> praiseworthy—think about such things. Whatever you have learned or received or heard from me, or seen in me—put it into practice. And the God of peace will be with you. (Philippians 4:8–9)

In these two verses, Paul gave two instructions on how to take our thoughts captive and renew our thinking. He told the Philippian Christ-followers to focus their thinking on right thinking. Look at the words he chose: true, noble, right, pure, lovely, admirable, excellent, and praiseworthy. In other words, think about the things that fit those words. Then he said ACT on these new thoughts. For me, I practice this as I memorize and meditate on Scripture because my natural thinking is not friendly to Jesus. Trusting Jesus is always about my thinking.

### Love

Trust always leads to affection. When I follow Jesus by seeing and hearing Him more and more clearly, my trust in Him will grow because my thinking about His life will change. Following leads to trusting and trusting leads to **love**. Follow—Trust—Love.

Love is a response to love. "We love because He first loved us" (1 John 4:19). Why do I love? Because I am loved. Why do I love like Jesus? Because Jesus has so loved me. When I am discipling someone or training someone to be a disciple-maker, I lead them to examine (thinking and seeing) all the ways we have been loved by God. We write them down, we talk about them all the time, we reframe our lives through the lens of God's love for us, and we respond in love to God and others.

### Imitate

Following leads to trust, trust leads to love, and love leads to **imitation**. Imitation is what happens when I love someone so much I want to be like them. Discipling someone or training a disciple-maker requires sitting face-to-face with Jesus (abiding in Him) because we want to be like Him. When I disciple someone (the best form of training for a disciple is to be discipled well), I teach them to sit face-to-face with Jesus for the express purpose of imitating Him. Our focus is to be like Him because we find nothing better than His life.

---

Side Note: We have been taught to sit with Jesus primarily for comfort and encouragement; transformation often seems secondary. Imitating Jesus happens when we sit with Him because we love Him and want to be like Him. Transformation must be our primary motivation for sitting with Jesus. We get comfort and encouragement, but what we are aiming at is the transformation of our old lives into Jesus Mission Lives.

---

### Bear Fruit

Following leads to trust. Trust leads to love. Love leads to imitation. Imitation leads to **fruit**. The transforming process of following, trusting, loving, and imitating transforms me into a fruitful friend and partner with Jesus. When I am discipling someone to bear fruit or training a disciple-maker to bear fruit, we work hard to build a mindset that Jesus is always at work. Jesus tells us this in John 5:17—"My Father is always at his work to this very day, and I too am working."

There is no place where God has not been working long before you arrive. Years ago I took a team of pastors to Africa. Some of these pastors struggled with the thought that they were bringing Jesus to Africa instead of joining Jesus in Africa. God is already at work next door, with your barista or your barber, at work or the gym. God is ALWAYS working and ALREADY at work before you arrive.

This fruit-bearing mindset that Jesus is already at work before you arrive is accompanied by the mindset that everywhere you go, you have been sent by God. When this mindset is in place and becomes more and more natural, you will bear fruit. The process of following Jesus by seeing and hearing Him will move you to trust Jesus because your thinking will be in line with His. Trusting Jesus opens the door to understanding every way in which you are loved by Jesus and can love like Jesus. When you love Jesus and sit face-to-face with Him, your desire to be like Him will grow, and you will begin to imitate Him. Jesus knew that the time for working the Mission of God was while He was alive; He saw Himself as One sent by the Father with a Mission—so Jesus bore fruit. This is your time to bear fruit.

All my coaches, in every sport I played, used the phrase, "Practice makes perfect!" We would repeat a drill over and over again until we didn't have to think about it. What I discovered is that practice does not make perfect—*practice makes natural.* When I am training a disciple-maker, I have them repeat words and actions again and again because I want disciple-making to be natural. I want those I disciple to be able to recognize that God is already there everywhere they go. He is already at work, and they need to know exactly what to do when prompted by God the Holy Spirit. ***Training makes The Jesus Process natural.***

One last thing and then a story from the Bible. The Jesus Process is not a single path to a fruit-bearing life; it is a process of knowing and loving Jesus that leads us to the Mission of Jesus and to bear the fruit Jesus chose us to bear (John 15:16). It is a repeated process with a specific outcome. Please forgive the run-on sentence below.

I follow, and as I do, I trust, and as I trust, I love, and as I love, I imitate, and as I imitate, I bear fruit, and as I bear fruit, I follow more closely, and as I follow more closely, I trust more deeply, and as I trust more deeply, I love with more passion, and as I love more passionately, I imitate more precisely, and as I imitate more precisely, I bear more fruit, and as I bear more fruit, the closer I follow … trust … love … imitate … bear fruit. Repeat, repeat, repeat, training, training, training. Now, on to the Bible story.

Peter and John were on their way to the temple when they saw a guy who had been lame from birth begging for money. (I am paraphrasing the story, but you can read it in Acts 3–4.) Stopping in front of him, they said, "Look at us, we do not have silver or gold, we have something better. In the name of Jesus, get up and live as a person who can walk." They then grabbed the guy and yanked him to his feet. Then, he started walking, leaping, and praising God!

They were in the temple, and this guy was still walking, leaping, and praising God, and drawing a lot of attention while he was at it. So Peter and John started telling the crowd about Jesus, and because they were talking about Jesus, they were soon arrested. Brought before the high council in Israel—the Sanhedrin—Peter and John were questioned: "Under whose authority/power did you do this miracle?"

They answered, "Jesus did it! There is no other way for people to be saved except by Jesus" (Acts 4:12). On the council, tensions were rising and tempers brewing. It was this same council that plotted for a couple of years to have Jesus killed, and when the time was right, they had Jesus arrested. These were the same guys who declared their allegiance to Caesar just to get Rome to approve Jesus's death. These were the same guys who had Jesus beaten and participated in His murder. These were the same guys who begged Pilate, the Roman governor, for guards to be placed at His tomb. These were the same guys who lied and bribed people to try and kill the news of the resurrection of Jesus (pun intended). These were the same guys who were now arresting two of Jesus's best friends for speaking and acting like Jesus.

When they saw that Peter and John followed Jesus, trusted Jesus, loved Jesus, imitated Jesus, and were bearing Jesus fruit, this is what they said: "When they saw the courage of Peter and John and realized that they were unschooled, ordinary men, they were astonished and they took note that these men had been with Jesus" (Acts 4:13). These men, Peter and John, had no formal training, but it was obvious to those questioning them (the council) that their master was Jesus. They were pursuing excellence as students of Jesus and practicing the way of their master. In other words, they were disciples.

Peter and John began **following** Jesus by seeing Him and hearing Him. What they saw and heard led to the kind of **trust** we read about in John 6, where Peter answered Jesus's question, "Will you also leave me?" by saying, "We have no other place to go, we believe you." Trusting Jesus led the disciples into a growing **love** for Him that led Thomas to speak for all the disciples in John 11, saying if Jesus were going to go to Jerusalem and die, then we would go and die with Him. This incredible love for Jesus caused them to **imitate** Christ, and this love was fueled by abiding, sitting face-to-face with Jesus so they could be like Him (read John 13–17). Finally, they went, and everywhere they went, their lives were lived on Mission for Jesus, **bearing fruit.**

For us to build a life fully immersed in the Mission of Jesus, we must train to become disciples of Jesus. In short, we make sure our master/teacher is Jesus. We make sure we are pursuing excellence as His students. We make sure we practice His way, His Mission, and His strategy. Disciples become disciple-makers by entering into the same process Jesus used to make His disciples: Follow—Trust—Love—Imitate—Bear Fruit.

Once again, training is a specific and repeated series of actions or activities designed to bring about a specific outcome. Jesus trained His disciples, repeatedly giving them actions and activities that transformed them into fishers of men, disciples who make disciples. This is what we must do too.

# Stepping into Jesus's Mission

## A prayer you can pray today:

*Jesus,*

*Thank You for the process You use to make disciples. Help me find ways to train for Your Mission. Show me what repeated series of actions I need to incorporate into my life to become well-trained in Jesus Mission Living. Give me insight on how The Jesus Process applies to my life. I appreciate how You intentionally train Your disciples.*

*Amen*

## Some questions to move you forward:

What is something you have trained for (a job, a sport, a hobby...)?

The specific outcome of Jesus's training is Jesus Mission Living. Training is a specific and repeated series of actions or activities designed to bring about a specific outcome. Where have you received or are receiving training for Jesus Mission Living?

Which part of The Jesus Process—Following, Trusting, Loving, Imitating, Bearing Fruit—has God been speaking to you about the most? Take a few minutes and share what He has been saying to you.

From The Jesus Process, what will you apply to your training to live a Jesus Mission Life?

- Following Jesus: eyes and ears.
- Trusting Jesus: renewed thinking.
- Loving Jesus: being loved.
- Imitating Jesus: sitting face-to-face with Jesus because you want to be like Him.
- Bearing Jesus-fruit: recognizing where God is at work as you go and joining Him there.

## A step to take as you go:

Choose a specific part of The Jesus Process (Follow, Trust, Love, Imitate, Bear Fruit) and, using a biblical concordance, find five verses or a passage of the Bible that you can begin to memorize. Here is a simple-to-use online concordance you can trust. Simply scan the QR code with your electronic device:

# Chapter 11

## Study Jesus

Several years ago, I decided I wanted to learn to smoke meat in a backyard smoker. I got the cheapest smoker I could find, got the books, and studied. My first attempt was a roast. I read everything I could on the temperature of the fire, the temperature of the meat when finished, seasoning the meat, and how to keep consistent temperatures for my first low-and-slow-smoked roast. Today, twenty-five years later, I can smoke a roast without studying how to smoke a roast. However, because I want to make every meal that I smoke amazing, I still read and study more and more every time I cook.

Just like studying has become an indispensable part of smoking meat, it is also an indispensable part of building a life of Jesus's Mission. One of the questions I ask people when talking about building a Jesus Mission Life is, "What are you studying about Jesus?" Usually, I get a blank stare at the use of the word "study." Sometimes people share with me a great book or two. Occasionally, I get an article they read or a journal or blog post that caught their eye. The most common response is they watch YouTube preachers. As conversations unfold, I find these video resources include more about politics and nationalism, fighting the culture wars, conspiracies, end times, or just a list of why someone else in Christian circles is wrong.

It is not often I hear a person answer, "I am studying Jesus in the Gospels" or "I am studying the life of Jesus." It seems to me that to build a Jesus Mission Life, the study of Jesus would be necessary. If our passion is to follow Jesus, studying the life, Mission, and words of Jesus would be a great starting place. This is another swing we gotta take.

## FLANNEL GRAPH JESUS

I grew up in church, and my first several years of what we called Sunday school were spent learning about the people in the Bible. The teacher had a flannel graph with images of Bible characters. Flannel graphs were made up of flannel cutouts of people and other important pieces of a story, and my teacher would put the images of a Bible character on a large flat board covered in flannel. These characters would stick to the board, and then Mrs. Brown, my Sunday school teacher, would tell the story surrounding the character. What can I say? There was no YouTube or video or internet back then. Flannel graphs were state-of-the-art back then.

In one story, I saw a little flannel boy named David who was surrounded by some flannel sheep and a few flannel shrubs, and across the valley was a much larger figure, a flannel Goliath. These flannel figures were moved, replaced, shifted, and changed to make the story flow. I saw a flannel Noah and a flannel Ark and a flannel Flood. There was a flannel Moses, a flannel Red Sea, and a flannel nation of Israel who crossed on dry land. A flannel Elijah called fire from heaven, and a flannel Daniel (who, by the way, looked a lot like flannel David) was in the lions' den. It was through this flannel storytelling that I discovered all the major people, places, and stories in the Bible. I also discovered Jesus this way too.

My teacher would put a flannel Jesus on the board next to a boy's fish and bread lunch, which was next to a flannel crowd and flannel disciples. There, Jesus fed 5,000. Then there would be a flannel Jesus next to a flannel boat with disciples and a flannel storm—Jesus walked on the water. There was a flannel Jesus next to a flannel blind man—Jesus healed the blind man. I learned the settings, the places, and the lessons through these flannel graph stories. I am not complaining, just telling you about my early Jesus-and-Bible-learning process.

What if my faith today only consisted of a flannel graph theology? Flannel Graph Theology is what happens when we become familiar with the stories, people, and lessons of the Bible but struggle to really see and know Jesus in the Bible. Flannel-graph stories, flannel-graph people, and flannel-graph lessons. Flannel Graph Theology means having some information about Jesus but not a total transformation of our hearts because of Jesus. Flannel Graph Theology makes me familiar with some miracles and some stories, and I learn these stories in light of how they apply to me. David kills Goliath, and God can slay the giants in your life. Daniel is in the lions' den, and God will shut the lion's mouth and keep you safe. Jesus walks on water, and Jesus can calm your storm. Jesus feeds 5,000 with a little boy's lunch, so bring your little to Jesus so He can use it. This is Flannel Graph Theology. Does this sound familiar? While many people in the church today do not experience flannel graph storytelling, there is much Flannel Graph Theology in the church.

Here is my observation: a Jesus Mission life cannot be built on a flannel-graph foundation. It is hard to write these words but it is necessary. Too many people who follow Jesus are following a flannel-graph Jesus. They know who He is, His stories, and some of His teachings but have never fully embraced Him or His Mission.

## FROM HERE TO THERE

If "here" is in the neighborhood of flannel-graph Jesus, and "there" is a Jesus Mission Life, how do I get there? One important way is to study Jesus. Study takes time, study takes work, but let me share with you some surprising benefits to our lives when we invest the needed time to study Jesus in the Bible.

*When I studied Jesus, He became my friend.*

In my mid-20s, I was able to attend the Billy Graham School of Evangelism. I sat listening to the first speaker, and I thought to myself, "I could give that talk." The second speaker brought the same response from me. The third, too. Then, the great African American preacher, the late E. V. Hill, got up to speak for the final session, and as he did, the Holy Spirit revealed to me my pride and arrogance and said, "You don't know Jesus like E.V. Hill knows Jesus. You don't know Jesus well enough to do that." He was right; I knew Jesus, but I did not know Jesus like E. V. Hill knew Jesus.

I sat in my chair and cried. I was ashamed of my pride and my arrogance, and I made a promise to God that day—I would do whatever I could to get to know Jesus better. As I collected more Jesus stories, more of Jesus's teachings, and more of Jesus's interactions, I started to love Jesus in a whole new way. I was no longer learning about Him just to share Him (a trap many preachers and pastors fall into); I was spending time with a friend. I laughed at His interactions with His friends; I cried when He was arrested and beaten; I felt pride when He loved the outcast; I cheered when He banished demons. I was actually a friend of Jesus, and He was truly my friend.

*When I studied Jesus, my hunger for the whole Bible grew.*

Because of my upbringing, I have always had a lot of Bible knowledge. Even though I could not retain information in literature or science, for some strange reason, memorizing Scripture and sports statistics came easy. I knew every person, place, and story in the Bible by the time I was twelve. I could quote hundreds upon hundreds of verses, and yes, I had an advanced degree in Flannel Graph Theology. Something changed in me when I truly studied Jesus, though. The better I knew Jesus, the clearer the rest of the Bible became. The Sacrificial Law from the Old Testament showed me Jesus. The Exodus showed me Jesus. The Creation accounts helped me meet my Creator and my Redeemer. The entire Old Testament came alive, and all the letters written by Paul, Peter, James, John, Jude, and whoever the guy is that wrote Hebrews came alive. Everything I read pointed me to Jesus and His Mission.

*When I studied Jesus, my worship of Jesus became more personal.*

When I say worship here, I mean music and more. Suddenly, the songs I sang and knew were more rich and deep. I found myself in worship services singing and praying differently. It was as if I could see that my friend Jesus was pleased to be praised. I found more connection in nature, more joy in others doing well, and I became less needy of the applause of others.

*When I studied Jesus, my ministry exploded.*

God has given me some pretty cool ministry opportunities over the years. Studying Jesus turned ministry from addition to multiplication. Studying Jesus transformed my ministry by making it about disciples making disciples, equipping disciple-makers, and giving away ministry. Studying Jesus helped me build a Jesus-centered ministry, meaning Jesus's strategy, Jesus's method, and Jesus's Mission. You might not be in vocational ministry, but we are all called to make disciples. Study Jesus to learn how He made disciples. Study Jesus to see how He loved others. Study Jesus and discover His Mission as your mission.

Before Starbucks moved into so many neighborhoods, there were a lot of drive-through coffee kiosks. There was one I frequented often, and it was there I met Kim. Kim greeted me each morning, and over time, I got to know her story. One morning, as Kim handed me my coffee, she leaned out the window and said, "I'm getting married; my boyfriend proposed, and I am so excited!" I responded with all the appropriate enthusiasm and excitement and then asked if she knew who was going to officiate the wedding. "I don't know, we are not church people." I smiled and let her know that I was church people, and we laughed. "Will you marry me?" she blurted, "I am already married, and you are engaged, but I will do your ceremony on one condition," I replied. "Name it," she said. "If you and Brad agree to meet me eight times to prepare for staying married, I will do your wedding."

Over the next four months, we met, growing the friendship between Kim, Brad, and myself. After the second meeting, they both prayed to receive Christ, and I spent the next three months discipling this couple. They started coming to church and became great followers of Jesus.

Before studying Jesus, I might have missed this opportunity, but I learned from Jesus that making disciples happens as we go, everywhere we go, even in coffee kiosks. Here are a few other benefits of studying Jesus:

*When I study Jesus, I discover that greatness is found in serving others.*

*When I study Jesus, I am compelled to love like Jesus.*

*When I study Jesus, I learn to disciple others.*

*When I study Jesus, I find the value of time with my Father.*

*When I study Jesus, I understand the cross I am to "take up."*

*When I study Jesus, I begin to value Jesus above everything else in my life.*

But there is one more thing I have discovered whenever I study Jesus, and it is BIG!

*Whenever I study Jesus, His Mission becomes my only mission.*

Jesus's Mission, if you remember, is to seek and save the lost by giving His life as a ransom for many. Jesus's Mission, once He died and rose again, was handed to all who were and would become His disciples. Everywhere you go, make disciples who make disciples whose disciples also make disciples. The study of Jesus made the Great Commission my only mission.

So, how does one go about studying Jesus? We study Jesus by immersing ourselves in the Gospels. I know, seems simplistic, but it is the way. Here is how I do it: I read them again and again and again and again and again. For years and years now, I have read the Gospels several times a year. At least once a year, I read one of the Gospels thirty times. For example, I read John 1–5 every day for thirty days. Then I read John 6–11 every day for thirty days. Then I read John 12–17 every day for thirty days. Then I read John 19–21 every day for thirty days. This habit, though it may sound tedious to you, has been life-changing. I encourage you to try it.

When I am studying Jesus, I also ask questions about how

He interacted with lost people and with His closest friends. I ask about how Jesus and His Father interacted. I pay attention to Jesus's words, I pay attention to His miracles, and to both who and how He loved.

A part of my journey has included extra reading too. Here are some resources I recommend:

*Along the Road: How Jesus Used Geography to Tell God's Story* by John Beck

*How to Read the Bible for All Its Worth, Fourth Edition* by Gordon D. Fee

*30 Days to Understanding the Bible, 30th Anniversary: Unlock the Scriptures in 15 Minutes a Day* by Max Anders

*Leading from the Middle: How the Leadership of Jesus Launched a Movement* by Leonard Lee (order at leonardlee.com)

*Christ from Beginning to End: How the Full Story of Scripture Reveals the Full Glory of Christ* by Trent Hunter and Stephen Wellum

The Bible Project (thebibleproject.com)

*Let's Read the Gospels* by Annie F. Downs

Commentaries by InterVarsity Press and Warren Wiersby

**Pro Tip:** Don't read everyone else's books and neglect to read the Gospels for yourself. Use these as resources, but dig into the Scriptures for yourself too.

## A prayer you can pray today:

*Jesus,*

*Thank You for the four Gospels I can use to study Your words, Mission, and life. Help me become diligent in studying You. Give me insight into Your heart, love, life, and Mission. I am so glad You want me to know You.*

*Amen*

## Some questions to move you forward:

What is something you have studied in your lifetime that has shaped you in relationships or activities?

When you studied, what adjustments did you make to your time, schedule, or life in order to study?

When you hear the term "study Jesus," what thoughts come to your mind?

Of the changes listed in this chapter that happen when we study Jesus, which one is most appealing?

Studying Jesus takes time. How will you adjust your time or reading to study Jesus?

What do you anticipate will happen in your faith as you study Jesus?

## A step to take as you go:

Choose a Gospel (Matthew, Mark, Luke, or John) and begin to read, and then re-read it for three months. Note how Jesus's words, actions, relationships with people, and relationship with His Father came from His own Mission to seek and save the lost.

# Chapter 12

## Preparation

I played JV football my sophomore year in high school, and the summer before my tenth-grade year came, I hit the gym hard. I was given a playbook to memorize, and every day, I engaged in a series of strength, agility, and endurance-building routines. I started preparing for a single mission—to win football games. Five days a week, my teammates and I would talk, train, laugh, play our jokes, and learn our plays together, all in preparation for a single mission—to win football games.

I was not a great football player, but I was surrounded by some really, really good football players, so when we were far enough ahead in a game that even I could not ruin the outcome, I got a chance to play. My coach would send in a play with one of the receivers, he would tell the quarterback, and the quarterback would tell the team. Whether I was first string or second string, my job was to be prepared for a single mission—to win football games. I did my job.

My point is this: no matter my skill, my talent, my role in a game, or my chance of playing, I was prepared for a single mission—to win football games. My preparation began before the season and continued throughout the whole season, and at game time, I was ready. I was never as good as the players before me, but I most certainly was as prepared as they were. Because I was a part of the team, I was prepared for a single mission—to win football games.

Those are a lot of words to prompt a question. Are you preparing yourself as a disciple of Jesus (Team Jesus) to make disciples as commanded by Jesus? The Mission of Jesus, as you have already seen, is central to every part of our life and faith. It is a gift God hands us when we follow Him; it is the gift of partnership with the Creator. Jesus was so confident His guys were ready that He told the Father, "Put them in coach; they are game ready" (John 17, paraphrase mine). You and I have the same mission that Jesus gave His disciples, and it is a mission that requires preparation. How can we prepare for this mission? I'm glad you asked.

Two words matter in how we relate to Jesus. Both are essential, and both are of great importance in our preparation for a Jesus Mission Life. The words are **integrated and dedicated.** As I write about these two words, you might be tempted to place some condemnation on yourself or another person for how these words are used in our thinking in preparing for the Mission of Jesus. Please hear or read these thoughts as an invitation and instruction. I think it might be helpful if I share it as a story.

## INTEGRATED

My early faith journey has always included the phrases "daily quiet time" and "doing daily devotions." These two nearly interchangeable phrases are how I was encouraged to spend time with Jesus each day. The plan was to get up each morning or find time in the evening before I went to bed to read the Bible and pray. Quiet times were usually from the Bible, and devotions were usually from a small book with a Scripture and a story. I had notebooks that gave me places to answer some questions like, what did it say? What did it mean? How can you apply it to your life? Some daily devotions even asked me to apply what I read.

Again, in my early faith journey, I was instructed to pray without ceasing, to memorize Scripture, to study Scripture, and to keep short accounts of sin throughout my day so I could stay close to Jesus. The daily devotional market was much smaller back then, so my choices seemed to be limited to Our Daily Bread, and if I felt like I could handle the pro level, I could read great theologians and preachers like

Charles Spurgeon or Brother Lawrence or Oswald Chambers. But, since I didn't feel all that pro-level in my faith and since my reading challenges were present but undiagnosed, I really didn't like reading that much. But I did like Jesus a lot, so I just read my Bible a lot.

I figured out that if I could mix into my day a verse, a prayer, and a few minutes of reflection on Jesus, I could **integrate** my devotional duties into my daily routines. The amazing and life-changing ministry called The Navigators provided little memory cards and Bible studies. I often paused to read and pray over a verse, keeping my sins confessed, and since it was the seventies, a giant Bible and a fish-shaped sticker became tools in an integrated time with Jesus. Guess what? It was very meaningful and helpful. If you have a primarily integrated (throughout the day) time with Jesus, well done, but keep reading. God has some amazing grace in store for you.

Today, my integrated time with Jesus has the aid of technology. I can listen to my Bible as I drive and play faith-based podcasts and sermons from my favorite Bible teachers. I have websites where prayers can be recited for me, and I can find anything I want on YouTube or Spotify. I can be treated to the best worship music as I drive, fly, or walk. I can put earbuds in and let my smartphone bring to me throughout the day grace notes of faith, songs, and truth as I mow my yard, do my chores, or enjoy my hobbies. I love that technology has opened up countless possibilities for integrating my time with Jesus throughout the day, giving me strength as I navigate my day.

Integrated time with Jesus accomplishes three key relational connections I need throughout the day. **First, integrated time reminds me that I am deeply and personally loved by God.** I need this badly, not because I forget the cross but because I get distracted and look away from the love of God as expressed in His goodness. This was what Satan did in the Garden of Eden to Adam and Eve. He distracted them and made them look away from the love of God. He made them doubt God's goodness by distorting the words and instructions God had given them. Satan painted a picture of God as petty and small, yet EVERYTHING about creation was good. God declared it good, but the lies and misdirection of Satan caused them to be distracted and forgetful that God is good. Integrated time serves to remind me that in a broken world, a broken Leonard is deeply loved by a good and perfect Father.

**Second, integrated time keeps me aware that God is present.** Jesus's final words were, "I will be with you always, right up to the very end" (Matthew 20:20, paraphrase mine). A study through Scripture shows a glorious pattern that when God sends us and commissions us to His Mission, He also goes with us. He is present right now as you are reading these words. He is working to help you filter them through the lens of grace and truth and then integrate what He will use most into a Jesus Mission Life. Above us, below us, behind us, and before us, God is with us! The stops we make along the way each day through prayer, Scripture, and serving others integrate our time with Jesus and raise our awareness of His constant presence.

Here is a really great reason the presence of God matters: Jesus wants us to live beyond our strength, and His Mission is beyond our strength. A. W. Tozer says, "God is looking for those with whom he can do the impossible—what a pity that we plan only the things that we can do by ourselves."[8] Integrated time with Jesus helps me embrace a life that can only be explained by the presence of God in my life.

**Lastly, integrated time with Jesus keeps me prepared for spiritual battles throughout the day.** The enemy of my soul, Satan, is prone to sneak attacks, direct assaults, and internal attacks. We are instructed to be aware of Satan's schemes and his lies. I need truth throughout the day, and integrated time provides this truth. Satan is an accuser and a liar; I need grace throughout the day, and integrated time provides this grace.

I was driving in South Africa several years ago, and it was quite the adventure. They drive on the opposite side of the road and the opposite side of the car. I had to give myself a morning pep talk just to help me navigate. Our team was driving late at night, looking for a hotel we had reserved, and none of the directions we had received were of much use. This was in the Stone Age when the cost of cell phones and internet on your phone required more money than a small country had, so I did not want to use my GPS. Unable to find my way, I decided to pay for the cost of using my phone's GPS because knowing where to go and how to get there was better than being lost in a foreign country. I used the GPS, paid the cost, and arrived safely at our hotel.

Integrated time with Jesus provides me with what I need to navigate moment by moment, where the battle is really being fought, providing me with step-by-step directions to a place I need to be. It serves as a GPS for the Jesus Mission Life I have been given by God.

## DEDICATED

In my first Bible class in college, I heard about Johnathan Edwards, the Wesley brothers, D. L. Moody, and other great and influential preachers. I loved it because I was training to be one of them. Their stories had common themes, and one of these themes was their **dedicated** time with God. These men were committed to getting up early, even before Jesus, and spending time on their knees in prayer, study, fasting, and more. Their commitment to dedicated time with Jesus was remarkable.

These guys hunkered down with Jesus for hours and hours and hours before the sun came up, before people arrived and meetings began, and they did it every day. Compared to them, I felt pretty pathetic. More than once, I remember feeling like I was failing when I compared my dedicated time with Jesus to their dedicated time with Jesus. All of them cited Jesus's relationship with His Father as their example. I had small seasons of success, spending a few weeks with an hour a day of dedicated prayer or an hour a day with dedicated immersion in the Scriptures, but then my pillow would win again. When I felt enough guilt or enough inspiration, I would try again.

Integrated time with Jesus was easier for me than dedicated time with Jesus. But over time, with a lot of discipline and hard work, both integrated and dedicated time with Jesus is how God prepares me for a Jesus Mission Life.

Over the years, I have come to understand more about dedicated time with Jesus. I can see that dedicated time with Jesus needs to be relational, not religious. I am not better because I gave an hour of dedicated time; I am changed because I spent an hour with a friend named Jesus.

**Dedicated time is where I get to stop long enough to actually hear from Jesus.** It is the voice of Jesus I hear in dedicated times that guides me through integrated times. I know because I recognize this voice so much better now. I am in deeply connected friendship with Jesus and know His voice, just as John 10:4 says, "My sheep hear my voice and follow" (paraphrase mine).

**Dedicated time is where God does surgery on my soul.** A few years back, I had concerns about my heart (actual heart) and ended up in the emergency room. Tests, more tests, and then needles and more tests. Each amazing nurse and doctor gave me **integrated** time. I was one of many patients, one of many issues, one of many concerns, and they moved efficiently through each patient. A doctor finally gave me **dedicated** time where I could ask questions, get answers, and find treatments going forward. I felt like I understood what was going on and how to move in the right direction. (It all turned out fine, by the way.)

The dedicated time with my doctor, unhurried and uninterrupted, allowed his expertise to be useful to my peace. This is what dedicated time with Jesus does. Dedicated time allows me to sit with the expert on my soul and get diagnosed, get treatment, get assurance, and get care specifically from God. The beauty of dedicated time is that it also acts as a preventative to emergency room visits for my soul. Dedicated time is how, together with Jesus, I am filled for the exciting and amazing Jesus Mission Life that God has gifted to me.

When I embraced the Mission of Jesus as my life mission, to make disciples wherever I go, my need for both integrated time with Jesus and dedicated time with Jesus came to the forefront of my life. For the first ten to twelve years of knowing Jesus, I was taught to be a good Christian. Good Christians have a morality checklist. Watch your language and avoid taboo things like movies, alcohol, tobacco, rock 'n' roll music, tattoos, and sinners. I was taught that good Christians have a checklist of things they do, like prayer, the Bible, and church. Good Christians have a theology checklist, too. I know; I had it and knew it well. Then something happened to me, and I was undone—**my WHY changed.**

Spending time in the book of Isaiah, something grabbed my heart and shook me to the core. You see, the "why" in my life was mostly about believing right and behaving right. I was driven by truth and morality. The "why" for me was about positioning myself to say truths to others; this is how we were encouraged to do "evangelism." The "why" for me was about being morally clean. For all of the right reasons in my heart, I wanted to be spiritually strong. I wanted to be an expert in Scripture. I wanted to be mature in faith. I wanted to speak the Gospel with authority. This is what we thought was the goal for every believer. Then, Isaiah wrecked me because, in Isaiah, I saw God and myself and His Mission differently. Here is what happened and what changed.

Isaiah 6 begins with an emotional and time-establishing statement: "When King Uzziah died ..." For Isaiah, this was a moment to remember because they were cousins. When his cousin King Uzziah died, something happened. He saw the Lord. Not at the funeral, not in the care of the people, not in the rituals of grief, he actually SAW Him in His splendor, and WOW! His glory! Read these words out loud; pretty spectacular.

> In the year that King Uzziah died, I saw the Lord, high and exalted, seated on a throne; and the train of his robe filled the temple. Above him were seraphim, each with six wings: With two wings they covered their faces, with two they covered their feet, and with two they were flying. And they were calling to one another: "Holy, holy, holy is the LORD Almighty; the whole earth is full of his glory." At the sound of their voices the doorposts and thresholds shook and the temple was filled with smoke. (Isaiah 6:1–4)

In real time, in full definition, in real sound, Isaiah saw God. His description is epic. Now, let me be clear. I have seen some pretty amazing things in my lifetime. I have seen a beautiful bride enter the building to marry me. I have witnessed two kids being born and enter the world. I have been to the Grand Canyon, the Himalayan Mountains, sunrise over the Atlantic Ocean, and sunsets over the Pacific. I have been a part of countless baptisms. I have sat in the front row and watched friends go from this world into eternity. But not one of these sights elicited the response Isaiah had when he saw God:

> "Woe to me!" I cried. "I am ruined! For I am a man of unclean lips, and I live among a people of unclean lips, and my eyes have seen the King, the LORD Almighty." (Isaiah 6:5)

Let's add some context here. In Isaiah 3 and Isaiah 5, the word *woe* is used eight times. Each use of the word *woe* is outward, directed toward other people and the mess they are making. It is directed to someone else, a people group whose practices and actions fall short of God's Law. This external pointing of the word *woe* is not uncommon for a fiery up-and-coming prophet who had gotten both a calling and a word from God. Then Isaiah 6 happens.

"Woe to me!" he cried. What a radical shift! From external to internal, from you to me, from shouting to tears, from "you are going to be ruined" to "I am ruined." Isaiah lamented before God, "My lips are unclean; the people I live with have unclean lips, and I am undone. Woe to me." Isaiah credited the change to one thing. "I have seen God," and in front of God, our "why" changes to our WHY.

God responded to Isaiah by sending an angel. A seraph took a coal from the altar and touched Isaiah's lips, saying, "you are no longer guilty; you are atoned for." The end. Well, not actually the end. It was the beginning of Isaiah's God-given mission.

It was from this place of Isaiah seeing God as He is that Isaiah was undone. From this place, there was a directional switch of the woes. From this place of Isaiah's confession and from this place of God's cleansing Isaiah, God spoke.

> Then I heard the voice of the Lord saying, "Whom shall I send? And who will go for us?" And I said, "Here am I. Send me!" (Isaiah 6:8)

God, from the throne of heaven, asked two questions: **"Whom shall I send?"** and **"Who will go for us?"** These are God's questions about God's Mission. This was not hypothetical pondering by God, "I wonder who will say the next message." These two questions are God saying, "I have much to do, much I want done, who shall I send? Who will go for us?"

God's plan to rescue the world involves us being sent. His plan involves us going. "My people are my plan to rescue the world, my people need correction (Isaiah's woes were not inaccurate) for them to fulfill My Plan of rescue, to move My Mission forward, I need someone to go. Who will it be? Who will I SEND?"

"Here am I, send me." These five words expressed the change in my WHY because, for the first time in my life, I could answer the question as if it were God actually speaking. "Who will go, whom shall I send?" This led me to "Here am I, send me." For the first time in my life, I was not preparing to be good; I was preparing to be sent.

I know now that my "why" changed to my WHY when I went from "woe to you" to "woe is me." It was in my woe-to-me moment when I heard God ask me, "Who can I send? I have something I want done. I have a Mission, and who will go?" The mission upon which God sent Isaiah is the same Mission God started before the foundation of the world. It is on this same Mission that God has sent me (and you). It was as if God were speaking directly to my heart and mind. "I have a Mission that started as a promise when Adam and Eve sinned. I have a Mission that was preserved with Noah and a flood. I set this Mission in motion with Abraham by creating a nation to bring Jesus into the world. I sent the promise I made to Eve in the garden, into the world when Jesus was born of a virgin. Jesus's life, death, burial, and resurrection defeated Satan and conquered sin and death. I handed this Mission to the Church. I gave to each believer the Holy Spirit to give them the power to take this good news, this gospel, to every tribe, tongue, and nation. Who will go? Who can I send?"

I could only respond with five words, "Here am I, send me." My WHY has changed from being a good Christian to being a sent Christian. When my WHY changed, two things shifted in me. First, how I prepared myself to be sent, and second, what I saw myself as being sent to do.

My whole life, I was told to read, pray, and do devotions or quiet times so I could live a morally excellent life. All my faith instruction was directed towards holiness, maturity, morality, theological accuracy, or just being a good Christian guy. When my WHY shifted from the good Christian guy to the Mission of God, my preparation changed. I was now preparing to be sent, not preparing to be good. Remember, though, I am for moral excellence and good theology.

Preparing to be sent carried a different responsibility. I was preparing to be SENT by GOD. This is HIS Mission. This is what He set in motion before the foundation of the world. My time with God changed because it turned into preparation for mission. My prayer life changed because I was preparing to be sent. My time in the Word changed because I was preparing to be sent. My silence, listening, meditation, and memorization all changed because I was preparing to be sent by a God who loves me more than I can measure. The question from God to Isaiah, "Whom shall I send?" became a personal question to me.

Over time, the habits surrounding this preparation made natural the thought that I am sent by God. This means that I never go anywhere I am not sent by God. The God who watches over me also watches over my neighbor, the barista, the server in a restaurant, the guy sitting next to me in church, and I have never entered a room that I was not sent by God. Long before I arrive, Jesus is at work in the people around me, and with this being true, I am sent to join Him in this work.

Preparing to be sent means I need a healthy dose of both dedicated time and integrated time with Jesus. Do you have both dedicated and integrated time with God? Is your time with Jesus about being a good Christian or being a sent Christian?

Preparation to be sent has opened the door to my relationship with Jesus and the Father in remarkable ways, but I never expected how preparation to be sent would impact my relationship with God the Holy Spirit. Jesus promised that God the Holy Spirit would prepare me for a Jesus Mission Life, and Paul wrote these words to help us understand that the Holy Spirit produces fruit within us that is expressed outwardly as we live.

> But the fruit of the Spirit is love, joy, peace, forbearance, kindness, goodness, faithfulness, gentleness and self-control. Against such things there is no law. Those who belong to Christ Jesus have crucified the flesh with its passions and desires. Since we live by the Spirit, let us keep in step with the Spirit. (Galatians 5:22–25)

My faith corner did not talk much about God the Holy Spirit, so

He was a huge mystery to me. This mystery was so big that, for the most part, it kept me away from Him. I was taught that the days of the miraculous were done now that we have the whole Bible. I was taught that God's primary voice was the Bible. I am not diminishing the Bible because everything that the Holy Spirit says will always match the Scriptures. I am not advocating my own personal interpretation. What I am saying is that my preparation to be sent impacted my relationship with God the Holy Spirit.

Paul, in Galatians 5, says that if I live in relationship with my flesh, I get on the naughty list in big and bold ways. My work to be a good Christian kept me aware of any behaviors that appear on the naughty list. I wanted to avoid this list more than I wanted to live on mission with Jesus. Here is the naughty list:

> The acts of the flesh are obvious: sexual immorality, impurity and debauchery; idolatry and witchcraft; hatred, discord, jealousy, fits of rage, selfish ambition, dissensions, factions and envy; drunkenness, orgies, and the like. I warn you, as I did before, that those who live like this will not inherit the kingdom of God. (Galatians 5:19–21)

When I was preparing to be sent, I started looking at a different list, the one in verses 22–23.

> But the fruit of the Spirit is love, joy, peace, forbearance, kindness, goodness, faithfulness, gentleness and self-control. Against such things there is no law. (Galatians 5:22–23)

Instead of seeing this list as the counterpart to the naughty list, I saw this list as a description of the person God prepares to send. I saw this list as a perfect description of Jesus, the One God had already sent. I saw this list as a beautiful result of friendship with God the Holy Spirit, the One whose friendship changes me and prepares me to be sent.

I found that God the Holy Spirit used my **integrated** and **dedicated** times with Jesus to fill my life with love, joy, peace, forbearance, kindness, goodness, faithfulness, gentleness, and self-control. The more time I spent with God, the more the fruit of God the Holy Spirit became His calling card on my soul and character. My relationship with the Holy Spirit prepared me to enter into any place, no matter the law, the rules, or the situation. The Spirit of God prepares me to make disciples everywhere I go.

Today, my dedicated time with Jesus is what God the Holy Spirit uses to strengthen and fuel my integrated time with Jesus. I want to finish this chapter on preparation by sharing a couple of helpful practices that God the Holy Spirit uses in my life, both dedicated and integrated, as we prepare to be sent by God to live a Jesus Mission Life.

## MY TOP FIVE DEDICATED FAITH DISCIPLINES

Dedicated time with God involves five basic practices in my life. Each one overlaps and each one is used by God to love me, help me love Him, and prepare me to be sent so I can make disciples everywhere I go.

### One—Scripture

Since the previous chapter included studying Jesus, I will only add here that my time with Jesus in the Bible is how I prepare for the right Leonard to be sent into the day.

This daily time is highly relational, meaning I feel like I am sitting with a friend. This dedicated time with Jesus in His Word is mostly just reading the Bible, not other resources, because something happens in the process. I read or listen and hear the voice of my Shepherd. I meditate and cherish the voice of my Shepherd. I memorize and hold fast to the heart of my Shepherd. I study (ask questions for clarity) and understand the intent of my Shepherd. I obey and submit to the authority of my Shepherd. I share and brag about the goodness of my Shepherd.

### Two—Prayer

When Merrily and I got married, we talked about everything and anything. Our conversations were fun, informative, silly, serious, and beautiful. But what I realized is that there were seven basic conversations that formed the foundation for all the rest of our words. If we were lacking in the seven, the rest of our conversations were more of an attempt to connect and not the result of being connected. The seven conversations were about:

- our marriage
- our finances
- our schedules
- our faith
- our work/ministry
- family and future (kids, jobs, careers, and life)
- our individual selves

We needed these seven conversations to have a prominent place in our marriage, and when they were present, we could literally talk about anything and everything—and we did. These conversations form the bedrock of love and trust, and still to this day, they serve us well. Do we have every one of them every day? No, but they are part of a rhythm that has kept us in love since 1988.

Here is the question the Holy Spirit brought to my heart and mind: "If these conversations form the foundation for the mission of building a life together with Merrily, what conversations with God would have the same impact in forming a deep friendship and partnership with Him?" I came up with six conversations I need to have every day with God so I can know Him and make Him known as a disciple who makes disciples.

- **I talk to God about God.** This is where I worship, appreciate, love, praise, and celebrate all I know and see in God.
- **I talk to God about me.** This is where I confess, cry, shout, and express my joy and fears, my frustrations and satisfaction in my

life, and my friendship with God.

- **I talk to God about those I love.** This is where I pray for my family and my friends. I pray for all those I love.
- **I talk to God about His heart.** This is the conversation where I talk with God about His heart for the world. It is where I pray for my church, my pastors, and the leaders in my life, and where I pray for God's work to be done in and around the world. This conversation is where I talk to God about my co-workers, my classmates, my neighbors, or teammates.
- **I talk to God about my plans.** This is the conversation I have with God about my plans and activities. It is where I look at the activities of my life, the decisions I need to make daily and for my future, too.
- **I talk to God about my heavy burden.** My heavy burden is the place where my heart and mind go first or most. It changes with time. Sometimes, my heavy burden is here for one season and then gone for a while. Jesus said that when I live out His Mission, I can ask anything, and He will hear me. This is where that "anything" is most expressed in my life.

Two things I know about prayer: 1) God always answers prayer. God ALWAYS answers prayer. All prayers get answers, but not all prayers get the answers we want. All prayers get the answers we need. 2) God's answers are based upon the truth that He knows what we do not know, He sees what we cannot see, and He is very fond of us.

These six conversations are dedicated and form the prayer foundation for my relationship with Jesus and for being sent by Jesus. They also help me integrate throughout the day, spending much time with Jesus. I suggest writing them down and using them as a prayer guide.

### Three—I Sit

Sit is an inclusive word that involves listening to Jesus, being silent in front of Jesus, waiting on Jesus, and reflecting on Jesus. This happens in my life only when it is a part of dedicated time. For me to sit, I need to put the phone and computer away. I need no help in being distracted; I am an expert in doing that. Sometimes when I sit, I am overcome by God's presence, and I will weep, laugh, rejoice, and even sing. Other times when I sit, I hear nothing but recognize that with God, silence is not as much of a test as it is us trusting each other to just be. Usually, in my sitting time, God speaks to me, and it is very specific. Because the Scriptures are so alive in me when I sit, He reminds me that He is, I am not, He can, and I cannot, He does what I cannot, and I lean into His arms and surrender.

#### Four—I Fast

For me, fasting is not a daily, dedicated time. When I do fast, the time is dedicated, and I fast for three reasons throughout the year.

**First, I surrender what I love to the One I love.** I give up something to Jesus as a sacrifice of surrender, saying you can have any and all of it. What might be a place of surrender God is calling you to?

**Second, I fast for focus.** I can easily get distracted, and fasting helps me with the discipline of focus. Focus in study, prayer, holiness, worshipping, and hearing are the main places for me. What might be a place of focus God is calling you to?

**Finally, I fast for God to move.** I will fast for God to change me and my character. I will fast for God to heal or free me from a habit or hurt. I will fast for God to restore someone to Himself. I will fast for God to move a mountain in our ministry or my life.

#### Five—I Rest

Those who know me, you better stop laughing. Resting is not about doing nothing but about doing what restores my soul. In my life, this could be writing, fishing, watching a show, having a conversation with a friend, or making a meal for my family or someone else.

So there you have it—the top five dedicated faith disciplines that

God uses to love me, to help me love Him, and to prepare me to be sent wherever He needs me to go. *I read my Bible, I pray, I sit, I fast, and I rest.* May these spiritual disciplines be useful to you too.

## MY TOP FIVE INTEGRATED FAITH DISCIPLINES

Integrated times with God consist of multiple relational anchor points throughout the day for building a Jesus Mission Life. They serve as reminders for a forgetful Leonard, refreshing the love and calling of God. These integrated times are fueling stations for a faith that burns a lot of fuel throughout the day and needs to be refilled.

### One—I Hunt

As much as I love actual hunting, I mean something different here. When I say "I hunt," it means I hunt for opportunities to speak Jesus's love and grace to others. These opportunities over the years often turn into simple words of grace or sharing the gospel. Sometimes, these opportunities turn into leading someone to follow Jesus or inviting them to connect at church. By searching for these opportunities to remind someone that they are seen, loved, and appreciated, even a small act of kindness is used by God to show His love. Hunting for opportunities has resulted in giving money to feed or meet a need of a stranger, buying groceries for a struggling mom, feeding a friend or neighbor, telling a story of hope to someone, or greeting people at church. The point is when you are sent by Jesus on His Mission, you gotta hunt. And since I believe God is already at work before I ever arrive any place, the hunting is very good.

Here are four places that catch the eye of this hunter. **Whenever there is pain,** God is working, and I can be His hands and His feet. **Wherever there is change,** God is working, and I can be His hands and His feet. **Wherever there is a chance for kindness to be expressed,** God is working, and I can be kind in Jesus's Name. **Wherever there is relationship,** God is offering relationship to others through me, and I can share Jesus. The words for this kind of living is "integrating hope," the hope I get when I sit in front of Jesus.

### Two—I Feed Wisely

When my dad was dying, my parents knew he would be with Jesus, and that would be better. They both knew it was time, and his race was ending. But their house was immersed in turmoil, and the Prince of Peace was hard to find. Why? The television blared 24/7 news. Bad news, really bad news, and the worst kind of news—gossip news. The constant feeding of Fox, CNN, and other news channels was not just on in the house, it was on the car radio, the computer, and in print being read.

I turned the television off and replaced it with jazz music and worship music. We talked about the God of Hope, not the hopelessness of our world. We prayed, and guess what? Behind the cloud of dust and debris that the negative information saturation of the media had created was the Prince of Peace. Jesus was just waiting for us to stop fighting against His peace by feeding unrest to our souls.

You do not have to be dying to feed wisely. In fact, I suggest being intentional about what you let your eyes and ears consume. When I drive and when I am out and about, if I am not being quiet, I feed my soul wisely. I will listen to the Scriptures, to music, to a great book. I make an encouraging call, download a helpful podcast, and listen or pray or reflect on my dedicated time as a part of integrated time with Jesus. If I do not choose wisely, I will feed a part of my life that will eventually devour me.

### Three—I Obey

When I decided to follow Jesus, the commitment was much bigger than I knew. Following Jesus actually brings a host of decisions that are made for me because of my friendship with Him. Because of my integrated times with Jesus and the connections we share throughout the day, I gain a clearer understanding and a more obedient heart as I live a Jesus Mission Life. Integrated time with Jesus strengthens me to love my enemies, forgive others, build good character, show kindness, and see others as more important than myself. Integrated time with

Jesus actually gives me a "want to" in these places where my faith and following fall short.

If you are building a checklist, please stop. I understand why, and even writing these words I was tempted to build one for myself. Here is a helpful way to reframe checklist thinking.

I love my wife, and loving her brings a host of commitments that express and communicate love. I love my kids, and loving them brings a host of commitments that communicate and express love. I do these things because of love—because I want to. Love makes me want to. Take a minute and think of the people Jesus told us to love—friends, enemies, people who are mean, people we do not know well—let's just say everyone else too. What kinds of commitments come with loving people as Jesus commanded? When I am driven by God's love, my checklists go away.

Being sent by the One who loves us impacts our attitude. Our actions, commitments, and decisions made by love are not burdensome; they are liberating when they come from a place of being loved and loving in return. Love turns "should" and "have to" into "I get to" and "want to." No shame, no guilt, just the joy of living fully in a friendship and partnership with Jesus. Obedience to God is how we submit to the One who has all authority and all power.

### Four—I Rejoice

Can I be so bold as to add to the word *rejoice* a couple of other words that live in the same house? I am grateful. I am thankful. Here is an observation. When I meet someone who is genuinely grateful, thankful, and rejoices, I want what they have. Not the syrupy or smarmy, putting-on-a-smile kind of happiness, but the person whose sight is fixed on Jesus. These people know something we all need to know. I am not talking about the person who refuses to deal with pain or setback, but rather the person whose pain and setback do not keep them from seeing Jesus. I like that person; I want to be that person. I choose to rejoice so I can see Jesus more clearly. I rejoice.

**Five—I Choose Humility**

> But He gives us more grace. That is why Scripture says:
> God opposes the proud but shows favor to the humble. (James 4:6)

Humility requires me to be teachable to God. James 1 reminds us that God has unlimited wisdom waiting for each of us. The catch? We need to ask and ask in faith. Asking in faith is not about me believing He will give me wisdom; it is me trusting that His wisdom is better than mine and the world around me.

I need to embrace being sent by God but remember that God only sends the humble. Proud people go, but the ones sent by God are humble. Read Philippians 2:6–11, and you will see that Jesus was humble.

Humility requires me to submit to others and to think of others first. Way harder to do than to write, but way more powerful when I do it than when I write it. The words "Choose Humility" are intentional. I really don't believe that God humbles you. I think as we live, we either respond to life, others, and God by choosing or not choosing humility. Now, that being said, as an act of love, God might humiliate you or allow you to experience humiliation in order to help you choose. Confession, I have been that person who, in the midst of humiliation, chose pride. Maybe you know someone like that too!

These five principles keep my faith integrated throughout the day. *I hunt. I feed wisely. I obey. I rejoice. I choose humility.* Integrated, dedicated time with Jesus shapes my perspective. Let me finish this chapter with some life-shaping verses from 2 Corinthians:

> But we have this treasure in jars of clay to show that this all-surpassing power is from God and not from us. We are hard pressed on every side, but not crushed; perplexed, but not in despair; persecuted, but not abandoned; struck down, but not destroyed. We always carry around in our body the death of Jesus, so that the life of Jesus may also be revealed in our body. For we who are alive are always being given over to death for Jesus' sake, so that his life may also be

revealed in our mortal body. So then, death is at work in us, but life is at work in you. (2 Corinthians 4:7–12)

In these sentences written by Paul, I get a truth, a reminder, and a promise:

### THE TRUTH

The Gospel is a treasure, and God placed it inside of me when I trusted Him and followed Him. His Mission is in me because the Gospel, the treasure, is in me.

### THE REMINDER

God's work in me and through me is about God. His work involves me because He is just good that way, but it always has been and always will be about Jesus. He places HIS treasure (the Gospel) inside this jar of clay (that is you and me) to show that all the power—the surpassing great power—to change a life, a family, a neighborhood, a city, a county, or a region comes from God and not us.

### THE PROMISE

When I remember I am NOT the treasure in this story, but the gospel is, I become resilient. I can be hard pressed on every side but not crushed; perplexed but not in despair; persecuted but not abandoned; struck down but not destroyed. This is so amazing because you cannot crush, make despair, abandon, or destroy the treasure or the one who carries the treasure when the one carrying the treasure knows they are the jar of clay.

When I forget that I am the jar and think I am the treasure, I can be crushed, in despair, struck down, and destroyed. In fact, I guarantee it. It is assumed that Jesus's Mission is our mission in this text, and Paul says the secret to a resilient life of mission is to be on mission as the jar of clay, not the treasure. EVERY stumble and fall I take in my life is when I put too much emphasis on the jar and not enough on the treasure.

I was speaking about the Jar and the Treasure while training a group of pastors and leaders in West Africa. One afternoon, as we talked about the Mission of Jesus and our call to make disciples who make disciples, a couple of women asked if we could have a conversation about the Jar and the Treasure. With the help of my translator, these two dear sisters began.

"Everything in our culture is about the jar."

"Tell me more," I said.

"Beauty, clothes, status, how many children, hair and braids, jewelry—everything pastor, everything!" They were becoming excited as they understood the Scriptures about the jar and the treasure. These Scriptures were beginning to reveal their freedom in Christ.

They continued, "These verses from the Bible are liberating for us, especially as women in this culture. In our culture, the work of the enemy is to make the jar more important than the treasure. Satan knows that we are most at risk when we worry about ourselves; this is how the enemy hurts us most. This is how the enemy keeps us off mission. This is what the enemy did to Adam and Eve. This is why our country is poor, and women are abused, and children are trafficked … ." For the first time ever, or maybe in a long time, these women could feel the grace of God that gave them a treasure, and they felt safe because they felt loved and held by God.

One of these amazing sisters looked at me and spoke truth. "You cannot crush me when I make my life about the treasure. You might be able to leave a scar, but you cannot destroy me. I am on mission and am carrying THE treasure inside me. I have the gospel, which is the power of God! We are going to go now to prepare the jar, the treasure is beautiful." With that, they turned and left.

Has there been any pushback in you as you read the words that remind us we are all intended by God to build Jesus Mission Lives? Have you thought, not me? Have you questioned your gifts, personality, talent, and calling as God invites you to be a disciple who makes disciples? Remember the trick of Satan is to make us think much more about the jar than the treasure. Could this be happening to you?

# Stepping into Jesus's Mission

## A prayer you can pray today:

*Jesus,*

*Thank You for sending me into a world that You love. Help me to see myself as sent and then to take time to prepare myself to be sent. Will You give me the discipline to build consistent dedicated and integrated times with You? I look forward to meeting with You each day.*

*Amen*

## Some questions to move you forward:

What is something people prepare for most every day?

God asks two questions of Isaiah: "Whom shall I send?" and "Who will go for us?" Where are some places God might be sending you?

Isaiah answered these two questions by saying to God, "Here am I, send me." If you answered these two questions with "Here am I, send me," how would that impact your preparation to be sent by God?

We prepare ourselves through both integrated time with God and dedicated time with God. Take a few minutes to discuss these two types of time with God in your own life.

Integrated time with God is how we relate with God throughout the day. How can you grow a more intentional, integrated time with Jesus throughout your day?

Dedicated time with God is a specific time you stop and sit without distraction just to be with Jesus. How can you grow your dedicated time with Jesus each day?

We are the jar, and the gospel is the treasure. How does seeing yourself this way influence living a Jesus Mission Life?

## A step to take as you go:

Take time this week to look at the expressions of integrated and dedicated time with God and set some time aside to practice one or more of these each day this week. Keep an awareness of how this impacts your preparedness to be sent by God.

Do you not know? Have you not heard?

(Isaiah 40:28)

# Chapter 13

## Perspective

I have a confession to make: I was that guy. You know, the guy who judged parents and kids in the store based on how noisy, whiney, or rude they were? I was the guy who had a ton of advice for these parents about how to raise kids; never mind, I didn't have any and had never raised any. At least I kept my opinions to myself. Whenever I share that I was "that guy" to a group, I ask, "Is there anyone else who was that guy or gal?" The room is usually filled with us.

After we laugh, my next question is, "How did your perspective change when you had kids?" Without exception, we all tell stories about how our experiences and real-life moments as parents changed our perspective. Having kids freed me from being "that guy" by changing my perspective.

Perspective is how we see something or someone, often shaping our feelings, our thinking, our actions, and our understanding in any given situation or relationship. Whether it is an event or it happens over time, we all have perspective-shaping-and-shifting moments. When Merrily was pregnant with our first kid, my perspective was limited to biology and seeing her change. Late-night taco cravings and certain smells didn't help at all, and we rearranged a room to host the new kid. These were some of the pieces of evidence that a new person was going to join our family.

One day, we went to the doctor, and they did a sonogram, and the sonogram showed us our daughter for the first time. In an instant, my perspective changed. With the printed photo, everything became real. Shortly after, I saw the baby kick, and my perspective shifted some more. Then, the day came, and I saw my daughter being born. Seeing the wiggly little blanket creature enter the world changed how I saw, what I saw, and how I felt and thought about most everything. Meeting my daughter and then my son a couple of years later changed how I acted and where my priorities fell. I guess you could say my perspective was changed.

A Jesus Mission Life for most of us will require a shift in perspective. This shift might not be what you think, so join me as I share how a shift in perspective fueled and continues to fuel my Jesus Mission Life today. My Jesus Mission Life ignited when I shifted my perspective on the Bible. Today I see the Bible radically different from the way I was taught to see the Bible.

You might be tempted to think that I am abandoning the truthfulness of Scripture, denying its authority, and adjusting the meaning of the Bible to fit my own lifestyle. I promise you, I am not. My belief in the authority and divine gift of the Bible has not changed, nor will it ever change. I believe with all of my heart and mind that the Bible is true and accurate. I believe that the Bible has everything God wanted us to have so we could become friends and partners with Him. The Bible is God-breathed, meaning inspired by God the Holy Spirit. The Bible is the authority for all who follow Jesus. I submit to it. I also would say my view of theology is pretty conservative. I left something out that you need to read to be convinced I am not a heretic; I am sure I just overlooked it.

The Bible is a single story about one main character—His name is Jesus. All the other characters and the story surrounding each of these characters are best understood in light of Jesus and His Mission. Here are some other perspective-giving-and-shaping thoughts on this subject.

The star of the Bible is Jesus. No one else, just Jesus. He is the

Beginning and the End, the Start and Finish, the Alpha and Omega, the Author and Finisher of our faith, the King of kings and Lord of lords. He is the Voice in creation (Logos), the Promise of rescue, the Creator and Redeemer. As Paul said in Athens, "In Him [Jesus] we live and move and have our being" (Acts 17:28). The Hero is Jesus, only Jesus, always Jesus.

Genesis to Revelation tells us the story of Jesus and the rescue Mission He has had since before the world was even formed. From creation to the final restoration, the Bible reveals who God is, what He can do, and His Mission. Jesus's Mission began before the foundation of the world. After sin entered into the world, God promised to bring a Redeemer into the world. God's power and Mission were revealed when He created the nation of Israel by calling Abraham. **The entire Old Testament is primarily about Jesus and His Mission.**

In the New Testament, the Gospel of Matthew begins with a recap of the Old Testament by providing us with the genealogy of Jesus. This recap traces how God created, directed, and preserved His people so that Jesus could enter the world. Mary, the mother of Jesus, is the fulfillment of the promise that a virgin would give birth to the One who would rescue the world from their sin. Matthew, Mark, Luke, and John give us four eye-witness accounts of the life of Jesus. These four Gospels reveal the Mission of Jesus. Each one tells us how Jesus equipped and trained His disciples for His Mission. All of them have a record of His death and resurrection and reveal the before-the-foundation-of-the-world Mission of the Lamb that was slain. Jesus is that Lamb.

The book of Acts, written by Luke, chronicles the birth of the Church and God's plan to take the good news about Jesus to Jerusalem, Judea, Samaria, and the uttermost parts of the world. The people who Jesus discipled and trained repeated this mission again and again, as did their disciples again and again. The shaping of God's people for mission is recounted in the letters written to churches and individuals by Paul, Peter, John, Jude, James, and the person who wrote Hebrews. Finally, the book of Revelation is the completion of God's Mission, made complete by Jesus, the only Hero of the story. **The entire New Testament is a book about Jesus and His Mission.** This is the perspective I hold about Scripture.

Today, everything I read in Scripture begins with Jesus and His Mission. I call this the Disciple Maker's Hermeneutic. Hermeneutics is basically the study of interpreting something that clarifies the meaning. Hermeneutics can be used in literature, music, arts, and other places too. In Bible College, I learned what we called Biblical Hermeneutics. This was the discipline of interpreting the Bible that led me to get the meaning from a text, from a collection of texts, or from a grand story.

I was taught to **define the written words of the Bible** in light of six lenses:

- The language in which it was written.
- The type of speech or literary style in which it was written.
- The historical context and culture at the time it was written.
- The audience who would have either read or heard these words.
- The accepted understanding in Jewish or Church history.
- What other Scriptures say.

Each of these lenses have subcategories and created for me a very useful tool. I was also taught to look for **ways to apply Scripture** through five specific lenses:

- The spiritual lens.
- The moral/ethical lens.
- The literal lens.
- The dual application lens (what I can apply today that also applied when it was written).
- The relational lens.

I loved having these tools to interpret the Scriptures, and this was one of the most helpful classes I took to build a life aimed at teaching Scripture. Gratitude and respect are my two most pronounced feelings towards my hermeneutics professors. But over time, my perspective shifted. Let me add some backstory to where this shift in perspective entered and another lens was added, one that became my primary lens and gave clarity to the discovery of meaning and application.

My faith history is a hard story to tell with clarity. The main reason is that the difficult parts of my story also included parts of the same story that moved me forward. I had an alcoholic and abusive birth father and an over-the-top loving stepfather, who I call my dad. I had a struggling mother with wounds deeper than I ever knew. She was a remarkable mom and person who made the best of whatever was handed to her. I was abused in heinous ways as a kid yet drawn into the healing work of the Holy Spirit through the Scriptures and by a clear calling to a Jesus Mission Life from my earliest years. I struggled in school but excelled in Bible classes and Scripture memory. I am a rule breaker but not rebellious. The work I do today was placed in my heart from early childhood. Each of these contrasting sides of my story has been used by God so clearly.

In my heart, there has always been clarity about my calling. My calling is to invite people to follow Jesus. It is to help them find Jesus and then teach them to follow Jesus so they can also invite others to Jesus, help others find Jesus, teach others to follow Jesus so they can … You get the point. I do not know why this has always been clear, nor do I know where I learned to do it except by reading the Bible and actually doing it. This is called disciple-making, and my calling is to be a disciple-maker and to train and equip disciple-makers.

I went to a public school in kindergarten where I was forced to be right-handed; they even tied my left hand down. By the way, I am still mostly left-handed. First through ninth grades were spent in Christian schools. Okay, let me add a word of clarification: fundamental

Christian schools. The word *fundamental* was not about education but about theology and morality. It was like being enrolled in a crash course to be a legalistic Christian. The summer between my freshman and sophomore years, I had the talk with the camp speaker I mentioned earlier, who told me, "Stop acting like you have a purpose, you don't have a purpose. God has a Mission, and you need to give your life to His Mission." (This story is in Chapter 6, Mission and Purpose.) I switched from a private, fundamental Christian high school of one hundred or so students to a public school of two thousand or so students. I knew no one there except my sister. Over the next three years, I made friends, and about one hundred of my friends met Christ. I started ministry at age seventeen as a junior high director.

My next step in answering my calling was Bible college, so off I went to study Greek, Hebrew, theology, ministry, church history, and all the things that help you become an excellent expository Bible teacher. I hated it; well, most of it anyway. I struggled to figure out why it seemed the faith corner where I lived cared more about theology and how other Jesus people were wrong than they did for lost people. I did not understand why we focused so much on behavior and the rules to enforce moral standards and so little on the transforming work of God the Holy Spirit. I did not equate knowledge with maturity like my surrounding community did, and I was not sure why. I didn't get why we talked about love but were so mean to people who needed God's life-giving and life-changing love. We talked about preaching the gospel as a Sunday sermon, not a daily life of loving God with all your heart, mind, soul, and strength and loving your neighbor as yourself. What I realized was that I did not fit in, and in this holy confusion, a shift in my perspective on the Bible and Jesus and His Mission began to surface.

It became really obvious that I did not fit in when I was sharing Christ with someone and was told by one of the deans, "You need to be preparing for ministry and not be distracted by spending time with sinners." It was obvious to me that we were looking at the same

Bible but with different lenses. That was a very significant perspective shift for me because I realized I saw Scripture differently. *I saw the Bible through the lens of Jesus and His Mission.* I knew that I didn't fit, so I left. I worked in the building trades to earn a living so I could do full-time student ministry and not need to be paid. I did one job to earn a living and the other as an answer to my calling until I was twenty-four when I joined the staff of Youth for Christ.

Let me make two statements here before I move on from the story. First, the people surrounding me in my fundamental Christian school days, the fundamental Baptist church I attended, and the fundamental Bible school I attended loved Jesus and loved and believed the Bible. And I am friends with many of them to this day. My story is not intended to make me look good and make them look bad. My story is about a much-needed shift in perspective on seeing and understanding the Bible. Second, I am where I am completely because of God's mercy and grace. My perspective on the Bible, Jesus, and a Jesus Mission Life is not from some sense of inner nobility or super wisdom; it is exclusively and fully the result of God's grace and mercy to me.

Back in the early eighties, I could not articulate clearly the shift in my perspective, but the change started to become more and more clear the longer I served with Youth for Christ. (Youth for Christ is a ministry that works on high school campuses, bringing the good news of Jesus to students who do not know Christ. Merrily and I served there for more than a decade.) My whole life, I had been taught that good theology, excellent morality, and real maturity were the pathway to mission. But when I realized that theology, morality, and maturity were actually the byproducts of Jesus Mission Living and not the pathway, Scripture came alive. This is the perspective I want to share with you, and I hope you see it and use it.

## THE DISCIPLE MAKER'S HERMENEUTIC

The Disciple Maker's Hermeneutic is what I teach to pastors and leaders around the world today. It comes from the perspective that the

Bible is a single story about Jesus, who He is, and His mission in this world. For the Bible to be most fully understood, it must be interpreted through the primary lens of Jesus's Mission. Here's how it works:

- Start with God's Mission. Everything in the Bible reveals the heart of mission that our Savior has and imparts to us.
- See Jesus as the Hero of the "Big Story" God is telling. Find where the story (small "s") fits within the Story (big "S") that God tells about Jesus in the Scriptures. I see Jesus's Mission in the story of the Judges, the story of Tamar, the story of Rahab, the story of Moses, the kings of Israel, Judah, King David, and so many more Bible characters and situations. These are the small "s" stories.
- Discern where the story fits in the Mission of Jesus—the Story.
- Discern meaning in the text. I use this filter to shape the text by seeing what God was doing in the grand Story.
- Discern the application of the text. Once the meaning is clear, the application becomes clear.
- Invite others to take their place in God's grand Story and singular Mission.

The way I was taught to interpret Scripture is still a very important part of my toolkit for study. I did not change this part, I just started in a different place. Reading and understanding our Bible through the Disciple Maker's Hermeneutic, the lens of Jesus's Mission, impacts our perspective of the Bible in five ways.

### One—When We Read Our Bible Through the Lens of Jesus's Mission, We Can See the Bigger Story that Our God is Telling

I have already written much about the Mission of Jesus and the importance of truly knowing Him, so I will not give a lot more space here. From a practical approach, this lens helps us see Noah, Moses, Joshua, and the nation of Israel at their best and worst as pieces of a single story pointing to a single person (Jesus) who has a single

Mission (Rescue). Reading the book of Judges, learning about the kings who rebelled, studying the call of the prophets, and knowing the battles that were won and lost help us see that the high cost of forgetting Jesus's Mission is to risk missing the Story God is telling altogether.

Seeing the Jesus Mission in the whole of the Bible opens our eyes to a much bigger Story. David beats Goliath—we say, "You have a Goliath, and God will defeat your giants." This is more than a story about giants; it is a story about God's promise to protect a nation He created to bring Jesus into the world. The story of Rahab hiding the spies is much bigger than hiding spies so the promised land could be taken. Rehab actually becomes a part of the genealogy of the Rescuer. The splitting of the nation of Israel under Solomon's sons and establishing Israel was used by God to strategically place His people around the world to spread the gospel after Jesus came nearly eight hundred years later.

Establishing Judah gave a place for Jesus to be born at just the right time. The exile to Babylon is why wise men from the East recognized the star pointing to Jesus. There are so many truths pointing to the Mission of Jesus from the Old Testament that to record them here would take several hundred more pages. These stories do not merely point to a big God; they actually tell the Story of His Mission. Included in the stories are the Law, the sacrifices required to appease the judgment of God, and the miraculous ways God provided for and protected His people.

### Two—When We Read Our Bible Through the Lens of Jesus's Mission, We Gain a Significantly Greater View of What It Means to Live a Jesus Mission Life

In Luke 14, large crowds were traveling with Jesus, and Jesus made a classic Jesus move when He clarified the cost of following Him. These people were not just looking for a sign; they had actually begun to travel along with Jesus. In that moment, Jesus told about a man building a tower making sure he had the resources to finish that tower. Jesus added another analogy about cost counting, saying that kings measure the strength of their armies before going to war. Jesus was saying to these travelers:

*Mission has a high cost.*

When I teach pastors in Africa or India to count the cost of mission, I often point them toward persecution and possible death. I tell them that their families might die, that they might starve, be beaten, and die of preventable diseases because they cannot afford medicine. The cost of Jesus Mission Living is high. Jesus teaches more than counting a cost; He says that what He came for has a cost—but Jesus and a Jesus Mission Life are worth it. Jesus is not asking if we can afford it. He is saying it will cost everything to follow Him. Will you pay it?

Our current faith culture in the USA often considers counting the cost as what we can afford to pay. A Jesus Mission View of Scripture invites us to be ALL IN—to sign the check and let the Jesus Mission Life fill in the amount.

### Three—When We Read Our Bible Through the Lens of Jesus's Mission, We Get a Better Understanding of the Context and the Meaning of Scripture

Hebrews 11 is called by many the Hall of Faith because the writer of Hebrews praises the faith of many Old Testament Bible people. We often read Hebrews as a lesson about faith, but try reading Hebrews 11 through the lens of Mission. When you do, you will see that every person mentioned entered into the rescue story of God. They were inducted into the **Mission Hall of Fame** by taking their place in advancing God's Mission. They did so by leading, preserving, and calling people back to God. These **Mission Hall of Fame** people were essential to making the grand Story of Jesus and His Mission unfold.

Reading Hebrews through the lens of Mission gives a broader insight and application to the lives of each character mentioned in Hebrews 11. Their faith was forward-looking to a city whose builder and maker is God. Their faith saw what God was doing as bigger than what was directly in front of them. In other words, God was working on something bigger. Guess what? God is still working on something bigger than what is in front of you and me. Here is just one of many examples of seeing the Bible through the lens of Mission.

In John's Gospel, Jesus prepares His friends for Mission. He let them know that He would be going away. He would die and rise again, but He would send God the Holy Spirit. He told His disciples that they would be His ambassadors for His Mission. During one moment, while walking to the Garden of Gethsemane, where He would be arrested, Jesus reminded the disciples that they would be hated. They would suffer, and the mission would be costly. Now scroll down to John 16:33, and you will find Jesus saying some really amazing and gracious words:

> I have told you these things, so that in me you may have peace. In this world you will have trouble. But take heart! I have overcome the world. (John 16:33)

Jesus gave a sneak peek into the cost that these disciples would pay for living Jesus Mission Lives. "I'll let you in on what is coming so when you see it, you can still have peace." Jesus wanted His friends to know that when all hell breaks loose while on this mission, don't be surprised. "You can find peace because I told you this was going to happen. You will not be blindsided; I am still in control." Jesus continued, "In this world and on this Mission you are going to have troubles. My Mission brings difficulty. But strengthen your heart with this truth: I win" (the whole context of John 12–18, paraphrase mine).

Whenever I hear this verse spoken today, it is used almost exclusively as a salve for the scratches of life and the ensuing comfort of Jesus. That is simply not the meaning, my friends. Jesus says that when we live a Jesus Mission Life, all hell breaks loose, but the gates of Hell cannot win! When on mission and when suffering because of the mission, He will give us His peace because He has overcome this world. This is a much better understanding of John 16:33.

The lens of Jesus and Jesus Mission Living is easily found in nearly every story, every character, and on every page of the Bible. We just have to change our lens to see it. Here are a few more illustrations that are 100 percent on Mission:

- "For me to live is Christ and to die is gain" (Philippians 1:21). Paul is saying that "to live is Christ" means living every part of his life for Jesus and His Mission.
- "Now to him who is able to do immeasurably more than all we ask or imagine, according to his power that is at work within us, to him be glory in the church and in Christ Jesus throughout all generations, for ever and ever! Amen." (Ephesians 3:20–21)
- "For we are God's handiwork, created in Christ Jesus to do good works, which God prepared in advance for us to do." (Ephesians 2:10)
- Second Corinthians 5—the whole chapter.
- John 12–21—all these chapters are 100 percent Mission.
- The Sermon on the Mount, the Parable of the Sower, most everything in Philippians, all of the book of Acts, and most of the rest of the New Testament are 100 percent Mission.

The more you use the Mission of Jesus as your starting place in interpreting Scripture, the clearer Scripture becomes. Every time Jesus tells someone to take up their cross, it is 100 percent Mission.

### Four—When We Read Our Bible Through the Lens of Jesus's Mission, We Can See More Clearly the People God Used and How He Can Use Us

"Sure, God could use them, but I am different." I cannot tell you how many times I have personally thought this, felt this, and heard this from someone else processing a great Bible story. Kill a giant? I think not. Walk on water? Not me. Part the waters? I doubt it. I could make a list, and for nearly every kind of people God uses, I am not on it. Can I say boldly that none of these stories were meant to intimidate our faith or shame us when we compare our lives with theirs? Quite the opposite is true.

When I read the Bible through the lens of Jesus and His Mission, I realize that God doesn't need perfect people to move His Mission forward. I see a fearful and depressed Elijah; I see David who loses control of his libido, his temper, and his family and still manages to be a man who "served God's purposes in his lifetime and then died" (Acts 13:36). Moses killed a guy, Abraham said his wife was his sister, Noah got boozed up and passed out one night, Jacob tricked his father into giving him his brother's birthright. Gideon hid in a wine press, Samson traded his strength for a cute girl, Peter denied Christ, and the rest of the apostles ran away and hid. There are more, many more.

All of these people and more were used by God to play a role in His Mission. These are **not** just stories where the good guy wins in the end. They are **not** stories with the moral that if we trust God enough, it will all work out. These are stories of God, of Jesus advancing His Mission. And the people He used to do it were, well, just like you and me, a mess. They were unmade beds.

We get some insight into their lives when we read Hebrews 11. In verse 10, the writer was speaking of Abraham when he said, "For he was looking forward to the city with foundations, whose architect and builder is God." Abraham, while living in the promise of God to be the father of many people and nations, the real promise of God was to bless the world through His Son. Jesus was the fulfillment of this promise, and Abraham is in the Mission of Jesus Hall of Fame.

The writer goes on to list many more members in this sacred hall, the Mission of Jesus Hall of Fame, and then describes them with these words:

> These were all commended for their faith, yet none of them received what had been promised, since God had planned something better for us so that only together with us would they be made perfect. (Hebrews 11:39–40)

The "something better" is Jesus, and these all died not ever seeing the Messiah, but they died knowing God, and they died being used in the Mission of Jesus. Why? God had planned something better for us that only together with them can it be made complete. This means that God uses messy, broken people to accomplish His Mission.

These imperfect people have been used by God in such a way that we know Jesus because of them. Our Jesus Mission Lives give their Jesus Mission Lives completion. God used them with His eye on us, and now God wants to use us with His eye on someone else. Do you know what this means? When we live a Jesus Mission Life, we, too, will have a place in the Jesus Mission Hall of Fame, if we will take it.

### Five—When We Read Our Bible Through the Lens of Jesus's Mission, We Get a Front-Row Seat to the Power and Sovereignty of God

My first movie at a walk-in theater was in January 1973. Before this, all the movies I saw were shown in drive-in theaters. But in 1973, I walked into the movie theater in a brand new shopping mall. As ten-year-old Leonard entered, drink in one hand, popcorn in the other, and pockets filled with red vines, I felt like I had arrived. Scanning the room, I made my way to the very front row, took my seat, and sat in wonder as I watched *The Poseidon Adventure* unfold larger than life itself. To me, it was the best seat in the house.

The front row, in many situations, is the row that provides the best perspective and is often considered to be the best seat in the house. When it comes to the Bible, no perspective gives me a better seat to see Jesus and to know His love, His power, and His grace than the front-row seat called Jesus's Mission.

Seeing the Bible through the lens of Jesus's Mission gives me a front-row seat to His power. There are some really amazing power-of-God verses in the Bible, but to me, few capture the power of God expressed in the Mission of God like Isaiah 40. Isaiah 40 points forward to John the Baptist and Jesus. It is what we call a Messianic (Jesus the Messiah) portrait in the Old Testament. Written nearly 600 years before Jesus was born, Isaiah says someone will come and point to Jesus, and once Jesus arrives, watch out! Because it is going to be epic.

Twice in chapter 40, Isaiah asks: "Do you not know?" "Have you not heard?" In verse 21, these two questions were used to set up the resounding truth that God, indeed, is powerful and has a plan. The power of God created and sustains the world. The power of God moves nations, princes, and kings, raising them and lowering them all for His plan. Do you not know? Have you not heard? Have you not been told this from the beginning? Isaiah is declaring that God has something He is doing, and He is powerful enough to do it. God knows the stars by name, so look to Him; He has not forgotten you. He has not forgotten the promises and covenant He made with Abraham. The promise? To use this nation Israel, to bless the world through Jesus. Do you not know? Have you not heard? Your way is not hidden from God, oh, Israel. God is still going to accomplish His plan.

The context of Isaiah is that he is calling God's people back to God to take their place in God's Mission, the one declared in Isaiah 9. Go read it! Jesus is coming, and He will pay the penalty of sin. In chapter 40, he assures them that God has the power to accomplish this plan.

In Isaiah 40:28, Isaiah asks again, "Do you not know? Have you not heard?" From creation to now, God has been at work, and it is work no human can do; they are too limited. But even with our lack of understanding, God takes His strength and power and gives it to His people for His Mission. Read the whole text here.

Do you not know?
Have you not heard?
Has it not been told you from the beginning?
Have you not understood since the earth was founded?
He sits enthroned above the circle of the earth,
and its people are like grasshoppers.

He stretches out the heavens like a canopy,
and spreads them out like a tent to live in.
He brings princes to naught
and reduces the rulers of this world to nothing.
No sooner are they planted,
no sooner are they sown,
no sooner do they take root in the ground,
than he blows on them and they wither,
and a whirlwind sweeps them away like chaff.

---

"To whom will you compare me?
Or who is my equal?" says the Holy One.
Lift up your eyes and look to the heavens:
Who created all these?
He who brings out the starry host one by one
and calls forth each of them by name.
Because of his great power and mighty strength,
not one of them is missing.

---

Why do you complain, Jacob?
Why do you say, Israel,
"My way is hidden from the Lord;
my cause is disregarded by my God"?
Do you not know?
Have you not heard?
The Lord is the everlasting God,
the Creator of the ends of the earth.
He will not grow tired or weary,
and his understanding no one can fathom.

He gives strength to the weary
and increases the power of the weak.
Even youths grow tired and weary,
and young men stumble and fall;
but those who hope in the Lord
will renew their strength.
They will soar on wings like eagles;
they will run and not grow weary,
they will walk and not be faint.

---

(Isaiah 40:21–31)

Seeing the Bible through the lens of Mission shapes how we see these Scriptures as well as how we use them. These Scriptures are so much more than a promise that the God who is looking out for you is really big and strong, and He will help you get through the hard parts of life. These Scriptures are about God fulfilling His Mission. They are about God keeping the promise to Adam and Eve, to Abraham and Sarah, to the beautiful people He created, the nation of Israel. These Scriptures are a bold and loud declaration that HE, and only HE, has the power and will to accomplish His plan. These Scriptures tell us that He has moved kings, nations, and people all to accomplish His Mission. These Scriptures are about God having no equal, and in one sense, they are the gates-of-hell-cannot-prevail-against-it statement that nothing can stop His Mission.

Do you not know? Have you not heard? The God whose plan is impossible for you includes you. He will strengthen you as you take your place, trusting in the Lord, and you will fly, rise, and run with unbounded and unending strength.

These words remind me of the friends Jesus sent on Mission. They had a renewed strength; they soared beyond anything they thought their lives would be; they ran and did not grow weary; they walked and did not faint. "Seeing the courage of Peter and John, they recognized they were not trained by anyone other than Jesus" (Acts 4:13, paraphrase mine).

Do you not know? Have you not heard?

It is impossible to read the Bible or study the Bible and not see the Mission of Jesus clearly, unless, of course, we have been taught to see something else. When I use the lens of Jesus's Mission, the Bible verses we use to give us a bump up in our faith walk become so much more because they speak of Jesus and His Mission. Let me finish this chapter on perspective with a thought and a story.

## THE THOUGHT

Jesus's battles with people were not about truth nearly as much as perspective. The people to whom Jesus came to read the same Scriptures He did but had radically different ideas on what they meant. He once said to the experts of the Scriptures, "You are in error because you do not know the scriptures or the power of God" (Matthew 22:29). These people knew all the verses and the Law but missed what God was doing because they didn't know the Scriptures or the power of God.

Seeing the Bible through the lens of Jesus's Mission has changed my perspective on the Bible, life, every relationship I have, my possessions, my needs, and just about everything else. Without the lens of Jesus and His Mission as my first lens, I run the risk of stepping into three spiritual landmines.

### Landmine One: Knowing Verses but Not Knowing the Scriptures

I was in Africa when a dear sister met me at the mission house where I was staying. In every sentence she spoke, there was no less than one or two verses she quoted. It was impressive but annoying, too.

After several verse-filled conversations, I asked, "Why do you only speak in verses?" Her response? "God's Word never returns void (a verse about Mission), and I want you to be blessed so I could be blessed." We spent several minutes talking about knowing a lot of verses but not knowing the Scriptures. We talked about the perception of power because it's possible to have a lot of verses memorized but not know the power of God. Her mission was to speak a blessing; I appreciate that—so she could get a blessing back may not be the highest goal. She missed the meaning of the Scriptures and created her own.

### Landmine Two: Personal Application Instead of Biblical Interpretation

If I do not get the interpretation right, most of my application will not be right.

### Landmine Three: Smaller Missions Instead of Jesus's Mission

If I am taught that God's Mission is my prosperity, be it emotional, spiritual, financial, physical, or national, then I am operating on a smaller, less rewarding, and eventually self-centered mission. Can I be honest? For the most part, you and I can fuel smaller missions without the Holy Spirit. If I apply some self-discipline and read some good and helpful books, I can find that I no longer depend upon God. The answers to Isaiah's questions, "Have you not seen?" and "Do you not know?" become a less resolute yes, and I run a great risk of missing the Mission and power of God.

## THE STORY

Reading and teaching the Bible through the lens of Mission brings the much-needed perspective for the Church and Jesus's followers today. Let me close with a story.

In my travels, I hear a lot of stories that reveal the cost of a life of Mission and the power of God through that life. Let me introduce my friend Samual (name and location changed for security reasons).

Samual grew up in a Muslim family, in a Muslim village, in a 75 percent Muslim country. His family was very influential, and he was the prized young man in his village. It was with great joy for the whole village when his marriage was announced, and he and his wife were seen as blessed. Those blessings increased as he added two children to their family, and if that were not enough, Samual was soon in line to become an Imam, a Muslim holy man. His daily prayers, his understanding of the Koran, and his following after the teachings of Muhammad all pointed to a bright future.

One night, after falling asleep, Samual was caught up in a dream. In his words, he could not tell if he was sleeping or in a trance. In this dream, Jesus appeared to him, saying, "I am the way, the truth, and the life; no man comes to the Father except by me." Shaken, Samual couldn't stop thinking about what he had dreamt. After about a week of struggling with this dream, he sought input from a Christian pastor.

"Samual, this is God's way of saying He loves you and wants a relationship with you. Would you like to know Jesus?"

For Samual, this was not a small question. With much to lose, he wrestled with the question, and finally said, "I wish to follow Jesus." Samual prayed and trusted Christ as his Lord and Savior, and that is when the trouble began.

Stopping the daily prayers to Allah and attending a Christian church was a very controversial decision. Samual began learning much about Jesus and the Bible, but what he learned was more of an apologetic to prove the Bible to be true and superior to the Koran. Samual had been a Christian for five years when I met him, and he was a pastor of a small church in a different village. As I listened to his story, Samual began to share how, soon after choosing to follow Jesus, his wife divorced him, and he lost his wife and his children because of his new faith in Jesus.

In addition to losing his wife and kids, Samual was also disowned by his parents and asked forcefully to leave his village. Samual's father adopted Samual's sons, and following Jesus cost him nearly everything. Over the years, Samual had several conversations with his ex-wife, kids, and parents. These conversations usually dissolved into an argument about which is better, the Bible or the Koran.

Pastor Samual attended my training on Reading and Seeing the Bible Through the Lens of Mission, and he devoured this training. More than once, he asked me a string of questions, seeking both an understanding of the training and how to use them in relationships and conversations. We spoke before the training, after the training, and during breaks, and it was obvious God was doing something in Samual.

I returned home, went to another country, did more training, and prayed that seeds sewn would bring a harvest of disciples who make disciples. Little did I know what was coming.

Shortly after I returned to the US, I got word that Samual had taken the training to heart. Samual asked to sit with his wife so he could share with her what he had been learning about the message of the Bible. When they spoke, the old arguments about the Koran and the Bible began to surface. Gently, he pleaded, saying, "I am not saying the Bible is better than the Koran; I am telling you how the Bible and Koran answer the same five questions." Samual invited her to compare these answers and decide for herself.

*Where am I from?*
*What is wrong with me?*
*How do I fix this mess?*
*What are the values by which I live?*
*What happens when I die?*

Side Note: As a point of reference, every religion, philosophy, tradition, superstition, and system is trying to answer the same five questions. Instead of arguing, we can share how the Bible answers them.

When Samual changed his approach, the arguing stopped, and God began to move in the heart of his ex-wife. She began to compare how the Koran answered the same five questions the Bible does. One evening, after another more peaceful and gentle conversation, Samual's ex-wife gave up everything to follow Jesus. It was not long after this that both of his kids made this same decision.

Finally, Samual's parents began to be drawn to the Bible and saw how God answers the same five questions the Koran did. One afternoon, Samual's mother and father committed their lives to follow Jesus, and now the entire family was at risk in their village. Samual and his whole family moved to a different village, and when they did, the entire village met Christ. All that changed for Samual was his perspective on the Bible. He now saw Scripture through the lens of Jesus's Mission. He shared how the Bible answers the five questions that every person is asking. Today, Samual and his family are restored and on Mission, training disciples to make disciples.

While Samual's story is not the exact story of every person whose perspective of Scripture begins with the Mission of Jesus, it is very common for so many of those we train to make disciples more effectively. You and I in the West have been taught to see the Bible through three primary lenses—theological, moral, and experiential. It is all too common today for people to read their Bibles primarily through the lens of personal application, usually before mission and meaning are understood. Working with pastors and leaders, application is often the starting place for the study of the Word.

It will take time to add this perspective of the lens of Jesus's Mission to your Bible reading discipline. If you make the choice to use the Disciple Maker's Hermeneutic, let me suggest you take a slip of paper with the question: "Where is the Mission of Jesus in this passage?" Use it as your bookmark for your reading. Once you establish this as a part of your process, you WILL see so much more in Scripture than you ever did before. I guarantee it.

---

Side Note: Many devotionals today serve a purpose to encourage us to remember that we are loved by God. They provide us with a reminder that God is for us, and I believe they have a place in our friendship with Jesus. Devotionals are meant to be a snack, not a meal. Taking your swings is not being disciplined in daily devotions; it is a commitment to study and immersion in the Scriptures.

---

# *Stepping into Jesus's Mission*

## A prayer you can pray today:

*Jesus,*

*Thank You for so clearly communicating Your Mission through the Bible. Will You open my eyes to see Scripture through this lens, the lens of Your Mission? Show me the places in Your Word where Your Mission is being accomplished by Your people. Give me eyes to see how You so powerfully made Your Mission happen. What a gift Your Word is to my Jesus Mission Life.*

*Amen*

## Some questions to move you forward:

Where can you see perspective influencing how people see life in today's culture? (politics, money, health, faith, etc.)

What is a place where our perspective influences our faith and mission?

Current culture interprets the Bible through the lens of "What it means to me" or "How it makes me feel." What is the danger of interpreting Scripture this way?

When we see the Bible through the lens of Jesus's Mission, we see Abraham, Moses, David, Daniel, Jeremiah, and every Old Testament character and story as one single Story about Jesus and His Mission. Thinking through these stories, take some time to discuss where you see Jesus's Mission in them.

Since the Bible is primarily about Jesus and His Mission, how does this perspective impact your understanding of the Bible?

Looking at the chapter, discuss why it matters that we see the Bible primarily through the lens of Jesus's Mission.

What are some ways you could shift your perspective and begin to see the Bible through the lens of Jesus's Mission?

Read Isaiah 40:21-31. What can you see in these verses that point you to Jesus's Mission?

## A step to take as you go:

Read Hebrews 11 and look for the places where God's people saw their lives through the lens of God's Mission. Write down a story or two and look it up in the Old Testament.

Ask and it will be given to you; seek and you will find; knock and the door will be opened to you. For everyone who asks receives; the one who seeks finds; and to the one who knocks, the door will be opened.

(Matthew 7:7–8)

Chapter 

# Clarity

He was the spiritual father of many pastors and leaders, and when he entered the room, people sat a little straighter. Pastor Jacob's every movement in the church where we were having our training was intentional and calculated to make sure he connected with every pastor attending. His Bible was worn, his notepad was filled, and his sandals were nearly as old as he was. When we were introduced, he spoke very little English, and between what I knew of his language and a good translator, we exchanged a proper greeting. When I began my training, he sat in the front row, took notes, and participated in every training exercise we did. But, for five straight days, he never smiled or acknowledged his opinion of the training.

As I wrapped up on the final day, Pastor Jacob stood and said, "I would like to say something." The room was silent; he cleared his throat and began to speak. "This is the first time in decades of ministry that I have had clarity about the Mission of Jesus and the Word of God. I do not know how much time the Lord will give me, but I will give the rest of my life to a Jesus Mission Life. Will you join me?"

Pastor Jacob experienced a clarity of mission. *Clarity* is the ability to see without obstruction and hindrance, to have understanding and focus. Clarity is to Jesus Mission Living what water is to fish. Without clarity, missional living also dies. Clarity matters.

The disciples of Jesus were people who often had clarity like muddy water. The Mission of Jesus was explained to them by Jesus Himself, yet they didn't grasp it, not until later. The disciples had a front-row seat to Jesus's ministry; they saw how Jesus fed 5,000 and 4,000, and yet when He spoke of the leaven of the Pharisees, they focused on forgetting to get bread. They heard Him say, "I am going to die," yet Peter pulls Jesus aside to tell Him to tone it down. They saw Jesus raise the dead but scattered when He died. Their lack of clarity often prompted the questions, "Where is your faith?" and "Do you still not understand?" But it wasn't just the disciples who saw Jesus in action and still lacked clarity concerning Jesus's Mission, as we see in this story in Mark:

> They came to Bethsaida, and some people brought a blind man and begged Jesus to touch him. He took the blind man by the hand and led him outside the village. When he had spit on the man's eyes and put his hands on him, Jesus asked, "Do you see anything?" He looked up and said, "I see people; they look like trees walking around." Once more Jesus put his hands on the man's eyes. Then his eyes were opened, his sight was restored, and he saw everything clearly. Jesus sent him home, saying, "Don't even go into the village." (Mark 8:22–26)

In this story, the people of Bethsaida brought a blind man to Jesus, begging Him to heal this man. It is important to know that Jesus had a strained relationship with this town. He fed 5,000 in Bethsaida. Jesus walked on water near Bethsaida, yet the people of this town were so hard-hearted that Jesus later said in Matthew 11:21, "Woe to you, Chorazin! Woe to you, Bethsaida! For if the miracles that were performed in you had been performed in Tyre and Sidon, they would have repented long ago in sackcloth and ashes."

Jesus took the blind man by the hand and led him outside of the city. Then He spit on the man's eyes. In Jesus's day, spit was considered medicinal, so this was not strange to them, nor was it disrespectful. "Do you see anything?" Jesus asked. The man replied, "I see men, but they look like trees." Jesus touched him again, and he could see clearly.

The obvious question is, why did it take two attempts for Jesus to heal this man? Was Jesus tired? Did Jesus just have a bad day or a poor connection to His Father? Actually, this moment is more about a lesson to Bethsaida and the disciples. I think we can get some insight from the context.

Along the shoreline of the Sea of Galilee and in the foothills were three towns that saw a lot of Jesus's ministry: Chorazin, Bethsaida, and Capernaum. These three towns were spread across approximately six miles, so what happened in one town quickly spread to the other towns. Located on the north and northwest sides of the Sea of Galilee, it was this region, specifically Capernaum, that Jesus chose to make His ministry home.

Jesus recruited at least half of His disciples from this region. Jesus worked many miracles, raised the dead, fed the masses, and taught the people again and again and again. But Bethsaida had rejected Jesus as Messiah and refused to embrace Him, His Kingdom, and His Mission. The city of Bethsaida, by this time, really should have seen Jesus with much more clarity than they did. But Bethsaida sees Jesus like the blind man sees people: fuzzy and unclear. Making the point even more clear about Jesus's relationship with Bethsaida, Jesus actually refuses to heal this man inside the city.

The Bible points out that Jesus led him by the hand outside Bethsaida. This act was a statement to the people in Bethsaida that they had missed something. In one very real sense, Jesus had put His hands on Bethsaida through teaching and miracles, but instead of seeing, they remained without clear sight. Jesus once more touched the man, and he was healed. Look at Jesus's next instruction: "Go home, do not even go into the city." Again, a message was being sent to Bethsaida: "You have been touched but still remain blind." This is also a message to the disciples. "You have been touched by Jesus, but you still only see shadows of a king, not the real Messiah."

Here is my observation: **Clarity sometimes takes a few touches from Jesus.** I know this was true for the disciples and also very true for me. The people who brought the blind man to Jesus wanted him to be healed. The disciples wanted him to be healed, and the blind man wanted to be healed. Heck, Jesus wanted him healed. Everyone was on the same side concerning this man's blindness. Jesus provided the touches for this man to see clearly. Jesus also provides the touches we need to see clearly. This is a patient and powerful Jesus, willing to touch this man's eyes twice. Jesus is also willing to touch our spiritual eyes as much as we need it.

Jesus has a Mission and commissions His disciples and each of us to make disciples everywhere we go. The Bible makes this Mission clear. Jesus Himself made this Mission clear. The early Christians made this Mission clear. Yet today, in the twenty-first century, when it comes to living a Jesus Mission Life, we are often like the blind man in the story who needed another touch from Jesus. He needed the second touch because he still saw men like trees. We still seem to see the Mission of Jesus like trees. We lack clarity, and we need a patient and powerful Jesus to touch our spiritual eyes again.

Power and patience do not usually go together. When I have power, I usually struggle with patience because I have the power to get what I want done when I want it done. When I lack power, patience is often forced upon me, and my waiting is not patient but simply impatient waiting. **In Jesus, perfect and unlimited power are combined with patience. I point this out because patience requires two things: clarity to see the bigger picture and love for the ones needing patience.** Peter writes about the patience of God and His Mission:

> The Lord is not slow in keeping his promise, as some understand slowness. Instead he is patient with you, not wanting anyone to perish, but everyone to come to repentance. (2 Peter 3:9)

Jesus sees something bigger here than a single blind man; He sees His Mission for an entire city, nation, and the world. People wanted to see what Jesus could do in the moment. Jesus wanted them to see the bigger picture of what God wanted done for the world. The people chose a miracle over the mission.

Jesus wanted clarity in their physical sight, but of more importance to Jesus is clarity in their spiritual sight. Jesus wanted them to see that what He came to do included healing, but what He came to do was much bigger than a healing. The people of this town wanted healing without mission. They wanted the benefit of Jesus's power without embracing Jesus or His Mission.

Honestly, sometimes I want a crown without a cross. I desire, at times, a kingdom without allegiance to the King or His Kingdom Mission. A Jesus who loves me, cares for me, heals me, and makes me see is sometimes more palatable than denying myself and taking up a cross. When I get this way, I see "men like trees," and I need another touch from Jesus. The good news is that Jesus has both the power and the patience to heal my spiritual vision.

I'd like to continue using the metaphor of Jesus's healing of the blind man to give five insights on gaining and keeping clarity so we can live a Jesus Mission Life.

## INSIGHT #1—A JESUS MISSION LIFE REQUIRES THE KIND OF CLARITY THAT COMES FROM MANY TOUCHES FROM JESUS

**The process needs Jesus**. *Process* is a word that is critical to clarity and Jesus Mission Living. This book has invested a lot of words for the purpose of connecting Jesus Mission Living to being immersed in the Scriptures, a vibrant life of prayer, and living in community with God's people. As simple as this sounds, it is difficult. Churches are filled with people who have Bibles, who pray, and even go to church and small groups but do not live a Jesus Mission Life. I am not beating these people up; I am acknowledging how difficult the process is.

One reason the process of Jesus Mission Living is hard is because we are broken. When we come to Jesus, we bring addictions. We bring to Jesus broken family structures, foolish choices we have made, and choices others made that harmed us. We bring all kinds of abuses—verbal, physical, violent, sexual, emotional, or possibly all of the above. When we come to Jesus, we bring the wounds of abandonment, parents who didn't love us well, and so much more. Where does all of this go when we come to Jesus?

When we come to Jesus, we bring Him our fears, our anger, and our shame. In ourselves we lack the ability to get past all of the baggage and the habits of our sin. Many of us are still surprised that there is an epic war going on inside of us, an internal war between our two natures, the one that is new in Christ and the one we were born with—our sin nature. There is a spiritual battle raging around us, too, as the enemy of God and His Mission is also the enemy of our souls every second of every day. I will say it again: I really need Jesus!

I need Jesus to keep me in the process, to strengthen me in the process, to complete the process in me. When Jesus gave the Sermon on the Mount, He taught His disciples about His Kingdom and the Kingdom Mission we are to embrace. "This is going to involve persecution and laying aside your own life. There needs to be a change of mission, from the mission to see Israel restored to the Mission of a new Kingdom—seeing the world restored. This new Kingdom and the King (Jesus) measure everything differently. So, to be successful, here is the process: I want you to ask, seek, and knock."

> Ask and it will be given to you; seek and you will find; knock and the door will be opened to you. For everyone who asks receives; the one who seeks finds; and to the one who knocks, the door will be opened. (Matthew 7:7–8)

The way in which Jesus uses the three words ask, seek, and knock could be better understood like this. Because the Kingdom has a new and different mission, ask and keep on asking; in fact, do not stop asking. Because in the Kingdom, you are salt, light, and children of the Father, seek and keep on seeking; in fact, do not stop seeking. Because the King of the Kingdom is speaking, knock and keep on knocking; in fact, do not stop knocking. Jesus understands we are in process and that the process requires us to continually ask, continually seek, and continually knock.

The process is about acknowledging that the One we follow can do what we need in the moment but always operates with a bigger mission than just us. Yes, His Mission includes us, but it is so much bigger than we are. I am not diminishing His love for each of us, quite the opposite. God is preparing a place for our "in process selves" to live a Jesus Mission Life. The new Kingdom Mission is beyond our ability to accomplish, so Jesus says ask, seek, and knock.

If we are to see with more clarity, we will need to live fully in a place where the touch of Jesus is constant; we do this when we ask and never stop asking, seek and never stop seeking, knock and never stop knocking. Let me add one more thought to the reality of the process. Jesus knows we will never be perfect. It is Jesus who instructs the ask-seek-and-knock process. We, on the other hand, get discouraged, frustrated, or we believe the lies that we are not good enough, we are not accepted, or we will be sent to the spiritual corner for failure. These lies convince us to ask and then stop, seek and then quit, and knock and then walk away. When we end up asking only a couple of times, seeking a few times, and knocking a handful of times, we will never find the clarity and the freedom and the strength to embrace and live the Jesus Mission Life. Jesus knows we need Him, and that is why He says, "Come and follow me; stay with me, and I will give you rest."

Paul understood the need for constantly asking, seeking, and knocking; he did this for the churches and people whom his life had impacted, his disciples. In the letter Paul wrote to the Philippians, Paul says he has three attitudes in prayer as he remembers the way these believers have built Jesus Mission Lives and communities.

> I thank my God every time I remember you. In all my prayers for all of you, I always pray with joy because of your partnership in the

> gospel from the first day until now, being confident of this, that he who began a good work in you will carry it on to completion until the day of Christ Jesus. (Philippians 1:4–6)

Paul is saying, "I keep praying for you every time I remember you. I am asking all of the time, seeking all of the time, and knocking all of the time for you." Here are the attitudes that characterize his prayers:

**Thankful.** He is thankful every time he remembers them. What an affirmation! He is thankful NOT because of their theology or morality, NOT because they have the most exciting worship, but BECAUSE of their Jesus Mission Lives. "I am thankful because you live in partnership together with me in the gospel."

**Joyful.** Their Jesus Mission Lives brought joy to Paul as he prayed. I can just see the smile cross his face and the tears of joy roll off of his cheek as he prays for these friends of his. Paul thought, "The Jesus followers in this city are on mission; they live the same life I have been called to—a Jesus Mission Life."

**Confident.** Paul prayed with confidence that what God started in them would be completed by Him. This is a statement of mission. "I am confident before God that the partnership you have will continue as long as you live because Jesus will keep touching you and giving you clarity."

### INSIGHT #2—CLARITY IS DIRECTLY IMPACTED BY WHAT I CHOOSE TO CARRY

What we carry has a direct impact on our clarity for building a Jesus Mission Life. In the Bible, the word *carry* appears many times, usually as a verb telling someone to carry something. People were told to carry water, a mat they had been lying on, a burden that was heavy on their hearts and minds. Jesus even instructed the man who was unable to walk to carry his bed and walk. Jesus invites us to carry our burdens to Him because He cares for us.

While returning from serving in India, our team's connecting flight from Paris to California had a nine-hour layover. The team decided that we would go see the Notre Dame Cathedral. The first question we asked was, "What do we do with all of these backpacks and carry-on bags? We cannot go see Notre Dame with all of these bags." The team rented a giant locker and put all of our bags inside. The relief of not having to miss the sights of Paris and the Notre Dame Cathedral because of what we were carrying was visible on our faces. We grabbed a map, our passports, some cash, and our cameras/smartphones, and we were off. Our ability to fully enjoy our little mission of seeing Notre Dame was directly impacted by what we put in the locker and what we chose to carry.

### What We Carry in Life Impacts Our Clarity for Jesus Mission Living

Each person reading this book carries something. Some carry the joys of being loved well by a spouse or a parent. Others carry the baggage of a family filled with addictions and strife. We carry the standards of a culture that tells us how we are to look, what we are to earn, and how we must accumulate more stuff, and these standards pressure us continually. In the religious world, we carry expressions of faith and morality that sometimes bless us and sometimes feel so heavy.

We carry shame, fear, and anger as undercurrents to our souls and minds; this is what sin did to people and still does to us. We carry confidence, false confidence, wounds that have never been shared, and some that we cannot stop talking about. We carry the responsibility of family, kids, work, our health, and, for many, aging parents. We carry a lot, and what we carry has a direct impact on our clarity for Jesus Mission Living.

### Cue Jesus and Two Thoughts About What We Carry

In the Gospel of Matthew, Jesus invites us to bring what makes us weary and burdened to Him. What if you made a list of what makes you weary and burdened and then took that list to Jesus in prayer?

> Come to me, all you who are weary and burdened, and I will give you rest. Take my yoke upon you and learn from me, for I am gentle

> and humble in heart, and you will find rest for your souls. For my yoke is easy and my burden is light. (Matthew 11:28–30)

The word *weary* means to have grown tired in the struggle. The word *burdened* points to physical burdens, emotional burdens, and burdens that are placed upon us by expectations around us. Jesus's invitation is to carry these things to Him. The people listening to Jesus found different messages about weariness and burdens in their culture. Carry your burdens. You have burdens because you failed to live to God's standards. Then, after these messages, the burdens would increase because of the expectations and rules being placed upon them by the religious elite. Jesus says, "Bring them to me, and I will give you rest."

When Jesus offers rest, He is saying that He will give you a breather, a moment to gain strength and examine if what you carry is what is best for you to carry. "I will give you rest." How does Jesus offer this rest? Look at the verses again, "Take my yoke upon you and learn from me, for I am gentle and humble in heart, and you will find rest for your souls. For my yoke is easy and my burden is light." Jesus is giving us three separate instructions about Jesus Mission Living:

**ONE—Bring your burdens to me.** Bring me what makes you weary. Bring me what weighs you down. I care about you, and I care about what you carry.

**TWO—Exchange what makes you weary and what burdens you for my yoke.** The yoke was used to bind two animals together in pulling a heavy load, creating an even weight and load. Often, the stronger oxen were paired with weaker oxen. This allowed the weaker oxen to work without being crushed by the load and to gain strength while being yoked together with a stronger ox. Jesus's strength is immeasurably greater than our strength, so He invites each of us to come with the burdens and weariness we have. Bring it to Him, and when you do, you are to set your burdens down, put His yoke on, and join Him in pulling what He carries.

The habit of many Christians is to bring what makes them weary and burdened to Jesus. This is what we are supposed to do. But instead of putting them down and putting on His yoke, we have a spiritual and cathartic show-and-tell with Jesus, and then just like that, we gather them up and go on our way. This habit eventually becomes a faith-draining rut for us.

**THREE—Learn from me.** Jesus does not want us to bring to Him our burdens, have Him lift our burdens from us, and then take all these burdens back. That is not taking His yoke. Instead, Jesus says, "Learn from me." Jesus is saying, "Bring that heaviness to me, exchange it for my yoke, and I will give you rest. Learn something from me now because my yoke is easy and my burden is light."

There is a way we are meant to live with Jesus. Our friendship with Him, the place where He gives us rest, is supposed to result in us becoming partners with Jesus. "Take my yoke. Learn from me." These are missional invitations. "My yoke is easy and my burden is light." This is not how it feels a lot of the time. When I talk mission, people groan internally and sometimes even externally. This doesn't feel easy or light. One honest person spoke up in the middle of a training and said, "Pastor, this is a hard and heavy burden you are giving us. On top of all the other burdens we carry, now we are to carry the one to live a Jesus Mission Life. Respectfully, we cannot do it." Yet, Jesus says His yoke is easy and His burden is light. I responded with Matthew 11:28–30, and we did a little Bible study right there.

---

Side Note: One reason Jesus Mission Living seems heavy is that we never actually put down our burdens. We bring them to Jesus, show them to Jesus, claim promises from the Bible, and then place them back in our suitcase and haul that suitcase all over "Paris." When we do this, we are saying, "Jesus, why don't you take my yoke upon you and help me carry it." This is not what Jesus wants to do; He wants something much better—"Learn from me."

---

Jesus's yoke is easy, and His burden is light for us because we are yoked with Jesus in Jesus's Mission. This is the mission we were meant to live. We were built to live a Jesus Mission Life that comes from a friendship and partnership with Jesus. Two things happen to my weariness and burdens when I bring them to Jesus, take His yoke, and learn from Him.

**First, much of what I carry either goes away or becomes irrelevant to my daily life.** What I need from others to help me with my burdens is no longer needed when they are no longer my burdens. Weariness and heavy burdens muddy the waters of Jesus Mission Living. It is true that if you try to carry your own burdens and then live a Jesus Mission Life, it is too heavy. Set them down, take up His yoke, and let Him teach you.

**Second, Jesus the Redeemer shows me His superior wisdom and strength by taking my mess, redeeming it, and then turning it into His glory.** Rothy's is a company that has figured out how to take recycled plastic and turn it into comfortable shoes. How great is that! Jesus does one better; He takes a broken marriage and uses it to care for someone else who is in pain. He takes our cancer and uses it to point others to Jesus. He takes our sin and forgives it so others can know the forgiveness of God too. Jesus redeems what makes us weary and burdened in life.

Like my team in Paris, leaving behind our baggage in a locker opened a door to a much less distracted and a much clearer experience of the Notre Dame Cathedral. What do you need to carry to the feet of Jesus and leave there so you can carry His Mission, yoked together with Him?

There are two crosses in every Jesus follower's life. One is the Cross of Jesus, and the other is our cross. The Cross of Jesus is where we stand, where we kneel, and where we are saved. Our cross is what we carry as a disciple of Jesus.

**Jesus's Cross has everything we need to follow Him and everything we need to help us carry our own cross.** The Cross of Jesus has our forgiveness and freedom from sin. The Cross of Jesus is where Jesus defeated Satan, making a mockery of him. The Cross of Jesus is where I find my value and am assured I am loved. The Cross of Jesus is where I find my mission and my WHY.

At the foot of the Cross of Jesus, there is completely even footing for everyone. All of us are completely broken as we stand at the foot of the cross. At the foot of the Cross of Jesus, I finally see me as God sees me, BECAUSE, at the foot of the Cross of Jesus is where I find JESUS! That is why Paul says he only boasts in the Cross of Jesus.

> May I never boast except in the cross of our Lord Jesus Christ, through which the world has been crucified to me, and I to the world. (Galatians 6:14)

Something is meant to happen at the foot of the Cross. At the foot of Jesus's Cross, we surrender to Jesus; we confess our sin; we receive His sacrifice for our sin. It is at this place we drop the baggage of our lives because, on the Cross, Jesus bore all the sin and pain-filled bags we carry. Because of Jesus's Cross, my chains are gone. Jesus's Cross accomplished everything I need to live free. All my spiritual needs are 100 percent met at the foot of the Cross. The Cross is where the world is crucified to us and us to the world.

There is so much more to say about the Cross of Jesus, but I will add one more thing: the Cross of Jesus makes clear the urgency and importance of the Mission of God and our living out a Jesus Mission Life. Read the accounts of Jesus's giving His life on the cross, and you will see clearly God's love for us and His Mission to rescue us. At Jesus's Cross, we are to leave our bags.

**Our cross gets picked up again as we navigate life without a mission.** When I finally understood Jesus Mission Living, I discovered that what I am to leave at the Cross of Jesus is meant to be replaced and I am to pick up another Cross. We are not to leave the foot of the Cross with nothing; we are to pick up our Mission-centered Cross and, from that day forward, follow Jesus. At the foot of Jesus's Cross, I take up my Cross and follow Him and His Mission.

Jesus knows something. When you carry a cross, you have no room to carry anything else. Carrying a cross requires letting go—letting go of your past, letting go of your sin, letting go of your pain, letting go of your mission, just to lift the one thing we have been told all disciples must carry—their cross.

When we sin, when we wander into doubt or fear, we are setting down our cross and picking up something else. Carrying our cross leaves no room for us to carry anything else. For those of us looking for a "what is my cross" explanation, your cross and my cross will ALWAYS be Jesus Mission Living. When Jesus said, "Take up your cross," He was not instructing us to pick up our past and carry it to the Cross; He was saying, "Get on Mission and carry the Cross that Mission brings."

I was sitting with a small group filled with Jesus followers, and the conversation turned to this very subject, "Take up your cross." One person said, "My marriage is my cross." Another said, "My work is my cross, specifically my harsh boss." Another said, "My rebellious child is my cross," and still another who was caring for an elderly mother said, "She is my cross." Finances, health, pain from an abusive past, or some form of overcoming the habits of sin have all been associated with the cross we carry. In reality, these struggles are about the Cross Jesus carried. What Jesus did on His Cross was to take my sin away and then make me His. **My cross, the one Jesus said to carry, is about being a disciple who makes disciples and lives a Jesus Mission Life.**

Jesus's words included teaching His disciples and those listening to follow Him, transforming them to a life of Mission. Jesus said to them what He says to each of us, "Follow Me, I will make you fishers of men" (Matthew 4:19). He said, "Whoever wants to be my disciple must deny themselves and take up their cross and follow me" (Matthew 16:24). Interestingly enough, Jesus's recorded spoken words He said when He walked on the earth, in context, are mostly mission-driven words. There is nothing else you can carry when you carry your cross; that is actually what you were meant to carry. "Set all that other stuff down, pick up your cross, and follow Me."

When we take up our cross, our responsibility is to lift and then to follow. Jesus's instructions are for us to pick it up and follow, not pick it up and tell everyone how heavy it is. Jesus said it would be heavy; He said to count the cost; He said, "This is what my disciples do—they pick up and carry their crosses."

### INSIGHT #3—CLARITY IN JESUS MISSION LIVING IS A SPIRITUAL BATTLE

While working with students, we had a crazy season where we worked with gangs. It was strange because we actually worked with Bloods, Crips, and Skin Heads, all at the same time. We had about a year where they would meet in my house, all together, and we would talk about Jesus. At my door was a box marked "Weapon Box," and we told them that they could not bring weapons into the house. Each night, as the meeting was about to begin, you could hear a knife, brass knuckles, a sharpened screwdriver, a small pipe, or some other weapon hit the bottom of the box. It was odd, to say the least.

One night, after a really great meeting on the life and love of Jesus, we ended up at a local fast food joint, and that was where the trouble began. A gang we were not connected to drove into the parking lot, got out, and started fighting with our students. I ended up taking a knife and a bat away from a couple of students, and that was when the gun came out. A small revolver was being brandished by a new student; then, it was fired into the air. I was working hard to get students out of there and ended up standing between the kid with a gun and a guy he wanted to shoot.

In moments like this, there is not much time to plan, read your Bible, or refer to the safety manual. No, in times like this, you say words like, "No!" "Stop!" "Get down!" And my personal favorite, "Jesus, help!" Aiming the gun at a rival gang, this young man pulled the trigger three times, and it never fired, a miracle in and of itself. Feeling like the entire event was all in slow motion, this was a pretty crazy night as crazy nights go. In the end, no one died that night, and the evening ended. Except it didn't.

What kept coming back to me was just how close we came to tragedy. How close we came to burying some kids, a staff person, or how close my kids and wife came to losing their dad and husband. Sitting by myself early one morning, confessing (Christian talk for complaining) to God my frustration of the night, the ripple effect of the event, and how broken our world is, I heard a sweet voice say, "What did you expect? This is a spiritual battle." Duh, I know that, but how quickly I forget that the enemy of God is also my enemy, and he hates any time a person moves toward Jesus.

Satan hates these kids, and the last thing he wants is for them to find Jesus, home, forgiveness, freedom, and everything else that comes with Jesus. The last thing he wanted was for these young men and women to have a mission that would rescue others from a life of violence and gangs. Of course, he is fighting hard; this is a spiritual battle! Paul the Apostle wrote at the end of his letter to the Ephesians these words:

> For our struggle is not against flesh and blood, but against the rulers, against the authorities, against the powers of this dark world and against the spiritual forces of evil in the heavenly realms. (Ephesians 6:12)

To carry our cross is a spiritual battle. It is a fight against a defeated enemy who is trying to keep as many of us as he can from taking up our crosses, from entering into a Jesus Mission Life, and from being ALL IN. Someday, God will wrap up everything, and we will forever be with Jesus, but until then, we have a mission—a Jesus Mission. That is why we keep on asking, keep on seeking, and keep on knocking.

By the way, what began that night with students ended in a murder, and three of our students were killed about a week later. I asked the dad if I could help with the funeral service, and his only requirement was that I was not allowed to bring any religion into it since his son was not religious. I explained that his son was a deeply troubled kid, and in truth, all of the death and trouble started with him. The dad knew, and pain at the thought flashed across his face.

I shared, "Right now, there is a gang war that is going to start and might start at the funeral. I would like to at least use the funeral to make one positive from your son's life and talk about forgiveness. Maybe if we can convince people not to retaliate, we can save other families from the pain you are experiencing." The dad was shocked at my boldness but asked, "What do you have in mind?" Digging in my pocket, I pulled out a small, thin one-inch aluminum cross. Showing it to him, I said, "This is the universal sign of radical forgiveness because when Jesus was on the cross, being murdered by others, He cried out for them to be forgiven."

The dad looked up, and for the first time since I arrived, there was something other than guilt, sorrow, and anger in his voice. "Let's share that!" "Okay, I will," I said. As I walked through the cross and everything that was defeated by Christ, his only response was, "Let's share that!" I said, "I have 300 of these; would you let me give these out to every kid who promises not to retaliate and be like Jesus when suffering a wrong?" Again, slightly hopeful something good might come from this tragic life, the dad said, "Let's do that!" I did, and there was no retaliation anywhere.

Sometime later, I was asked how I did it; how I kept gangs from fighting. My response was easy: "I didn't do it; Jesus did. He fought this fight on the cross, won this fight with an empty grave, and invited me into this spiritual battle." We (the several hundred people who prayed for me through this moment) entered into a spiritual battle through prayer, fasting, and a clear focus on the mission.

## INSIGHT #4—CLARITY HAPPENS WHEN I CHOOSE JESUS MISSION LIVING ABOVE ALL ELSE

"There are none so blind as those who will not see." Jesus did not say this, but He said words like it. More than once He spoke about the people whose spiritual sight was their real blindness. In His confrontations with the religious elite, Jesus told them they were blind guides leading the blind. In case you missed it, those are fighting words.

Jesus's most hostile opposition was from people who would not let tradition go. They rejected Jesus, even in the face of His teaching, which had more authority than anything they had seen or heard. Tradition blocked their clarity of Jesus's Mission. The people who rejected Jesus did not do so from a distance. They were eyewitnesses to His miracles; they heard Him explain Scriptures, saw how He loved people, and witnessed the freedom He brought to others who followed Him. Even with all they saw and heard, they chose tradition over Jesus and His Mission.

They did not ignore Jesus; they were threatened by Him so much so that they broke their own laws to justify killing Him. Their love of their own culture, power, and traditions served to rob them of clarity, to keep them blind. Their pride and envy made them arrest Jesus. God created them for His Mission, and instead of embracing Jesus's Mission, they held tightly to their cultural expressions of faith and ended up rejecting Jesus and His Mission.

How easy it is to let my own culture influence how I embrace Jesus and how I build a Jesus Mission Life. Science has trumped Scripture for many people of faith. I recently had a friend tell me that they believed everything in the Bible except the creation story. Science was the reason given. Politics and nationalism have distorted Christian loyalty and divided people of faith. I regularly hear Jesus people equate the Bible and the Constitution of the United States of America as nearly equal. They are not even close, my friends. Jesus followers have told me they are afraid to talk about Jesus because talking about Jesus might lead to hard and controversial issues of race, gender, sexuality, poverty, abortion, and other issues that live in the categories of biblical values and social and human rights.

Embracing Jesus and His Mission is counter-cultural. Jesus is the King of His own Kingdom. His Kingdom knows truth, love, mission, loyalty, worship, and commitment differently than the world around us. Of course the truth of His Kingdom is difficult for the culture surrounding Jesus's Kingdom to accept and embrace. Jesus's Kingdom is scandalous because of grace. Jesus's Kingdom is radical because of truth. Jesus's Kingdom is reckless because the entrance requirements are never earned, just granted by faith.

In the collision of kingdoms that is happening all around us, people of faith lament the moral and ethical decline of the culture. Our lament is sometimes more about the decline of culture rather than a person spending an entire lifetime never knowing the grace and forgiveness of God. Our grief is too often more about what we have lost than a person living all of their years never knowing they are loved by God, desired by God, and invited by God to find true freedom in Christ. People are angrier at those they perceive as taking from them the safety of their Judeo-Christian culture than they are with Satan, who longs for them to be separated from God in this life and through eternity. The struggle to embrace Jesus's Mission as our own is because too many of us think the mission is about morality in our nation and not eternity.

Jesus's disciples followed Jesus, listened to Jesus, and loved Jesus, but the clarity of Jesus Mission Living did not happen from a distance. Their clarity came after they jumped into the deep end of Jesus Mission Living, and it was in the deep end that they discovered in every way, it was all true.

I wish reading this book would make you a disciple who makes disciples whose disciples also make disciples. I wish the clarity of

Jesus's Mission answered all your questions, and with the answers, your fears went away, and for the rest of your days, you lived a Jesus Mission Life. I wish, but it just doesn't work that way. The clarity comes when we make Jesus's Mission priority number one.

I made this very statement to a group of Jesus-loving and church-going Christians, and the question I was asked, "What does that look like in the twenty-first century?" I said, "What if you don't like the answer?" Or worse, "What if you knew the answer and looked for a different answer because you don't like the one we have?" Like a good preacher, I told them a bad joke.

There was a man who fell over a cliff and grabbed ahold of a branch, holding on for dear life, he began shouting "Help, is there anyone up there?" After a while, he heard a voice, and it said, "I am Jesus, and I have heard your cries, see your need, and I am here to help." "Oh, thank you, Jesus, I am almost out of strength; I am so glad you are here to rescue me. What do you want me to do?" Jesus replied, "I want you to trust me." "I do, I really do trust you," the man said in desperation. Jesus said, "I am so glad you trust me; I want you to let go of the branch, and I will catch you." There was an awkward pause, and it was interrupted by the man, "Is there anyone else up there?"

I know; bad joke but great truth!

Prioritize your life around Jesus's Mission. See Jesus's Mission as more than attending church, being in a small group, giving a percentage of time and money, and being nice. Embrace every part of your life and all your circles of influence as the mission field for a Jesus Mission Life. To guide me to the most honest answer, **I ask three big questions** with a lot of clarifying questions:

**Do my words reflect a Jesus Mission Life?** Do I speak life to others? Do I speak about Jesus to others? Do I speak grace and truth to myself and those around me? Who do my words sound most like—Jesus or my culture?

**Do my finances and resources reflect a Jesus Mission Life?** Is my goal to spend less so I can give more to the Kingdom? Is there any place of real sacrifice in my giving? Do I see God as the owner of all I have? Am I a good steward of God's resources? Do I use my resources of time to advance the Kingdom?

**Am I making any disciples?** Is there a person I am discipling? Am I walking with another person in their faith journey? Are my gifts and talents adding to other disciple-makers?

**Here is a bonus question:** How do you want God to answer these three questions for you when you are standing in eternity?

Jesus's invitation to a Jesus Mission Life is not a detailed roadmap to peace and safety; it is an invitation to live the life we are meant to live. This life, the Jesus Mission Life, brings clarity as we go.

## INSIGHT #5—CLARITY STAYS WHEN I KEEP THE PATH CLEAR

Hiking in the mountains can be some of the most breathtaking moments in nature for a person. I have spent countless hours in the Sierra Mountains in California hiking, hunting, fishing, and camping. Paying attention to the trail is how you keep from getting lost because people can become disoriented and easily lost when the trail is hard to find. Hikers help each other by building what are called rock cairns, a stack of several rocks that mark a trail that is hard to see.

More than once my bearings have been adjusted to the right direction and my feet to the correct trail by a small stack of rocks, a rock cairn. Cairns are not hard to see if your eyes are trained to look for them, but if you are not trained, then you will discover that you can walk right past them.

I took a group of students backpacking, and a couple of the guys who had never spent a night under the stars saw a rock cairn. Their first instinct was to knock it down. I told them about these important little stacks of rocks and made them rebuild them. When they agreed with the importance of these rock cairns and rebuilt them, two mission-living results took place. First, they began to see themselves as following a path. No longer were they looking for the path of least resistance or the straightest line; they followed a well-worn path. In the Twenty-Third Psalm, King David reminds us that God leads us in well-worn paths of what is right for His own name's sake. Second, they saw themselves as restored to a mission bigger than themselves. They now were a part of helping others find the way, too.

Jesus Mission Living can easily feel like a wilderness hike. It is beautiful, requires some strength, invites you to see places that can only be seen when you actually hike the trails, and requires directional markers to keep you on the path. Here are four "rock cairns" for keeping clarity in Jesus Mission Living.

**ONE—God's Word.** When the Bible is viewed through the lens of Mission, it accomplishes two life-altering tasks when I read it. The Bible shows me where my feet are; it is a lamp to my feet. More than once, I have seen my footing for life and Mission revealed by simply reading the Bible. My motives, my struggles, my trust, and the love I have for Jesus are illuminated by the word of God. Sometimes, the lamp reveals the danger, and other times, it reveals the solid foundation.

The second life-altering task the Bible accomplishes is to show me where my feet are supposed to go. "Your word is a lamp to my feet and a light to my path (Psalm 119:105). I love that the word of God is a "light to my path." A tool and gift from God, one that reveals where I stand and then shows me where to go, must be an intrinsic part of Jesus Mission Living.

**TWO—Confession and repentance.** Sin has a way of knocking over the markers we need to navigate a Jesus Mission Life. *Confession* means to agree with God about our sin—agree sin is wrong, agree sin damages us, agree with what God says sin actually is, and agree that our sin is forgiven by God through Jesus. When we ignore sin, the rock cairns—the markers for the Jesus Mission Life—get trampled, hidden, and knocked over. When I confess and agree with God about my sin, the Holy Spirit restacks the markers I need to live a Jesus Mission Life.

*Repentance* means to turn and go the other way. In one real sense, my confession is how the rock cairns are rebuilt, and repentance is how I return to the path He has already marked out for me. This is my paraphrase of Ephesians 2:10: "You are my exquisite and hand-crafted masterpiece; I have made you for plans that I marked out for your life, long before we were ever friends." Confession and repentance are how I stay on mission and how I return to mission when I stray. This is the impact confession and repentance have on Jesus Mission Living.

Sin in my life knocks over the rock cairns that God has placed in my life by destroying the clarity God is consistently bringing to my life. Sin makes my navigation more uncertain. Sin brings doubt as to God's love, His ability to use me, and His wisdom in choosing me. It also makes it so much more difficult to see the path forward in building a Jesus Mission Life. I had a youth leader tell me, "Leonard, your sin will make you uncertain of your calling. Keep a short account." He was right, and I applied his words by making immediate confession, true repentance, and reminding myself of the grace of Jesus. I applied his words by running from temptation. I applied his words by putting myself in relationships with others who know me and can ask me about my sin.

**THREE—Centering ourselves with Jesus's Mission.** Life gets hectic sometimes. How is that for an understatement? When people feel overwhelmed, the advice to "center" is often given. Through breathing exercises, meditation, or positive thinking, the idea is to calm the body and mind in a stressful situation. These tools can work to bring calm to our hearts and minds, but I believe what is often needed more than a calming-centering moment is a missional-centering moment. A missional-centering moment is when we make a choice to embrace the noise of mission, a Jesus Mission Life, because it is what we are made for. Some struggles are good, and we are built to do hard things. The problem is not the difficulty of life but how we make our lives difficult with things that, in the end, do not matter.

Peter wrote in his first letter (1 Peter 4, go read it) that when we suffer, when we struggle, we are blessed by God and bring glory to Him. But not if our struggles are coming from our own foolish behaviors or smaller mission living. Peter reminds us that it is the centering of our lives on Jesus's Mission that serves like markers, rock cairns, as it were, that shows us how to live in deep friendship and partnership with Jesus Himself. It is only when our lives are truly centered on Jesus's Mission that the peace of God captures us, guards us, and invades our hearts and minds in ways that are beyond our comprehension.

In my own life, there are two important mission-centering choices I make each day. **First, I choose to see myself as sent by God everywhere I go.** Being sent by God is such an honor to claim, and when I see myself as sent, the path becomes less entangled with fear, doubt, my past, or my pain. God knows what His Mission is, and He knows me, and yet He still sends me and you, too. **The second centering choice is the constant acknowledgment that not only does He send me, He goes with me and before me.** I never arrive somewhere that He is not already there working. I never arrive alone either: "I will be with you always, until the very end" (Matthew 28:20, my paraphrase).

**FOUR—We need to stay on the path.** I keep the path clear by deliberately choosing to keep it clear. Most of what gets in the way of me living a Jesus Mission Life was put there by me. My thoughts clutter the path. My priorities misaligned will keep me Mission adjacent. My disciplines, what I choose to carry, and how I feed my own faith all serve to clear or clutter the path. The Spirit of God produces in me the ability to use self-control and keep the path clear.

There is a cloud of witnesses who have gone before us (Hebrews 11–12), and these God-following people have placed rock cairns through their action-oriented faith and obedience to God. Each cairn is strategically recorded by God to help us know Him and then navigate the Jesus Mission Life. Study Jesus, study the characters in Hebrews 11, study the apostles, the women who followed Jesus, the faithful people throughout the past nearly two thousand years, and you will see that many of them left a stack of rocks to mark out a pathway for us.

Sometimes the best thing to do is jump. I do not like heights that much. Years back, I was speaking at a youth conference. Each day we would go and tackle some adventure, and on this day, the challenge was a forty-plus-foot jump into a deep pool of water. One kid jumped, then another and another, each one enthusiastically embracing the challenge by jumping almost without hesitation. Then came the speaker's turn (that is me, Mr. I Am Afraid of Heights). Everything in my body said, "No, jumping is dumb." Everything in my mind said, "Do not jump." Soon, those who had gone before me were cheering me on, shouting, "You can do this!" "You got this!" "Come on!" "We believe in you!" Standing on the edge of the rocks, fear and anxiety ran wild through my body. But because those who had gone before me did not actually die, I found the courage to jump. On my way down I could hear the cheers, felt the rush of adrenalin, and muttered bad words under my breath. Coming out of the water, I was pumped. First, I was still alive, and second, I did it! I jumped!

Could it be that what we need is not more information but the actual faith to jump? The Mission of Jesus requires faith, and faith requires action. So jump! Let me close with this thought.

When my kids were little, we played the jump-to-dad game. You know, the game where your kid stands on something and then, with encouragement, jumps into dad's arms? I would get myself set and then encourage my kids to jump into my arms. The encouragement? "Your dad's arms are safe, and you can trust him; go ahead and jump." I found my kids' eagerness to jump was connected to the height and distance they were being asked to jump. What I also found was that their willingness to jump was connected to trust in their dad. "You can jump because I love you. You can jump because I will catch you. You can jump because I caught you last time. I have the size, strength, desire, and skill to catch you when you jump. Trust me and jump."

Give your life to the Mission of Jesus; live a Jesus Mission Life. Jump. Become a disciple of Jesus who carries their cross and bears the yoke of Jesus. Jump. Find ways to make a disciple, who makes a disciple. Jump. Love others like Jesus loved. Jump. Embrace the Jesus Mission View of the Bible. Jump. Rearrange your life around a Jesus Mission Life. Jump. Take time to become trained as a disciple-maker. Jump. These words, and possibly this whole book, feel like you have been invited to a giant rock ledge, and you are being asked to jump. To add to the tension, you cannot see the bottom; you do not know how far down you will go, but you can hear the voice of Jesus.

> Then Jesus came to them and said, "All authority in heaven and on earth has been given to me. Therefore go and make disciples of all nations, baptizing them in the name of the Father and of the Son and of the Holy Spirit, and teaching them to obey everything I have commanded you. And surely I am with you always, to the very end of the age." (Matthew 28:18–20)

In other words, **JUMP!**

When asked to jump, some of us will love the adventure and jump immediately; others of us will take a bit more cheering. When it comes to Jesus Mission Living, I hear my Father say, "Jump," and I tend to jump quickly. Others hear "Jump," and it takes more cheering. I think if you are the "takes more cheering" person, your jumping takes a much greater act of faith, trust, and courage than mine.

Our Savior invites each of us to Jesus Mission Living. I jump first because God wired me that way, not because I have a greater friendship with Jesus. I jump when clarity is at its highest in my life. Some of you jump after much cheering because that is how He wired you, and I so admire you for jumping. You demonstrate gigantic faith, and I thank you. I pray all of us will jump into our Father's arms and embrace a Jesus Mission Life. His arms are safe, and He will catch you. Jump.

# Stepping into Jesus's Mission

## A prayer you can pray today:

*Jesus,*

*Thank You that You heal spiritual blindness. I need You to keep touching my eyes so I can see clearly. Will You help me choose Jesus Mission Living above all else and to keep the pathway clear? I am so grateful You are willing to touch my eyes again and again.*

*Amen*

## Some questions to move you forward:

When was a time when personal clarity made a difference to you in any part of your life?

Clarity in building a Jesus Mission Life means to see clearly that Jesus has a Mission, and we do too, when we follow Him. How clear is this becoming to you as you read and process this book?

Where in your journey of building a Jesus Mission Life do you experience a lack of clarity or great clarity?

From the story of Jesus healing the blind man outside of Bethsaida, what can we learn about Jesus, His Mission, and missional clarity?

Remember the five statements on clarity: clarity sometimes takes a few touches from Jesus; clarity is directly impacted by what I choose to carry; clarity happens when I choose Jesus Mission Living above all else; clarity is a spiritual battle; and clarity stays when I keep the path clear. Which one stands out to you most? Why?

Take a few minutes to share something that God might want to "touch" in your life to give you the clarity needed to continue to build a Jesus Mission Life.

## A step to take as you go:

Take the five statements about clarity in building a Jesus Mission Life and choose one to bring to Jesus in prayer. Ask Jesus this week to give you specific verses, actions, and relationships that help with clarity.

All this I have spoken while still with you. But the Advocate, the Holy Spirit, whom the Father will send in my name, will teach you all things and will remind you of everything I have said to you. (John 14:25)

# Chapter 15

## "I Will Send My Spirit"

In 2002, I took my first trip to India. It was almost thirty days, and by far, the most difficult part of this trip was saying goodbye to my kids. Merrily understood the calling and mission; they did not. We all cried, and I handed them both gifts. We hugged, said I love you, and promised to be back soon. Then I drove away.

On the way to the airport, I thought of Jesus saying goodbye to His disciples. The hugs, possible gifts, the promise to return, and the pain in their hearts as Jesus said, "I am going away, and you will not find me." I also imagined the joy in their hearts when He said, "I will come again."

In the space where Jesus is right now, sitting on the throne at the right hand of the Father, we have been given the same gift the disciples were given. The same promise that God the Holy Spirit would come and we would not be left as orphans. What a promise for them and what a promise for us!

God the Holy Spirit is the promised gift from God. During the tension of Jesus's last night, Jesus told the disciples that when He goes away, the Holy Spirit will come and will be their chief partner in living out Jesus Mission Lives. Walk with me through Jesus's promise in John chapters 13–17.

It was evening of the last night of Jesus's life. By 9:00 a.m. the next day, Jesus would be hanging on a cross between two thieves, fighting for His breath, and by 3:00 p.m., He would be dead. Having already been threatened and escaped an attempted stoning for His words, Jesus knew that everything but the Mission is about to change. Here is what Jesus knew.

Jesus knew that His time had come. He knew that He had come from the Father and would now return. He knew the disciple who would betray Him, the disciple who would deny Him, and the disciples who would scatter because of Him. Jesus knew the road to the cross would be a road filled with hate, scorn, abuse, and torture. He knew He would die. Jesus told His friends plainly, "I am going to suffer and die," but the words were too much for them. He knew He would rise again, but they all struggled to understand. (I would too.) Jesus knew that He had prepared His friends to live Jesus Mission Lives and that after the resurrection, He would return to the Father and be seated at the right hand of God where all things in heaven and earth would be subjected to Him. Jesus knew that one day, you and I would give our hearts and lives to Him. Jesus knew that God the Holy Spirit was on His way!

However, back in Disciple Town, when it came to grasping the moment, the disciples went between "What the heck?" and "What the heck!" It was not until after the resurrection of Jesus that their understanding of these final moments before the cross began to make sense. Jesus's words were heavy, "I am going to be arrested, dragged in front of the authorities, and then killed." "I am going away." "The world hated me, so the world will hate you." Jesus's promise in all of this? "God the Holy Spirit is on His way."

You have been reading a book that says the singular Mission of Jesus is the rescue of people from their sin. He gave Himself as the Lamb slain before the foundation of the world. This book says that the singular Mission Jesus gave His Church is to make disciples who make disciples, whose disciples also make disciples. Then, this book has the audacity to say that the singular Mission of a Jesus follower, a disciple as it were, is to make disciples, too, meaning your singular Mission is to live a Jesus Mission Life.

Reading this book might have challenged you to make more of the Mission of Jesus in your own life. Your reading might have given you as many questions as it answered. It could be what you read jumpstarted within you the hunger to be singular in your focus on a Jesus Mission Life. Possibly, you disagreed and decided to investigate further. Maybe you just got mad.

I think most of us reading have been trying to figure out what living a Jesus Mission Life might look like in our own lives in the twenty-first century. I know that I tend to do what the disciples did about two thousand years ago. I ping pong between "What?" and "What!" Here is what Jesus knew about His friends then (His disciples) and His friends now (you and me): **Apart from God the Holy Spirit, it is impossible to live a Jesus Mission Life.**

This is why Jesus went to such great lengths to tell His disciples, "It is going to get rough out there on a Jesus Mission Life, but I will be with you, always and in all ways to the very end of the age through the Holy Spirit" (paraphrase mine). Let's discover the depth of Jesus's promise of God the Holy Spirit coming; indeed, God the Holy Spirit is here.

Before we get to the promise, let me tell you why the role of the Holy Spirit is last in this book. I put this last because Jesus seemed to put it last. Jesus's training of His disciples could be summed up like this: follow me; training for Mission; more training for Mission; more training for Mission; here are the keys to drive the Mission; I am dying and going away, so let's make sure you can actually live a Jesus Mission Life; oh, and let me tell you about God the Holy Spirit—He will be your partner in Jesus Mission Living. Of course, all of this training for Mission was in the context of the best and most amazing love the disciples and the world have ever seen.

While all of the work of Jesus Mission Living is supernatural, we have to do our part here in the physical world in which we live. We are

His ambassadors, given the very words and Mission of Jesus. What we do here in this life shapes and impacts eternity. It took the disciples a long time with Jesus to understand that what they did in the physical world made a difference in the spiritual world.

It was during the last twelve to fifteen hours of Jesus's life when Jesus promised His disciples that the gift of God the Holy Spirit was coming. It was evening, and the Passover meal was in full swing, as you might remember from earlier in this book. What was being said and done in that room had never been said and done in the nearly fifteen hundred years of celebrating the exodus of the nation of Israel from slavery in Egypt. The disciples, fresh off a huge wave of love and truth from Jesus in the form of washing their feet, listened to Jesus speak. John 13–17 give us a close-up view of Jesus and the disciples' evening. John 13–14 took place in the upper room, where the Passover was celebrated. John 15–16 took place as the disciples and Jesus walked to the place where Jesus would be betrayed. John 17 is the prayer Jesus prayed to the Father for the disciples as they would soon be living Jesus Mission Lives. Someday, I might write a book on Jesus's last night, but for this book, let's look at a few bits and pieces from these moments.

## JOHN 13

> **I am telling you now before it happens, so that when it does happen you will believe that I am who I am.** Very truly I tell you, whoever accepts anyone I send accepts me; and whoever accepts me accepts the one who sent me. (John 13:19–20, emphasis mine)

When my football coach would give us the fourth-quarter sideline chat, his first words were, "All eyes up here; look at me." His goals were that none of us miss anything he was going to say and that we hear it all together. This is how I read the tone of the evening and the potency of Jesus's words. "Look at me, all eyes up here. I am telling you what is going to happen so when it does, you can find strength in who I am. In a short time, it will look like I have lost, and the Mission is over; IT IS NOT!"

Jesus goes on to tell them, "You are going to be sent, and whoever accepts the ones I send (you) accepts me, and whoever accepts me, well, he accepts my Father (Mission). I want you to recognize in the next several hours, days, weeks, and for the rest of your lives that this was a planned part of accomplishing My Mission. The better you understand this, the more you will live a Jesus Mission Life" (paraphrase mine). We learn in Acts 4 that they got what Jesus was saying. I encourage you to read all of Acts 4 and then see how they prayed in verses 23–31.

> After he had said this, Jesus was troubled in spirit and testified, "Very truly I tell you, **one of you is going to betray me.**" (John 13:21, emphasis mine)

This statement really caused a lot of external and internal whispers between the disciples. "Is it me, is it him, who will do this unthinkable act of spiritual treason? Ask Jesus who." And even when Jesus showed them by dipping the bread and giving it to Judas, they still didn't know. Then Peter says, "Not me, I will die before I betray you."

---

Side Note: I think Peter meant it with every ounce of his being. It is just that without the Holy Spirit, we cannot deliver on the commitments we make to Jesus.

---

> My children, **I will be with you only a little longer.** You will look for me, and just as I told the Jews, so I tell you now: **Where I am going, you cannot come.** (John 13:33, emphasis mine)
>
> Simon Peter asked him, "Lord, where are you going?" Jesus replied, **"Where I am going, you cannot follow now, but you will follow later."** (John 13:36, emphasis mine)

If I was in this room with Jesus, the last thing I would want to hear is Jesus say, "I am going away, and when you look for me, you won't find me." Peter responded with such Peter-like curiosity, "Lord, where are you going?" Peter's question began by respectfully calling Jesus "Lord." This shows Peter knew what Jesus said about Himself was true. The question itself shows that Peter was trying to understand the truth that Jesus was going away.

Jesus honors this sincerity by saying, "You will join me later. In the time I go away until we are together again, there is work to be done. I am giving you my Spirit for this work." These words would serve the disciples later when the cost of Mission and the hunger to be with Jesus collided.

I was recently asked, "Pastor Leonard, why doesn't God just take us to heaven when we get saved?" I smiled and showed them these words from John 13–17. We have a mission from God Himself, and we are here to live out this Jesus Mission Life. I like the words of Paul in Philippians:

> I eagerly expect and hope that I will in no way be ashamed, but will have sufficient courage so that now as always Christ will be exalted in my body, whether by life or by death. For to me, to live is Christ and to die is gain. If I am to go on living in the body, this will mean fruitful labor for me. Yet what shall I choose? I do not know! I am torn between the two: I desire to depart and be with Christ, which is better by far; but it is more necessary for you that I remain in the body. Convinced of this, I know that I will remain, and I will continue with all of you for your progress and joy in the faith, so that through my being with you again your boasting in Christ Jesus will abound on account of me. (Philippians 1:20–26)

Paul, while in prison for his Jesus Mission Life, writes that he knows that by life or by death, God's glory and Mission will advance. To live, well, that will be Jesus and His Mission, and to die, that will be Jesus and Mission accomplished. "I want to go, but it is better that I stay. So I will stay with you, I will stay on Mission, and together, we will show that Jesus Mission Living is always worthwhile."

Our conversation ended with the encouragement to choose a Jesus Mission Life for as long as we live—to live a Jesus Mission Life as we go, everywhere we go. This is God's will for each of us.

## JOHN 14

Still reclining around the table, Jesus preempts the wrong questions with words of hope and Mission. "I am going away to prepare a place for you. I will also return to get you, and we will be together again. Don't let your hearts be troubled by these things I am saying and what is unfolding; you can trust me" (vv. 2–3, my paraphrase).

After more conversation, Jesus boldly said that because of who He is, no one can come to the Father except by Him. From this truth, Jesus comforted His friends, saying they knew Jesus was the Way and they knew the Father. Jesus told His friends that knowing the Father opens the door to Mission success. With belief in Jesus and the Father, Jesus told His friends that they could do what Jesus had been doing. "You guys will do even greater things than these once I get back to the Father" (v. 12, paraphrase mine). The disciples are promised Mission success by knowing the Father and are given the promise that Mission prayers receive answers from the Father.

Okay, get ready for it; Jesus is about to put the final piece of how to live a Jesus Mission Life in front of His disciples in the form of the promise of God the Holy Spirit.

> If you love me, keep my commands. And I will ask the Father, and he will give you another advocate to help you and be with you forever—the Spirit of truth. The world cannot accept him, because it neither sees him nor knows him. But you know him, for he lives with you and will be in you. I will not leave you as orphans; I will come to you. (John 14:15–18)

Jesus's words here in John 14 are more of a missional statement than a moral statement. "If you love me, keep my commands" is best understood in the context of Jesus Mission Living. Love for Jesus because of the love of Jesus is what drives mission. Through love, we obey Jesus's commands to love like Him. We are being prepared to be sent. It is as if Jesus is saying, "When you enter into the loving obedience of Mission, I will ask the Father to give to you God the Holy Spirit. He will help you and be in you and with you forever." Dang, this is so good, isn't it? Jesus was building up to this moment as He celebrated Passover with the disciples, and in this room, He kept saying that there was a mission—His Mission. "I want you to take over when I leave. It will be costly, it will be hard, and it will be worth it. But to make sure you succeed in this Mission, I am going to ask the Father, and He will say, Yes! He is going to send you another advocate" (vv. 15–16, paraphrase mine).

The words "another advocate" have a rich understanding, pointing to someone who would do for the disciples what Jesus did for the disciples. Not replacing Jesus, but partnering with Jesus in the disciples' friendship with God and Mission from God. Jesus is saying, "God the Holy Spirit will be my deposit, guaranteeing that I will come to get you; you will not be orphans (v. 18, paraphrase mine).

---

Side Note: We often act like we are orphans and beggars, as if our troubles mean God is not here or that we have to beg Him to help. We groan and say words like, "I sure wish I could learn what God is trying to teach me so this trial will end." At times, we treat God the Holy Spirit as a divine butler appointed to make sure the "good life" promises being thrown about our culture to Jesus followers actually happen. This is still an orphan mentality, just an orphan with a butler.

---

An orphan in the days of Jesus had no mission for life beyond survival. They had no hope, strength, mission, meaning, or options. Their destiny was in the hands of others, and a life of slavery or worse was the "next" reality for them. But orphans knew this was not supposed to be. Orphans longed to be adopted because they knew that healthy families would provide them value and a mission. Jesus said that He would NOT leave us as orphans.

Reading a book like this, if read with an orphan mentality, will keep you from seeing how Jesus's promise of the Holy Spirit matters to the Mission of God. Jesus is saying, "Do not act like you have no one, no strength, no hope, no power, no Mission—YOU ARE NOT ORPHANS BECAUSE YOU HAVE GOD THE HOLY SPIRIT IN YOU. This is a part of my plan, and it is very good." I depend on this promise from Jesus as I live a Jesus Mission Life.

> All this I have spoken while still with you. But the Advocate, the Holy Spirit, whom the Father will send in my name, will teach you all things and will remind you of everything I have said to you. Peace I leave with you; my peace I give you. I do not give to you as the world gives. Do not let your hearts be troubled and do not be afraid. (John 14:25–27, emphasis mine)

Over the years, I have mastered a small prayer. I use it regularly when I am speaking, traveling, meeting new people, answering questions about Jesus and faith, solving conflicts, and discipling others. This might be my most prayed prayer:

*"Jesus, in a few minutes, I will be saying words. Will you put them in my mouth?"*

Because I see myself as sent wherever I go and because I see myself as an ambassador of Christ and His Mission, because I believe I am to relay the very message of God, this has become my prayer. Second Corinthians 5:20 says that God has made us ambassadors who speak the very words of Jesus to lead people to be reconciled to God.

This is exactly what God the Holy Spirit will do! He will teach us as we discover more and more about Jesus, and then He will remind us of the words Jesus spoke so we can speak them too. Oh, and one more bonus—PEACE. We get the Peace of God with the Spirit of God. What a generous God we have! I think peace is the word of choice here because nothing can disrupt our lives quite like being a disciple-maker.

Jesus's Mission Living stretches us to build lives best measured by eternal weights and scales, not earthly weights and scales. This life stretches us as we build bridges beyond our comfort zones and quite often beyond our knowledge. This life stretches us as we love people who don't look, think, or vote like us. This life stretches us to deny self, take up a cross, and follow the One whose cross ended in a real, true Cross. Jesus says when God the Holy Spirit comes, we will get peace, a supernatural peace. This peace is not like the world gives; it is a different kind of peace, and as we live a Jesus Mission Life, this peace keeps the trouble that builds in our hearts and around us from derailing us.

---

Side Note: We often seek peace as confirmation of the will and leading of God. We say, "I knew it was God because I had so much peace." I have heard this about marriage, work, financial decisions, moving, having kids, what school to attend, what church to attend, and even where to serve in the church. "I trust this is God's will or plan because I have such peace."

---

The Bible actually says the fruit of trust is righteousness. Trusting God to lead us can give us some of the least peaceful moments because trusting God stretches us past the life we live to the life we were made to live. The Jesus Mission Life is not peaceful; it is quite challenging and disruptive, but it is the right life. The fruit of trust is doing right.

The fruit of doing right is peace. When I do what is right, the presence of God brings peace to the life He has given me. I find no peace in pushing myself to right living, but I find great peace in right living. If you are feeling the weight of a Jesus Mission Life, and if this weight is disruptive to your peace, there could be a reason and a solution. **The reason: It is not God's peace you seek but rather the absence of any real internal conflict.** You might just be feeling disrupted by the Holy Spirit. Jesus said His peace is different, not like the world's peace. **The solution: Get into the Mission and let God the Holy Spirit give you God's Peace. Trust Jesus, do what is right, and receive Jesus's Peace through the Holy Spirit.**

A final thought on why I think this is true. The world's peace encourages us to do what makes us happy. The world's peace wants us to find a safe and secure path, to find what feeds us in the moment, and to get loved by someone who fills a need. The world's peace is fleeting because it is something we have when life feels great and leaves when life is hard. God's Peace says, "You were made for Mission, built for eternal significance, and I am with you. Trust me, do what is right, and I will give My Peace to you" (my paraphrase). God's Peace is not something you find but rather something God gives through the Holy Spirit.

## JOHN 15–16

Earlier in this book, I spent time in John 15, so let me summarize here and then quote Jesus. The Father has a Garden, and He is the Gardener. "I am the True Vine, and there is no other vine that can sustain a Jesus Mission Life. I chose you to bear fruit and fruit that remains. We are friends, we are partners, and we have work to do" (my paraphrase). Now let's skip to the end of John 15.

> When the Advocate comes, whom I will send to you from the Father—the Spirit of truth who goes out from the Father—he will testify about me. And you also must testify, for you have been with me from the beginning. (John 15:26–27)

In light of everything Jesus has said and done in John 13–15, Jesus starts verse 26 with the confidence-building and promise-bearing word "WHEN." I love this! Not if, not in case, not by chance, if it gets really tough … no, Jesus says WHEN. Jesus is saying, "You guys are the next part of the plan, disciples who make disciples, Jesus Mission Living, and you have a partnership with God the Holy Spirit guaranteed." WHEN.

When the advocate comes, "whom I WILL send." Again, how amazing and assuring are these words from Jesus? "I WILL send Him." Let's keep going. This is such a Jesus Mission Living confidence-building bunch of sentences. "He WILL testify about me." What comforting words. There was nothing the disciples wanted to hear more than hearing about Jesus. God the Holy Spirit will testify about Jesus. The reason God the Holy Spirit will say so much about Jesus is because they are going to use so many words to also testify about Jesus.

## JOHN 16

Jesus is turning the corner to drive home the Jesus Mission Life these disciples were now going to live. Jesus told His friends, "I do not want you to fall away, so I am giving you this next revelation. What is next is going to require you to be all in. As you make disciples, you are about to be treated with hatred and brutality. They will kick you out and kill you and think they are serving God while doing it. These are not people who know me or the Father" (vv. 1–3, paraphrase mine).

Jesus added, "I did not tell you this from the beginning because I was with you, but now that I am going back to the Father, you need to know." I believe Jesus is pushing His friends to be all in, to move fully into the Mission of Jesus, to fully embrace the kingdom of God—to be ALL IN. "I am leaving, but you are sad when you should be glad. My leaving is the 'next' step in My Mission."

> But very truly I tell you, it is for your good that I am going away. Unless I go away, the Advocate will not come to you; but if I go, I will send him to you. When he comes, he will prove the world to be in the wrong about sin and righteousness and judgment: about sin, because people do not believe in me; about righteousness,

> because I am going to the Father, where you can see me no longer; and about judgment, because the prince of this world now stands condemned. (John 16:7–11)

"It is good for you. I am going away, and this is good for you." If I were sitting in that room, the only way for me to believe that Jesus's going away and the Spirit coming was good for me would be to fully embrace the Mission of Jesus as my own mission. Then, I would be leaning into both friendship and partnership with Jesus. When He comes, the world will gain an understanding of what is right, what is wrong, and who Jesus is. This is what the world needs, and it cannot happen until God the Holy Spirit comes. Jesus continues with these words:

> I have much more to say to you, more than you can now bear. But when he, the Spirit of truth, comes, he will guide you into all the truth. He will not speak on his own; he will speak only what he hears, and he will tell you what is yet to come. He will glorify me because it is from me that he will receive what he will make known to you. All that belongs to the Father is mine. That is why I said the Spirit will receive from me what he will make known to you. (John 16:12–15)

"You are going to get more truth, but the truth you get will be from God the Holy Spirit. He will guide you, meaning it will be done together. He will be with you to guide you into this truth. You can trust Him because the Spirit is getting all of what you discover from Me" (paraphrase mine).

Let me pause and observe two things here. First, look how the entire God Head is involved in Jesus Mission Living. Jesus continues to care, to give, and to lead. The Father is at work, keeping us and sealing us as belonging to Jesus. God the Holy Spirit indwells and teaches and guides and strengthens the disciple to make disciples in step with Jesus Mission Living.

## JOHN 17

Often called the high priestly prayer of Jesus or the real Lord's prayer, which I certainly understand, I feel that in light of John 13–16, a more accurate title of this section of Scripture might be the Missional Prayer of Jesus. From start to finish, Jesus is talking to His Father about what He has done, what He came to do, and what the Father wanted done. Jesus's prayer reveals how His work of making disciples glorified the Father. Jesus declares that the unity He and the Father expressed, although driven by love and honor, came from their shared Mission. Jesus prayerfully declares that this unity is how people will become convinced that Jesus really is from the Father. How does all that Jesus prayed in John 17 become a reality? The answer is found in our friendship and partnership with God the Holy Spirit.

I am about to get in trouble here but stay with me. I believe in the full work of God the Holy Spirit in the life of the believer. I believe I am a Spirit-filled follower of Jesus, and in my daily life as well as in my ministry, I experience both the power of God and the presence of God. God's Spirit has lifted my hands in praise and moved my feet in celebration. Please stay with me; we are going to get real for a few paragraphs.

I was training a group of pastors in West Africa, and each day, the meeting would begin with a few pastors shouting, "Come Holy Spirit! Come Holy Spirit!" again and again and again. The rest of the crowd, leaning into the chant, were animated and jumping up and down. They were clapping and having both physically visible and vocal expressions as a response to what they perceived as the presence of God the Holy Spirit. One woman began to do what the crowd called speaking in tongues; this was usually the cue for others to join in. Another man entered into a trance-like posture and shook. It was not long before the whole room was affected. This was not the first time in my travels that I had seen this, but on this day, I felt led by God the Holy Spirit to say something.

Our training topic on this day, as luck would have it (not luck but God), was God the Holy Spirit and how He is our primary partner in Jesus Mission Living. Now, standing in front of these dear friends, I commented, "What in the world was that?" The room sat in silence, stunned because of the challenging tone of my question. One pastor replied, "It was the presence of God's Spirit moving in us." Another pastor described it as a visitation of the Spirit, preparing them to receive the Word. Each comment brought agreement and murmurs.

I asked a series of questions. "Why do you need that experience to receive the Word?" "Why does your expression of God's presence with you look like the pagan and witchcraft rituals in nearby villages? Why are you begging God's Spirit to come when the Bible teaches you He is already here?" I added a few more pretty challenging questions, and the room went completely silent.

One pastor slipped up his hand to ask a question. "Pastor, do you not believe in the Holy Spirit?" The room groaned in approval of the question, and the whole room wanted an answer.

"I DO!" I said with a smile. "I really do, but when I read the Scriptures and see what I just saw, I am confused." I asked for permission to proceed with our training and to return to the conversation we were having. "I promise we will come back to talk about both what we just experienced and God's presence." We paused, I prayed, and then we started training.

During this day of training, I walked them through John 13–17, showing them from the very words of Jesus the ways in which Jesus described the work of God the Holy Spirit in Jesus Mission Living. They took a ton of notes, they asked questions, and we laughed a lot. As we wrapped up our training for the day, we circled back around to the question, "Do you not believe in the Holy Spirit?"

We reviewed what I saw, the experience they had to start the meeting, and what Jesus said about the Holy Spirit. "My dear brothers and sisters, I told you this morning that what I saw was confusing. The reason it is confusing is that this morning when we began our first session with repeated shouts for the Holy Spirit to come and all of the trances, the slapping of walls, and the other expressions you exhibited, I struggled to find any of this in Scripture. In addition, the things we found in Scripture today, the words Jesus spoke about God the Holy Spirit, I do not see anywhere in your lives."

The room was quiet again, and then I spoke softly. "I would like to ask you the same question, 'Do you not believe in the Holy Spirit?' You ignore what Jesus actually said about the work of God the Holy Spirit in you, and you create experiences that look more cultural than biblical. Yes, God does miracles. Yes, the supernatural is real. Yes, the gifts of God's Spirit are real. But not to the exclusion of the daily work of Jesus Mission Living." We spent the next ninety minutes in a fun and helpful conversation about Jesus's words concerning the Holy Spirit. When we were done, the room clapped and cheered.

Why the story, Leonard? This is an extreme picture of how so many people treat the work of God the Holy Spirit. We tend to think of God's Spirit as providing an experience in worship. Saying something when the preaching is good. Giving us sort of a nudge when we sin or comfort when we are hurting is what we often expect from Him. He does this, by the way. Sadly, too few Jesus followers know the power of God's Spirit to build a Jesus Mission Life. We leave a dynamic time of prayer and worship declaring the richness of the Spirit, and rightly so, but then go throughout our day unaware that HE is leading us to share Christ with others, to say words that HE will give, to love people that HE already loves. Revival does not happen when we worship or when we linger in worship. Revival is not created by praising Jesus on the steps of the capitol and calling out governmental leaders. Revival, true revival, is when we learn to live every moment in step with God the Holy Spirit and live a Jesus Mission Life.

We know God the Holy Spirit strengthens us, guides us, leads us, teaches us, reminds us, and seals our relationship as sons and daughters until the day of redemption. God the Holy Spirit unites us, convicts us, encourages us, and protects us. God the Holy Spirit indwells us, prays on our behalf, and provides us freedom and liberty in Christ. God the Holy Spirit transforms us into the image of Christ, producing the fruit of the Spirit in us as we walk with Him.

Let us not forget that God the Holy Spirit is on Mission too. He is good, and He is God. It is just as supernatural for God to heal a body as it is for Him to provide the words to invite someone from spiritual death to life. The Holy Spirit IS our chief partner in building a Jesus Mission Life and in making disciples wherever we go. Do you believe in the Holy Spirit?

It is supernatural that all who know Jesus have been given spiritual gifts. Supernatural abilities to lead, serve, speak, administrate, give, and so much more. These gifts are given to bring about God's Mission in the world and fullness in the Church. Who decides which gifts we have? According to Paul, God the Holy Spirit is both the decider and giver of the gifts. These are not random assignments; He takes into account who you are, and how you are wired—how you have been made.

This is really important to know because in knowing, we can all take our place in Jesus Mission Living. I am a preacher; I am comfortable on a stage, making speeches, developing ideas and talks, and opening the word of God. I am an extrovert, and I am comfortable saying hello to strangers, engaging in conversations with people I do not know, and finding ways to share Jesus. This is how God made me, and the Holy Spirit takes into account my design as He gifts me.

The Holy Spirit knows you and how you are made and wired. With careful consideration, He gifts you accordingly, not for a different mission but for a different role in the same Mission. He supplies what you need to live a Jesus Mission Life in the way you are designed.

Sometimes, we look at our personality and think we are not qualified when it comes to Jesus Mission Living. Our task is to choose Jesus Mission Living and receive the gift of God's Spirit to be your chief partner in making disciples who make disciples.

There is an invitation at the end of this book. It is an invitation to find and follow Jesus. If you have felt drawn to find Jesus and then to follow Jesus, this is also the work of God the Holy Spirit. I added a few paragraphs for those who would also embark on the journey of living the Jesus Mission Life. I close this book by telling you a secret.

Regardless of where I have spoken, who I have led, what I have given, and where I have served, the most effective and life-impacting and life-changing decision I have made is to be a person who lives a Jesus Mission Life. I have found my WHY! There is nothing that has caused more growth and maturity in my life than living a Jesus Mission Life. There is nothing that has helped me know Jesus better, love Jesus more, and grow my faith and trust in Jesus more than living a Jesus Mission Life. I have found the most personal and deep love that Jesus has for me and for those around me when I live a Jesus Mission Life. And you know something? You will too.

# Stepping into Jesus's Mission

## A prayer you can pray today:

*Jesus,*

*Thank You for sending the Holy Spirit. I know that without Him, I could never live a Jesus Mission Life. Help me keep in step with Him and become the kind of person You send, one who bears the fruits of love, joy, peace, patience, kindness, gentleness, faithfulness, goodness, and self-control. I appreciate the way You transform me and then send me.*

*Amen*

## Some questions to move you forward:

What has been your understanding of who God the Holy Spirit is?

How did this chapter add to your understanding of the person or work of God the Holy Spirit?

How important to living a Jesus Mission Life did Jesus say the Holy Spirit would be?

What are some ways in which the Holy Spirit will be our partner in living a Jesus Mission Life?

Has the Holy Spirit ever given you words to speak? Share this story.

When was a time the Holy Spirit gave you courage, comfort, or strength?

Share a time when the Holy Spirit prompted you to live a Jesus Mission Life.

## A step to take as you go:

Take time to read John 13–17 each day this week. Have a piece of paper or a place to make notes about the amazing partnership with God the Holy Spirit as promised by Jesus.

“Come follow me,
I want you to truly live.”
—Jesus

## A NOTE TO THE READER

Before I ever start writing, I pray for people who might read these words and be drawn to embrace Jesus, the Creator and Redeemer. Maybe this is you, and you are drawn to commit your life to Jesus. This is God the Holy Spirit speaking to you, so make sure you listen.

Jesus loves you so much, and wants to be your friend and for you to join Him in the life He has already prepared for you. This incredible life is LIFE here on earth and LIFE forever in heaven with Him. This is His Mission: to rescue us from sin, death, and the brokenness sin has created in our lives. His invitation: "Come follow me, I want you to truly live." How can Jesus give such a powerful invitation?

Jesus Christ was sent by the Father to seek and save the lost (all of us) and to give His life as a ransom for any who will come. It had to be Jesus; it could only be Jesus, and here is why.

Jesus lived a perfect life without sin. His closest friends said there was no sin in Him; my closest friends would say the opposite of me. Because Jesus was sinless, His life perfectly met all the standards of God. In other words, Jesus's life satisfied God's holiness.

Jesus's death was the only death of a 100 percent innocent person. So when He died on the cross, His death satisfied all the justice requirements of God. Jesus literally paid the penalty of all sin, which is death, when He died on that cross.

Death and the grave could not hold Jesus, and He rose again from the dead. When He did, His resurrection sealed forever the satisfaction of God brought about by His sinless life and His death. In rising from the dead, Jesus made it possible for you and me to know God and to be forgiven of our sin.

What God asks each of us is that we respond to Jesus in faith. The great news is that when we respond to Jesus—His life, death, and resurrection—by faith, we are made alive and new, adopted into the very family of God. Our sins—past, present, and future are forgiven—and we are restored to God.

The faith response we make is to turn from sin to Jesus. The Bible's word for this is to repent. When we repent, we are confessing we have sinned and are asking Jesus to forgive us, to live in us, and we are committing our whole lives to follow after Him. We are receiving the gift of God, which is eternal life with Him. This new life is provided by the life, death, and resurrection of Jesus.

A great prayer of faith in response to Jesus is as follows:

*Dear Jesus, I believe you lived and died and rose again. I believe that your life, death, and resurrection satisfied before God what sin, my sin, has broken. I confess to you that I have sinned. I know that my sin has made me fall short of the life and friendship we could have. I am turning away from my sinful ways to follow you. Will you forgive me? Will you come and take up residence in my life? Will you help me follow you forever? Thank you for your grace-filled love. Amen.*

If you prayed that prayer, all of heaven rejoiced and celebrated you and your new friendship with Jesus. This is just the beginning of a Jesus Mission Life. Feel free to contact me at leonardl@4-gen.net and share your new life in Christ. Finding a community of people who love Jesus is important too. When you do, send me your address, and I will send you a book to assist you as you begin in this friendship and partnership with Jesus.

**Maybe you read this book and already know Jesus.** You are discovering His perfect love for you, and in response to His love, you love Him, too. I have been praying for you.

It is possible that the words of this book nudge you, maybe even push you, challenge you, or dare I say, bring conviction to your soul to build a life of Mission and to become a true Great Commission follower of Jesus. Here is where I suggest you begin.

Confess to Jesus the gap between your mission and His Mission, either in heart, mind, or action. Repent and simply ask Jesus to make you a disciple who makes disciples. He never says no to this.

I suggest you act immediately on this prayer in three ways:

1. **Ask God to help you find the person you were meant to disciple.** This is actually how Jesus found and chose His disciples.
2. **Take your swings.** Get some training and get some practice in making disciples. Through a local ministry like Youth for Christ or Young Life, you can work with students and be trained to make disciples. Ask your church if any training is available for you to become a disciple-maker. Reach out to us if we can help. (info@4-gen.net)
3. **Get to know Jesus better and better.** One way to do this is to read Matthew, Mark, Luke, and John a lot. If you read three chapters a day, you can finish all four Gospels in a month. Try this for the next six months.

With much prayer and love,

Leonard

# APPENDIX

## Leverage: Finding the Power Beyond Your Own Strength

1. **Leverage WHAT YOU KNOW.**
   a. Using the space below, make a list of everything you know. For example: Do you know how to read? Do you know how to farm? Do you know how to fix meals? Do you know how to repair roofs? Do you know how to write? Do you know numbers? Do you know how to teach, tutor, sing, or play an instrument? What do you know?
   b. Circle anything on your list that someone else might also need to know.
   c. Put a star next to anything you circled if you know someone personally who needs Jesus who might also need to know that specific thing you know.
   d. Write the name of that person next to your circle and star. Pray for each name, asking Jesus for an opportunity to use what you know to love others.
2. **Leverage WHO YOU KNOW.**
   a. Using the space below, begin to make a list of people you know. For example, teachers, pastors, people who sing, people who are great cooks, business owners, car repair specialists, coffin builders, farmers, athletes, seamstresses, artists, political leaders, soldiers, officers of the law, craftsmen, and so on. (Put their names by each one.)
   b. Circle any name of a person who is a phone call away, meaning you could contact them, and it would not seem strange.
   c. Put a star next to anyone you know who would also be willing to talk about following Jesus or helping them help others follow Jesus. Pray for that person.

d. Put on your list between five to ten names of people you need to know.

3. **Leverage WHAT YOU HAVE.**

   a. Using the space below, make a list of everything you have. For example, a pot to cook in, a plot of land to farm, a roof over your head, a car to drive, a phone to connect with people, a chicken that gives eggs, and so on.

   b. Circle anything you have that can be used to love someone else in the name of Jesus.

   c. Put the name of someone next to what you circled. Pray for these people.

4. **Leverage YOUR OBSTACLES AS OPPORTUNITIES.**

   a. On the following page are two columns. One column is for "Obstacles"; the other column is for "Opportunities." Answer these questions: "What obstacles do you face?" Maybe words like religion, time, money, education, skills, and food apply here. Now, what opportunities do these obstacles provide?

   b. Take your list of people from the "What You Know," "Who You Know," and "What You Have" lists, and see if you have any ability to turn an obstacle into an opportunity for that person.

| OBSTACLES | OPPORTUNITIES |
|---|---|
| | |
| | |
| | |
| | |
| | |
| | |
| | |
| | |
| | |
| | |
| | |
| | |
| | |

5. **Leverage YOUR CULTURE.**

    a. Using the space below, what are some built-in cultural expectations you can use? For example, some cultures cannot say no to the hungry. Some cultures value work ethics. Some cultures value generosity. What does your culture value?

    b. Make a list of your cultural expectations. After each list, ask the following question: "What can I leverage from this expectation or value?"

    c. What does your culture celebrate and why?

    d. What does your culture punish and why?

    e. What does your culture expect from men, women, children, old people, and young people? When does someone become an adult in your culture? What are the religious practices of your culture?

# NOTES

**CHAPTER 3**

[1] John A. Beck, Along the Road: How Jesus Used Geography to Tell God's Story (Grand Rapids, MI: Our Daily Bread Publishing, 2018).

**CHAPTER 4**

[2] The Walt Disney Company, "Our Mission," https://thewaltdisneycompany.com/about/.

[3] "Vision and Mission Statement Comparison: Chick-fil-A vs. Boeing," Empowered Leadership, https://empoweredleadership.com/blog/vision-and-mission-statement-comparison-chick-fil-a-vs-boeing#:~:text=Chick%2D%20Fil%2DA%20Vision%3A,at%20winning%20and%20keeping%20customers."

[4] https://corporate.walmart.com/purpose.

[5] The Lord of the Rings: The Fellowship of the Ring. New Line Cinema/WingNut Films, 2001.

**CHAPTER 5**

[6] Tracy Ebarb, "Nonprofits Fail: Here's Seven Reasons Why," September 7, 2019, NANOE, https://nanoe.org/nonprofits-fail/.

**CHAPTER 8**

[7] JAWS, directed by Steven Spielberg (1975; Beverly Hills, CA: Universal Studios, Video Release 1980), VHS.

**CHAPTER 12**

[8] A. W. Tozer, "A Man of God: Everything by Prayer" sermon series, YouTube, December 3, 2018, https://www.youtube.com/watch?v=75LunLW2mMg.

## ABOUT LEONARD LEE

A lot of people say I am fearless and a little bit crazy. I promise you I am not. Why do they say this? Because my focus on the Mission of Jesus makes me look crazy and fearless. In 1966, I met Christ, and since that day, the focus of my life has been to help people find and then follow Jesus. Over the years, this focus has driven me to work long hours in one job so I could do ministry in another for free, to work with at-risk students and gangs. (Yes, Bloods, Crips, and Skinheads would come to my house each week and find out about Jesus.) This focus compelled me to plant two churches where more than a thousand people met Christ. Since starting ministry work in 1980, I have never had only one job but rather several at a time to make ends meet. In 2011, this focus caused me to launch the 4GENetwork, a ministry dedicated to making disciples who make disciples. (www.4-gen.net)

As of today, the 4GENetwork has trained close to 400,000 pastors and leaders from six continents, about 100 countries of the world from more than 250 denominations, and we are just getting started. Our work has taken me to places where the only thing to do at night is lock yourself in a room in a compound surrounded by concrete and razor wire. We have trained pastors in regions of Africa that when they hear a motorcycle pass by, they drop to the ground because riders have often delivered bombs via motorcycles. We have fled in the dark of night to new regions, and much of our training is carried out in clandestine locations. I swear to you that I am not crazy—I'm just really focused on seeing people meet Jesus through well-trained disciple-makers who make disciples.

I also write books and host a podcast called Say Yes & Become. You can find them at www.leonardlee.com. I also speak around the country and the world and would love to speak at your church or ministry. You can connect with me at www.leonardlee.com or leonardl@4-gen.net.

Growing up in Northern California, I spent a lot of my time hiking, camping, fishing, hunting, and driving my 4X4 Bronco and Jeep over boulders and mountains. I almost always like sleeping outside more than inside. I love to cook on my smoker all kinds of amazing foods to share with my neighbors and friends. In 1989, I married my best friend, Merrily, and we have been blessed with two really fun and great kids. My favorite thing to do is spend time with Merrily, drinking coffee, talking, watching a movie, eating food, and sharing life together in our Tennessee home. My undergrad degree is in Theology and Ministry, and my master's is in Leadership Development. I am on the five-yard line of my doctorate in Transformational Leadership.

Thank you for taking the time to read *A Jesus Mission Life.* I am beyond grateful! I pray you were as blessed reading it as I was writing it. I hope you will join me on a Jesus-worthy adventure as you build your Jesus Mission Life. Trust me—you will never be the same again. Only heaven will be able to measure the eternal impact.